AF443690

Custom
Gunstock Carving

Custom Gunstock Carving

Philip R. Eck

STACKPOLE
BOOKS

Published by
STACKPOLE BOOKS
5067 Ritter Road
Mechanicsburg, PA 17055

Printed in the United States of America

10 9 8 7 6 5 4 3 2 1

First edition

Color photographs by Doug Nicotera

Library of Congress Cataloging-in-Publication Data

Eck, Philip R.
    Custom gunstock carving / Philip R. Eck. — 1st ed.
      p. cm.
    ISBN 0–8117–0348–7
    1. Wood-carving. 2. Gunstocks. I. Title.
    TT199.7.E514 1994
    736′.4—dc20
                                         94–25803
                                                   CIP

To my mother, Theresa

Contents

 Author's Note

IN MEMORY OF FRED EMMEL, A FRIEND AND A TRUE gunsmith's gunsmith, the first to encourage this writing.

Although the primary subject of this book is carving, it contains enough information about stock finishing to enable coverage of carvings and the completion of a total stock. For those who wish a more comprehensive study of stock finishing, I highly recommend *Gunstock Finishing and Care* by A. Donald Newell.

My permission is given to any who wish to use the designs in this book for personal or professional carving. All designs are reproducible if you carefully follow the instructions. Good luck, and remember, you can enjoy the carving process just as much as the finished product.

PREFACE

THIS BOOK PROVIDES COMPREHENSIVE, IN-DEPTH, practical instruction to all aspiring gunstock carvers. You need not be an accomplished artist or craftsman to produce a successful carving; all that is necessary is a serious desire plus patience, practice, and common sense. If you have the desire to carve but have never attempted a carving, or if you failed in an initial attempt, this book provides the information necessary for success. It will also help those who have already carved with some degree of success to improve their work.

When displaying my work at gun shows, I am often approached by people interested in learning to carve and others who have tried and failed. Many of the latter have returned with samples of their work for advice on what went wrong or how they might salvage a botched job, and suggestions for their next attempt. I made notes on the most asked questions, and this book evolved from those notes.

Some carvers who possess an exceptionally high degree of natural ability have never studied but have become successful strictly through trial and error with nothing but hands-on execution. No matter what degree of natural ability you may have, however, the road will be a lot less bumpy if you take advantage of reference material such as this book. This will save you countless hours of trial and error plus a great deal of frustration, and may save a potentially good carving from a disastrous fate that can occur from but one serious mistake.

The carver is a creator. He or she creates beauty, a work that will endure, one that may well be admired by future generations just as many today marvel at the craftsmanship of those before us. I hope the following statement will be as inspirational to the reader as it has been for me.

The real heartache in life is knowing you had the potential to do something but never tried.
—author unknown

Proper Working Conditions

DISREGARD ANYTHING YOU MAY HAVE HEARD OR read to the contrary: There are no advantages to carving at a kitchen or dining room table versus working at a permanent workbench in a more suitable area of the home. Although many carvings exhibiting quality workmanship have been produced at the kitchen table, it is a fact that those who work at a temporary carving station will face many inconveniences that those who use a permanent workbench will not. If you simply do not have the space for a permanent work area, you can make do with a temporary work station, but if you intend to do a significant amount of carving, I strongly suggest that you set up a permanent workbench in a remote area of the house.

PRIVACY

Carving takes an enormous amount of concentration. You need to be able to work for long periods of time in comfortable surroundings without distraction. If you live in an active household, family members or roommates may try to be considerate, but it is unrealistic and unfair to expect others to alter their way of life to accommodate you. I advise setting up a workbench in a basement, attic, or spare room, where you can close the door and have a noisefree environment. In addition to the advantage of privacy, such a work area can be left undisturbed; it won't be necessary to clean up right away, set

up each time you wish to resume carving, or pack up and move your project suddenly. Truly, the only real advantage to working at a kitchen table is its proximity to the coffeepot.

A beginner especially needs privacy. In the early stages of learning, mistakes due to distractions and poor work habits are most prevalent. The carver needs to apply 100 percent attention to the work at hand, and any distraction may lead to disaster. Experience does allow a degree of liberty, but a simple jump or flinch still can result in a major error. While I carve, I keep a radio playing to cover unexpected or irritating noises that may occur even if the workbench is set up in an out-of-the-way spot. I place the radio at the far end of the room, tuned to a soft music station. On several occasions, such as when a crew was working on a section of roadway just outside my window, I used a headset with the radio to cover up noise from outside. There are several models of lightweight headphones that can be worn comfortably for long periods of time.

WORKBENCH

You do not need to have a professional-quality workbench, just something sturdy that has a large surface. What has served me well as a workbench for a number of years is a 6-by-2½-foot heavy-duty folding table, the type used at exhibition and craft shows. It provides a working surface of 15 square feet, which is more than adequate. It is important that the surface of the work area provide ample room to maneuver a stock in any direction so that you can work on any given section or angle of a carving with comfort and ease. You will need to cover your work surface with a pad to protect the stock. Without a pad, serious damage can occur. You can easily fashion a suitable pad from a 12-by-48-inch piece of ½-inch-thick foam rubber. Cover this with upholstery plastic or vinyl, and sew or glue the overlapping seams of the covering at the edge of the foam rubber. This covering allows easy cleanup of wood shavings during and after carving.

Keep all tools out of the stock pivot area but within easy reach so that you won't have to stand when you need a particular item. I have three shelves mounted to one side on the wall within arm's reach. They are 2 feet long and 10 inches deep and are spaced 10 inches above one another. On these shelves I keep stains and other materials. Directly in front of me and 12 inches above the tabletop, I have another shelf of the same size. This originally served as a mount for a light, and then I discovered that the top was ideal for holding my most frequently used carving tools. The surface area of the table is large enough that I can keep sharpening stones at one end yet still out of the stock pivot area. Beneath the table, to the left, I keep a file cabinet for organizing customer information.

LIGHTING

Do not take lighting for granted. Don't settle for existing lights, because they may not be suitable. You should have two sources of lighting, placed at a 90-degree angle to each other. One light should be directly in front of you, shaded to cast its glow just below eye level. Place a second light to your left if you are right-handed, or to your right if you're a lefty. I use a front light that is an 18-inch, double-tube fluorescent, designed for use on a kitchen counter. The second is a 60-watt incandescent soft-white bulb set in a low-profile table lamp. Many people will dispute using a fluorescent light, and I agree that it is not suitable for some types of work, such as checkering, but it is excellent for carving when used in such a two-light arrangement. The fluorescent provides a flood of light that casts a soft, discerning shadow from one direction. The incandescent casts a different type of light that creates a deeper shadow from another direction. The shadows created by the two different types of light give form to the carving as you make deeper cuts in the stock.

This lighting arrangement eliminates visual distortions likely to occur when using only one light. I feel the combination of fluorescent and incandescent light increased the quality of my work and reduced the strain to my eyes. If you do not wish to use a fluorescent, the light placed in front should be a 75-watt, soft-white incandescent bulb in a low-profile shaded lamp. The side light should be a 60-watt standard incandescent bulb, also in a low-profile shaded lamp.

A gentleman once brought a stock he had carved to me at a gun show where I was displaying my work. He asked if the stock could be salvaged. I learned that his only source of light had been a low-wattage lamp placed in front of him. He clearly had no concept of working conditions or layout, and he had paid the price for his lack of knowledge. A single source of light will cast a dark shadow and cause everything to look distorted shortly after the initial parting-line cuts are made. In reality, there is no distortion, but the illusion is created and grows worse as the carving becomes deeper. In an effort to correct what appeared to be wrong, he removed more wood. The removal of additional wood resulted in actual distortion. Had the carving not been so deep, it may have been able to withstand a touch-up, leaving it somewhat presentable and not a total loss. As it was, nothing could be done to correct the mistake short of inlaying another piece of wood into the entire area and recarving it.

For gunstock carving, an overhead light is not recommended at any time, either for a primary or a secondary source. Do not even turn on an overhead light while you are carving. Never use a colored light.

2

TOOLS

MANY TIMES OVER THE YEARS I'VE HEARD THE words, "You carved these gunstocks with those tools?" and other stock carvers I know have heard them too. Those who view my tools appear surprised that I don't use tools that require an engineering degree to use. One couple seemed to feel sorry I couldn't afford better. Most people expect the tools of this trade to be similar to those used by cabinetmakers, but that is not the case.

A gunstock carver's tools are chiefly a hodgepodge collection of items that have been lying around for years and others that were resurrected from a scrap pile. These were then altered for this type of carving. My tools are definitely not fancy or expensive. Even when done professionally, stock carving can be undertaken with little more than pocket money for basic essentials. Flea markets and yard sales offer excellent opportunities for picking up tools and essentials that can be adapted for the trade.

BASIC SET OF TOOLS

This list of tools is by no means absolute, and you do not need to duplicate all of them unless you intend to do a large amount of carving. A sizable number of well-carved stocks have proved these tools' value, and I am certain they will serve others as well.

I've seen carvings done with nothing but an ordinary jackknife. Most were not that well done from a professional viewpoint, but some ranged from respectable to very good. I've often wondered how much better the very good ones might have been had the carver used more tools. The goal of carving is quality workmanship; don't settle for anything less. In the descriptions that follow, I indicate which tools I feel are absolutely necessary for the beginner. If you do not know some of the items by name, familiarize yourself with them by studying the photograph of tools that accompanies this section.

Magni-viewer

After my first attempt at stock carving, I have not made a single cut without a magni-viewer. This particular model is equipped with a replaceable, scratch-resistant 2X magnification lens. With this tool, you can trace and transfer a pattern to a stock and make intricate cuts more easily and precisely. The tool reduces eyestrain, and the lens housing blocks out everything but what you are viewing and keeps your focus on the carving. If you have exceptionally good eyesight, you may be able to make do without this item, but otherwise it is a must. It certainly is a must if you intend to do professional work regardless of how good your eyesight might be. You can obtain this item from a number of sources, but your best bet for a quality product is a hobby shop or jeweler supply store. There

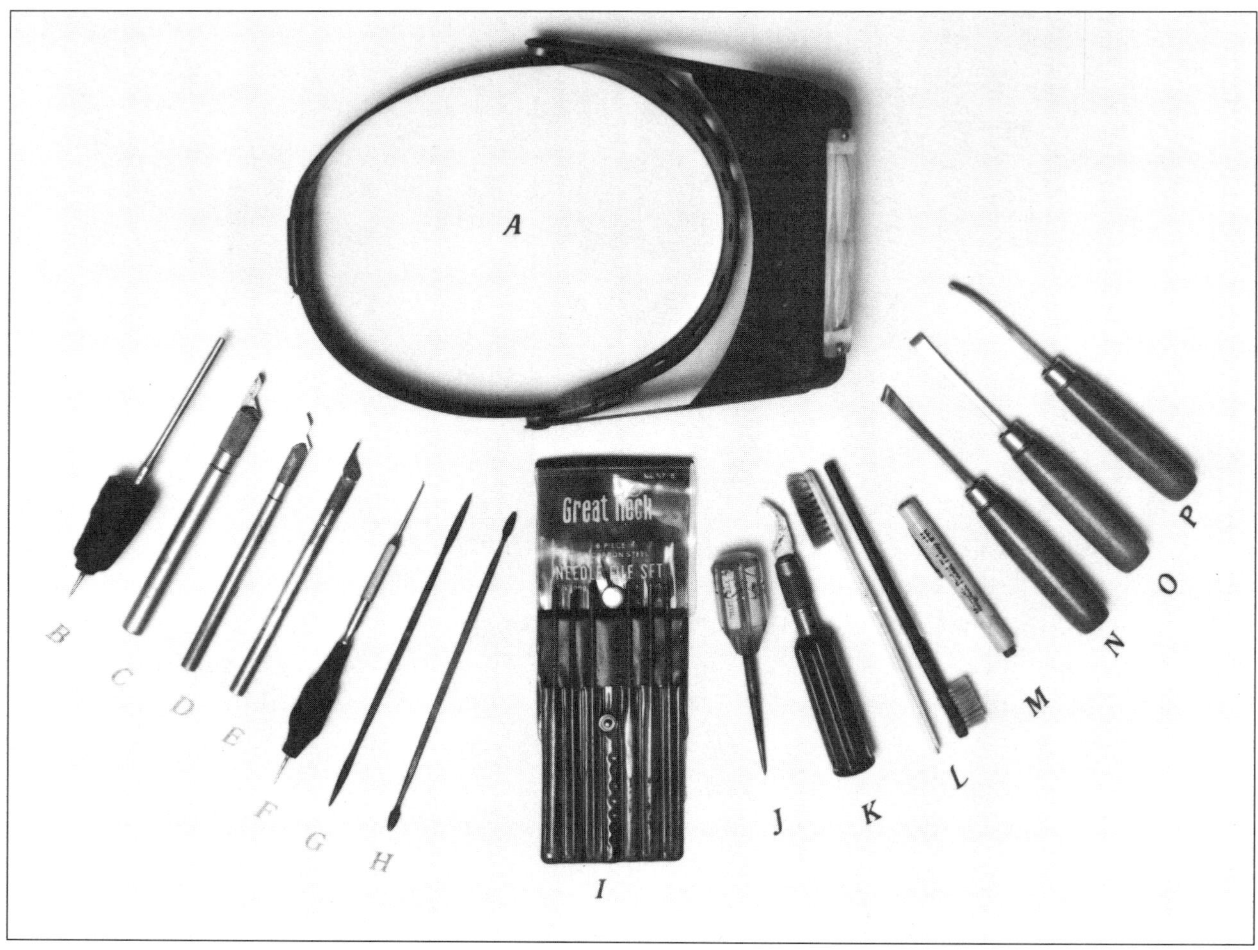

Basic set of tools: *A, magni-viewer; B, dental tool for design transfer; C, X-acto knife with wide grip; D, X-acto knife with narrow grip; E, X-acto knife with altered blade; F, dental tool for scraping and picking small areas; G and H, file rifflers; I, mill file set; J, scratch awl; K, X-acto knife with hook-bill blade; L, toothbrushes; M, magnet; N, skewed chisel; O, straight chisel; P, bent chisel.*

are several styles available, ranging from fixed-lens to variable-power, with a range of prices to match. I prefer a fixed-lens magni-viewer with a lens housing section that can be lifted while the headband stays in place. This allows me to position the headband at another spot or angle on my forehead should it become uncomfortable during a lengthy carving session. For anyone who wears eyeglasses, a clip-on type is available at jeweler supply stores.

X-acto Knives

Standard X-acto knives are readily obtained at hardware stores, hobby shops, craft shops, and art supply stores. You can make do with just one of these knives, but I prefer to have at least three on hand. With three, I don't have to stop to sharpen or change a blade as often, or be disrupted while I'm working on an area that calls for complete concentration.

The knives marked *C* and *D* in the accompanying photograph have the same type of blade, but the handle of knife *C* is thicker in diameter. Knife *D* is my favorite; I use this one for the bulk of my carving. I occasionally use the other knife to brake monotony and get a different feel when I'm carving for long periods of time. The smaller handle size of knife *D* is the size recommended if you will be using just one knife. The smaller-diameter handle will allow

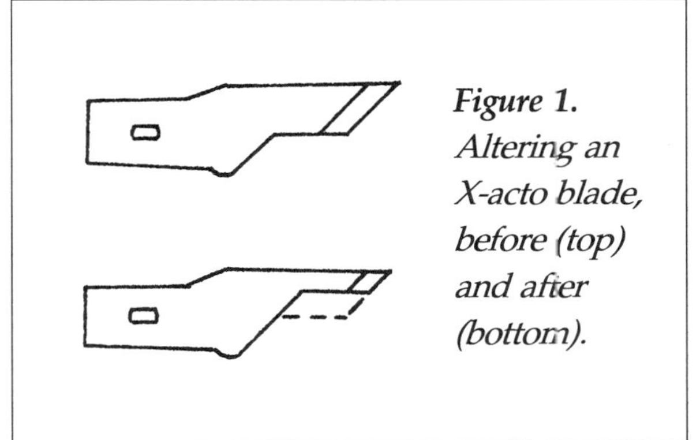

Figure 1. Altering an X-acto blade, before (top) and after (bottom).

cuts to be at angles that the larger handle will not.

The only knife blade I use is the X-acto #16 slant-blade. It is perfect for initial parting-line cuts and does extremely well when used in chisel-like fashion to remove background wood from large areas. Take note of the blade in knife *E*. It too is a #16 slant-blade, altered to the shape shown. I use the *D* handle with this blade. I wish the blade came in this shape, but such is not the case. I used a Dremel tool fitted with a carbide disc to modify the blade. You can use a mill file, but this will take a considerable amount of time and effort. The blade's reduced size allows access for detail work in difficult areas and is particularly useful in making outline cuts in tight curved areas. It's also very good in high-detail work such as feathers and facial features. Altered or unaltered, the #16 slant-blade is the gem of the entire X-acto line.

Dental Tool for Design Transfer

For transferring the design from the pattern paper to the gunstock, I use a dental tool that I modified with a mill file, removing a slight angle from the tip and forming a point. Then I smoothed the point and gave it a final polish with emery paper. This tool needs only an occasional touch-up to maintain its point. I occasionally use this tool to stipple in limited or hard-to-reach areas.

Although the tool produces a smaller stipple than is usually seen in larger accessible

areas, the combination of large and small stippling blends together nicely. To do this, stipple the larger areas first with the larger stippling tool, then stipple the more confined areas with this smaller tool, allowing the smaller marks to run in with the larger stippling. Place these smaller marks on the higher areas surrounding the larger marks; they should decrease in depth and number as they extend into the larger markings. Generally, it's only necessary to extend into the larger markings no more than $1/8$

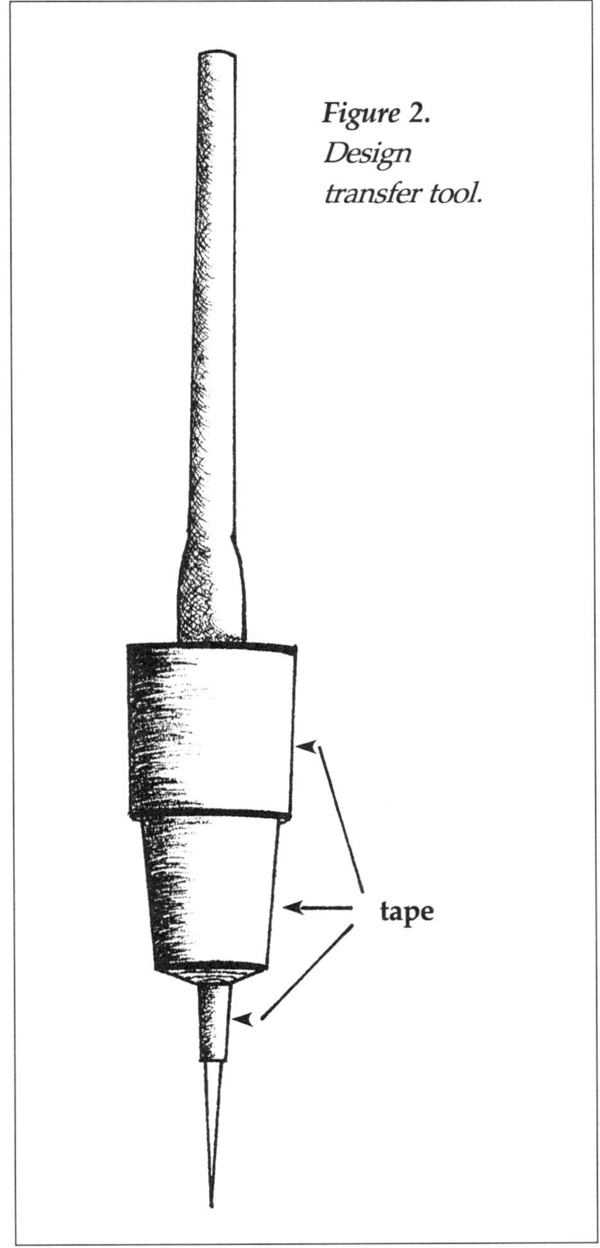

Figure 2. Design transfer tool.

inch to ¼ inch. This is best judged by appearance rather than by a set rule.

The tool's handle is about the thickness of a ballpoint pen, so it can become uncomfortable to work with for any length of time. I found that wrapping the tool with masking tape gives a firm, comfortable, controlled grip during long periods of use and greatly reduces or eliminates finger cramping.

You will need this tool or something similar to transfer the design to the stock. There are other ways to transfer designs, but I have found none so precise as the puncture method. Flea markets, military surplus stores, scrap yards, and of course, dentists, are the best places to find dental tools. Your dentist might give you this tool at no cost. A similar tool, with a wooden handle, is available at ceramics and plaster craft shops. It is also easy enough to make your own tool. To do so, use a 5-inch length of $^3/_8$- or ½-inch wooden dowel. Drill a hole in one end of the dowel about half the length of a large sewing needle and large enough in diameter to allow insertion of the needle without force. Run about 2 inches of thread through the eye of the needle, leaving an inch on each side. Dip the

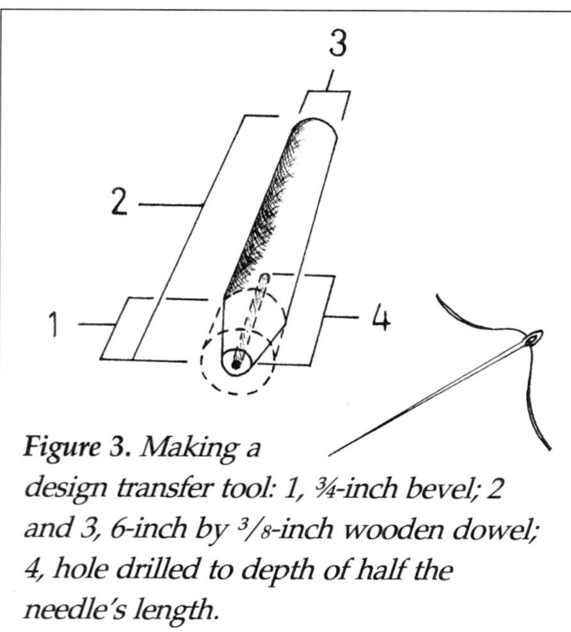

Figure 3. Making a design transfer tool: 1, ¾-inch bevel; 2 and 3, 6-inch by $^3/_8$-inch wooden dowel; 4, hole drilled to depth of half the needle's length.

threaded half into epoxy or good glue, such as carpenter's glue, and insert that end into the hole in the dowel, turning the needle while you do so. Add more glue if necessary to ensure that the area around the needle is solidly filled. Wipe off any excess, and let the dowel stand overnight in an upright position. You can temporarily use tape to make certain the needle remains straight while the glue hardens. Then remove the temporary tape and trim, shape, and tape the handle as shown in figure 2. When not in use, insert the needle into a cork or like object to protect the point.

Dental Tool for Scraping

I use a second dental tool as a pick, chisel, and scraper in areas that are very difficult to reach with ordinary tools. I used a Dremel tool to modify the cutting edge, then finished it with a stone. The final length of the blade is slightly less than $^1/_{32}$-inch. Although this tool can be done without, it makes carving gunstocks a lot easier, and I highly recommend that it be among those in your toolbox.

File Rifflers

File rifflers can be purchased at shops dealing in hobby woods, exotic woods, and materials used in furniture making, as well as hobby shops and jeweler supply stores. Do not confuse them with rasp rifflers, which are too harsh for use on gunstocks. Of the two shown, riffler *H* is the workhorse. I use it to remove took marks, to point up design side walls, and in some instances for final shaping. Riffler *G* is not as suited for final shaping; I use it strictly for removing tool marks and high spots in the background. These tools are not essential, but they make gunstock carving easier and faster.

Mill File Set

I use mill files for the same purpose as the rifflers, but on a smaller scale. Their size and variety of shapes allow better access to the more

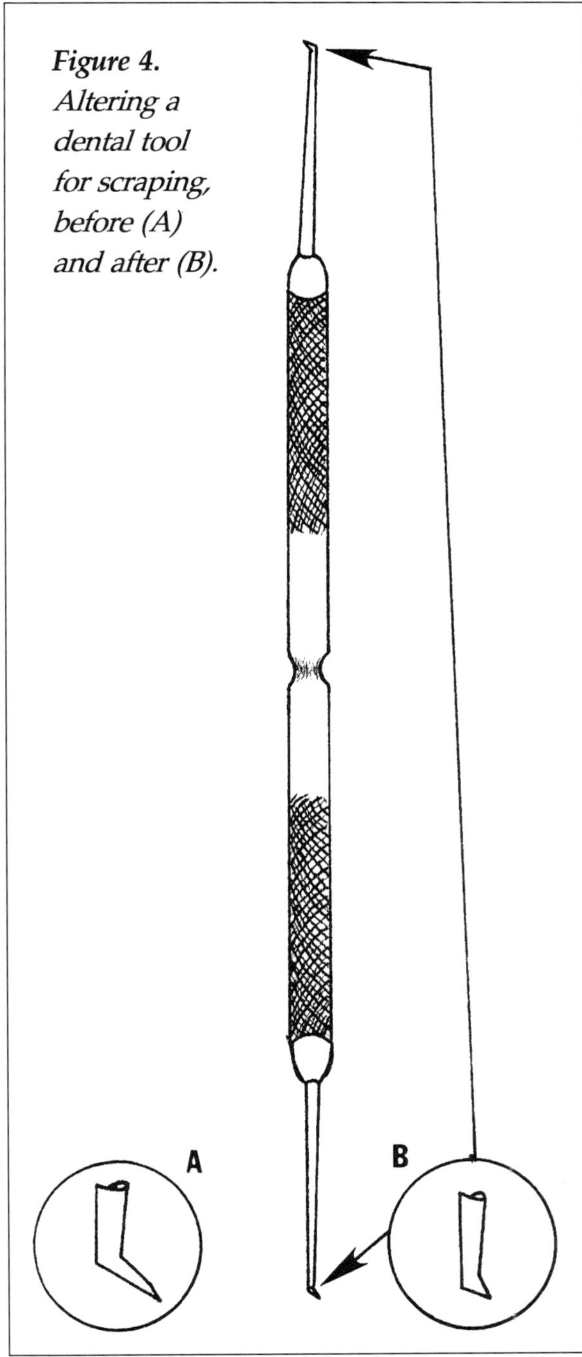

Figure 4. Altering a dental tool for scraping, before (A) and after (B).

difficult areas and help in shaping specific areas of the design. I consider a mill file set to be a must.

Scratch Awl

Chances are you already have this item lying around the house somewhere. If not, you can pick one up inexpensively at a discount hardware store or a flea market. For stock use, you'll need to round off the awl's sharp point slightly, using emery paper or a mill file, so that it will take a bit of pressure for the awl to indent wood. This is a necessary tool.

Hook-Bill Knife

The hook-bill is a type of X-acto blade that excels in the incised work common to carvings on flintlocks. Otherwise, this blade is seldom used, and it is not a necessary tool unless you intend to work on black-powder rifles such as the Pennsylvania long rifle.

Toothbrushes

The toothbrush no doubt is used for more things other than its original purpose than any other brush made. I recommend having two toothbrushes in your tool kit: one to brush the area clean of shavings during the carving process, and the other to apply stain or remove excess wet finish after the carving is complete. So that you don't confuse the two, use toothbrushes of different colors. These are must items.

Magnet

An ordinary magnet, although not absolutely essential, is useful to have on hand to clean up steel-wool fibers from the carving and surrounding work area.

Assorted Carving Tools

I also own a set of six Garrett Wade carving tools sold under the name Henry Taylor. Three are shown here. They are exceptionally good tools imported from England. I bought them on a day when I felt like being nice to myself. For their exceptional quality, they are not all that expensive, and they deserve looking into should you decide to add some special tools to your kit. Chisel *N* is a skew chisel. It serves the same functions as the slant-blade knife but on a much larger scale. I have found this tool to be excellent for removing large amounts of wood from background areas and have begun to use it more and more; it has really become a favorite. Chisel *O* is a straight-chisel, and *P* is a bent chisel. Each has a straight cutting edge at 90 degrees to the handle. The shank of the bent chisel curves slightly upward. This chisel is seldom used in any woodcraft profession, but it serves well in getting to areas where the shank of a straight chisel would touch wood and cause damage to that area. All three chisels are easy to work with and hold a fine cutting edge for long periods of extensive use. Though they are not necessary, I highly recommend them.

These are the tools that I use. They include everything I find necessary plus other items that save time or effort. After you have done several carvings, you can better decide what tools best serve your purposes.

In addition to working tools, there are several materials that you should have on hand at all times. All carvers will need the items on list A, and those who will be stock-carving on a larger scale will need those on list B as well. The items that have not yet been discussed will be explained in the text as they appear.

List A

Steel wool (000) or (0000)
Sandpaper (fine and extra fine)
Masking tape
Tracing paper
Workbench pad
Stock protection pads
Stain (optional)
Stock finish
Combination varnish and lacquer remover

List B

Chisels
Sharpening stones (coarse, medium, and
   fine)

Slip
Strop
Pantograph or Magna-Jector
Drawing pens and pencils
Assorted stains
Spray gun or finish application brushes
Drawing display photo albums

CUTTING EDGES AND SHARPENING

Every carver should fully understand what takes place when a tool begins to enter wood so that he will realize why it is important to maintain the highest degree of sharpness on all cutting edges at all times.

No matter how sharp a cutting edge may be, there is always some degree of crushing before a blade enters the wood and during its progress through the wood. Wood will offer resistance to the blade trying to enter it, and this is responsible for the crushing. The cutting edge of the tool determines how much crushing will take place. With a dull cutting edge, there is a larger surface area meeting the wood, and the force behind it results in a higher degree of crushing before entry of the blade. With a properly sharpened blade, less surface area of the cutting edge bears onto the wood, resulting in less resistance, less crushing, and easier penetration with less effort. Torn edges, chips and rough surface areas result from dull cutting edges. Also, with a dull edge, when the carver applies pressure, the tool is more prone to skip or ride into another area and result in damage.

It is imperative, therefore, to take the time to sharpen tools properly at the very first indication of dulling. Trying to save time by not giving attention to tools when they need it is simply not worth the potential for disaster. A dull cutting edge will produce shoddy workmanship and many possibilities for irreparable damage.

The bulk of your carving will be done with the X-acto #16 slant-blade knife, and its sharpness is of prime importance. If you intend but an occasional carving, you likely will be replacing dull blades with new ones and thus will not be too concerned with sharpening knife blades. If you intend to do a large amount of carving, on the other hand, you will want to sharpen dull blades as a means of keeping costs down and to ensure that your blades are up to desired standards at all times.

Knife blades are ground equally on both sides. The degree at which the bevels are ground will determine the sharpness and duration of the cutting edge. Most everyday knives

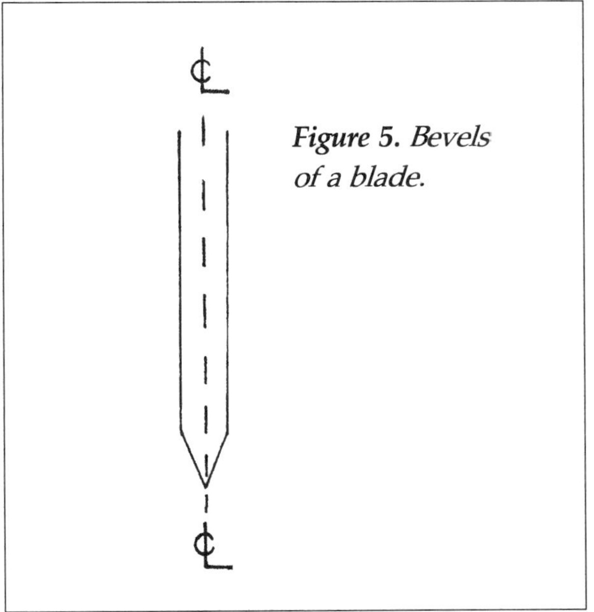

Figure 5. Bevels of a blade.

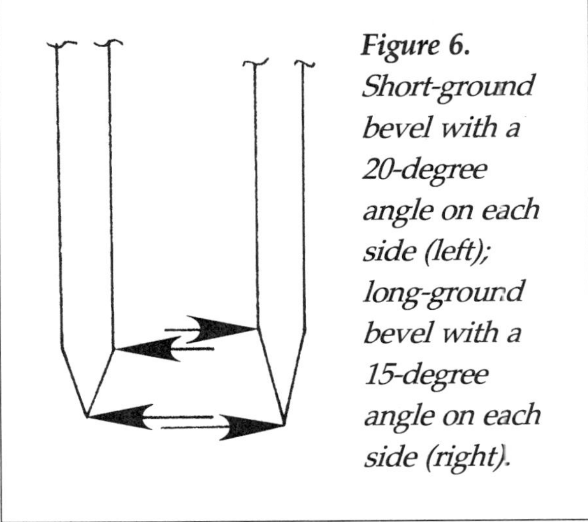

Figure 6. Short-ground bevel with a 20-degree angle on each side (left); long-ground bevel with a 15-degree angle on each side (right).

are ground with bevels at an angle of 20 degrees. Hobby and carving knifes and other tools with cutting edges, including those for stock carving, are generally ground closer to 15 degrees, referred to as long-ground. A 20-degree angle on a cutting tool or blade is termed short-ground, and it is generally insufficient for woodworking. A tool or knife that is long-ground will have a cutting edge that is far superior for stock carving, but it does not hold an edge as well and has the decided disadvantage of needing to be sharpened more frequently. All that is needed to bring back the edge during use, however, will be to strop it a few times. Stropping also will give the desired edge to a new X-acto blade. In either case, you will need to constantly touch up your blade to maintain the edge during the course of carving. To restore an older blade, one or two runs over a fine stone followed by five or six passes over a strop are generally all that is needed.

Even with this treatment, there will come a time when a knife blade has to be replaced. This is because the blade is shortened with each sharpening. Nevertheless, a single blade will give many hours of service on numerous stocks before you will have to replace it.

To sharpen the X-acto #16 slant-blade, there is a fairly easy method you can use so you do not have to be overly concerned with getting the degree of the bevel exactly right. Place the blade at full depth in the knife handle. Hold the handle so that the cutting edge and blade housing lie flat against the stone at a 90-degree angle to the stone's length (fig. 7). Place your index finger so that the tip of the finger rests on the blade at the point where it enters the handle, while your thumb and middle finger hold the handle securely just behind the index finger. In this position, the end of the handle will be resting in the remaining two fingers. Now raise the handle just high enough with those two fingers to permit the blade housing to clear the stone,

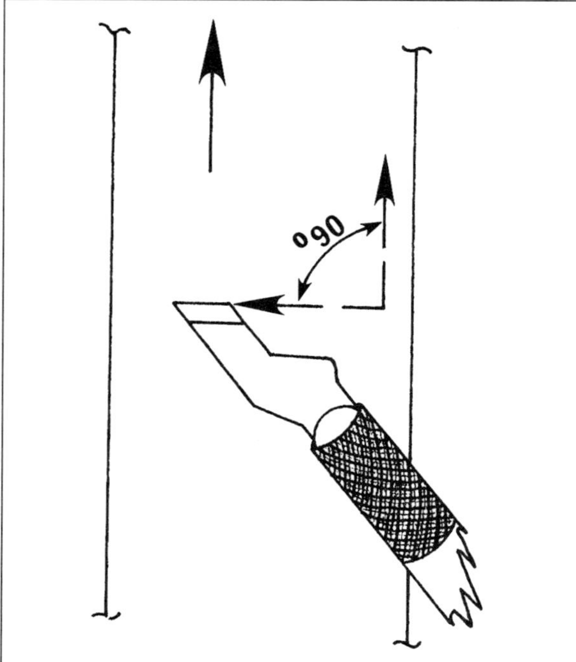

Figure 7. Arrows depict direction of stroke and cutting edge of blade at a 90-degree angle to the stone.

allowing only the extreme edge of the blade to be touching. This will create a tripod effect with the blade, tip of the thumb, and tip of one finger touching the stone (fig. 8).

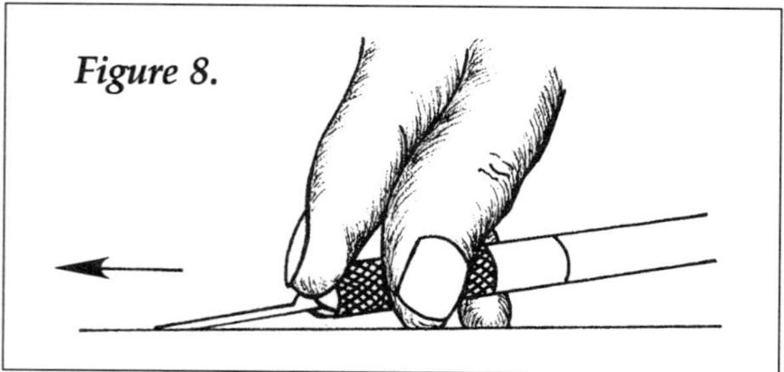

Figure 8.

Make sure the stone is well oiled. With just slight pressure on the finger resting on the blade, push forward as though trying to shave a very thin slice from the stone. When sharpening a cutting edge, always do so by pushing away, never drawing the blade toward you. Do not apply excessive downward pressure on the blade. Apply just enough pressure to the cutting edge to ensure that it remains in contact with the stone. Stop the stroke before the blade

reaches the edge of the stone. Repeat this procedure with the blade's opposite side. Always alternate strokes; the aim is to take off equal amounts of metal on both sides. With a very dull blade, repeat this procedure until each side receives ten to fifteen strokes using a medium-grade stone, followed by four or five strokes with the fine-grade stone. If the blade is not too badly dulled, you will need only the fine-grade stone. This will produce a long-ground bevel to the blade.

After the blade is sharp, strop each side alternately, five to ten strokes. Once a blade has been sharpened in this manner, the proper angle will be set in. To return the cutting edge to its peak of sharpness during use, all that will be necessary is to run the blade over a strop a few times when it appears to be dulling. Only an occasional run over a stone will be necessary. This procedure will become second nature after you have done it several times.

Sharpening Stones

If you intend to do a sizable amount of carving, you will find it necessary to have a good set of oil stones, as you will be using tools that will be nearly impossible to maintain without them. It's best to have three stones: coarse, medium, and fine grades. A single all-purpose stone will not be sufficient to achieve the needed cutting edge. The coarse stone is used to form an angle on a new tool that does not meet requirements or to reshape the angle of a well-used tool. The medium stone is used to remove burrs and to

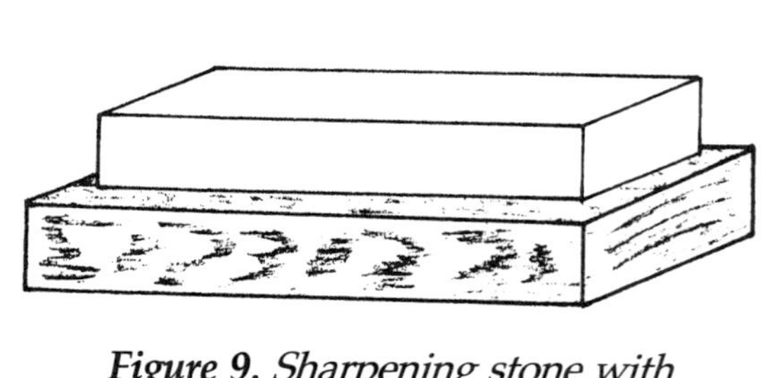

Figure 9. Sharpening stone with wooden base.

polish areas left rough by the coarse stone. It, too, can be used to shape a bevel, but with greater effort than the coarse stone, as it does not remove metal as quickly. The fine stone is the hardest of the three and is used to put the finished edge on the tool.

When purchasing a sharpening stone, inspect it very carefully. Though many brands are known for quality, quality does differ from stone to stone regardless of natural origin or brand. Do not accept one that has flake loss or a chip. I recommend using stones that are seated in a base. Many come in a wooden case with the stone seated in the bottom half; this holds it securely while in use. A ½- to 1-inch-thick stone measuring 6 by 2½ inches is a good size to work with in this type of setup.

For the past ten years, I have been using a setup with similar-size stones adhered to a triangular wooden block. I can turn this block to expose whichever stone I wish to use. I've found this setup extremely convenient.

The triangular stone-holding block extends at each end beyond the length of the stones. This enables the extended portions to rest in slots cut into the top portions of the vertical posts that are attached at each end of the base. The two stones not in use prevent the holding block from shifting during use, as they fit between the vertical posts. The unit shown features Washita oil stones of good quality and can be purchased at retail stores that deal in hobby woods and furniture-making tools. Before investing in individual stones, consider the triangle setup; it is nearly the same price.

When using stones, don't be a miser with oil, but don't use so much that it drips off. Use just enough to cover the stone without having it run over the sides. Oil serves to keep small particles of steel from becoming embedded in the stone. The cleaner the oil, the better the abrasive quality of the stone and the less chance of fouling its pores. The cleaner the stone, the quicker and better the cutting edge produced.

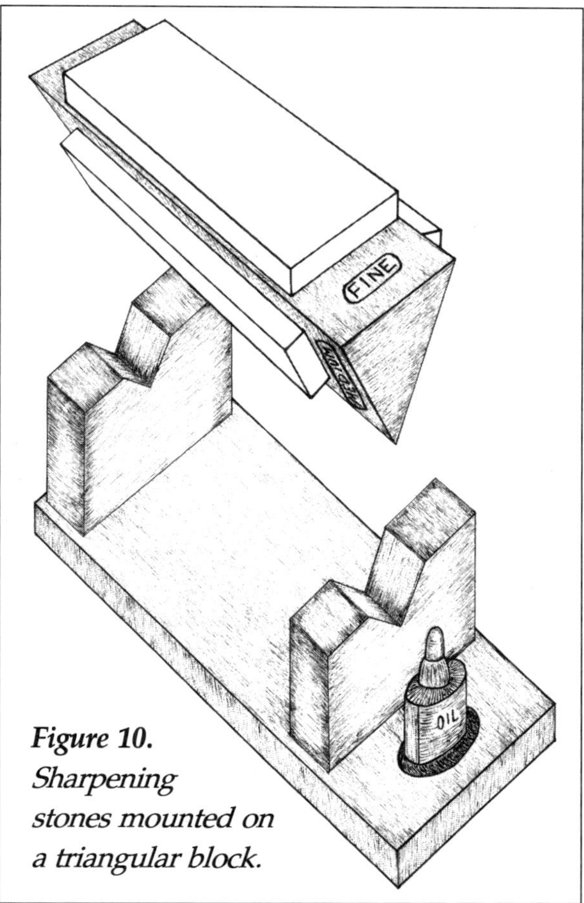

Figure 10. Sharpening stones mounted on a triangular block.

Most carvers sharpen every cutting tool in their arsenal before beginning a new project, rather than doing so when the need to use a particular tool arises. Depending on the number of cutting tools you may use, this can mean a rather lengthy sharpening session, during which the stone will have to be wiped clean and fresh oil applied numerous times. It's good practice to flush and wipe the stone two or three times after all tools have been sharpened. When the stones are not in use, be sure to wipe them clean and cover them to keep off dust and dirt. For ideal storage after a thorough cleaning, wrap a lightly oiled cloth around the stones and cover this with a thin plastic sheet draped over the top.

GOUGES

Store-bought carving tools have been ground to a bevel that is called a set-in, or proper ground, angle. Their sharpness, however, can be improved by a combination of light honing and stropping. This will improve the cutting ability by polishing the beveled surface and removing burrs. There are numerous shapes to gouges and chisels, and each type will require its own method of honing and stropping.

In most instances the bevel on a newly purchased tool will be 15 degrees. This bevel should be maintained until you try the tool. If you are not satisfied with it, the bevel can be changed by honing to a different bevel. The desired change is accomplished by raising or lowering the handle of the tool to a slightly higher or lower angle than the original angle and working the gouge toward its edge. If you don't have much experience sharpening tools, use moderation; alter the original set-in bevel by raising or lowering the handle of the tool to only a slightly higher or lower angle than the original angle. To alter the bevel, use the same procedure as sharpening, but hold the tool at the desired angle instead of the existing one.

If the bevel is set in at the desired angle, use a fine-textured stone to hone the outer bevel. Make sure the surface of the stone is well covered with oil, then hold the gouge at an angle that allows the bevel to lie flat on the surface of the stone (fig. 11). As you move the gouge along the length of the stone, twist it (see arrows) so that the entire bevel is worked. It's important to maintain the same angle for the bevel during the twisting process and to hold the shank of the tool at a 90-degree angle to the length of the stone. Otherwise an unevenness will develop along the cutting edge, leaving areas of dullness. Do this procedure slowly to ensure better control over both the angle of the bevel and the degree the shank of the tool is held to the stone. It's important not to overdo the twisting motion; this will round over the corners, which will affect the manner in which the gouge cuts. Honing should continue until all of the beveled surface has been polished and there are no flat spots along the cutting edge.

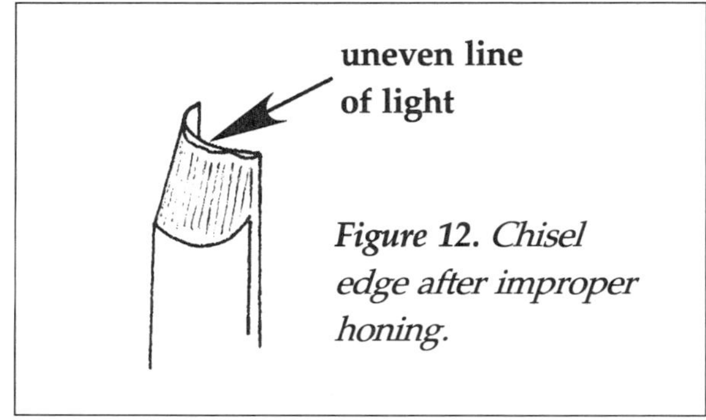

Figure 12. Chisel edge after improper honing.

Another practice is to sharpen the gouge much like the chisel by pushing toward the cutting edge while performing the twisting motion. While this does give faster results, I've found that there is a tendency to lower the handle when nearing the end of the stone. This is referred to as "rolling," a serious fault that is to be avoided, as the bevel will become rounded instead of having a uniform straight slant along its entire curve. Here, too, care must be

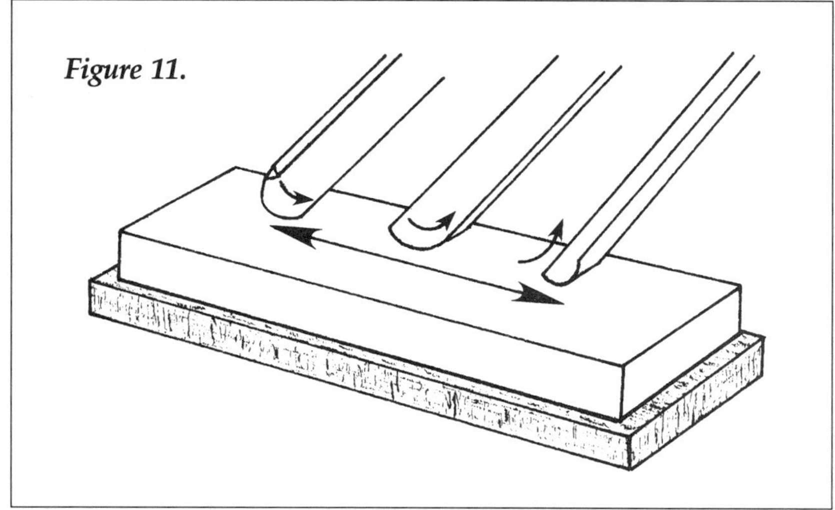

Figure 11.

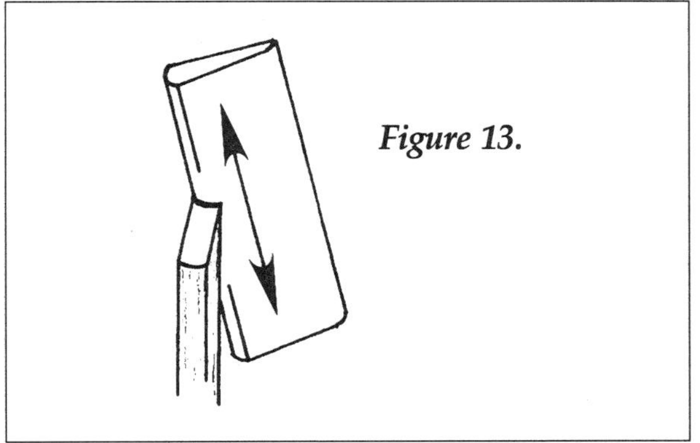

Figure 13.

taken not to overdo the twisting motion. I recommend to those who have this tendency to hone the outer portion of the gouge by performing the twisting motion while holding the tool at the proper angle to maintain the bevel and the shank at 90 degrees to the stone and to move the tool back and forth along the stone's length instead of in the direction of the cutting edge.

Some carvers have a block of hardwood running the length of the stone that enables them to rest the shank of the tool on the block

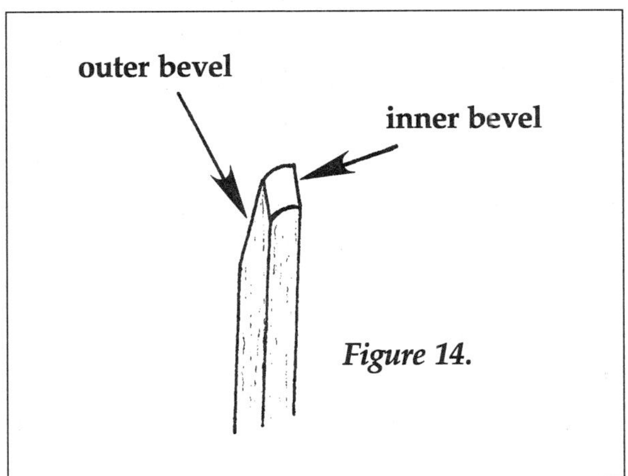

outer bevel

inner bevel

Figure 14.

while the bevel of the gouge is resting at the proper angle on the stone. With both hands on the tool, they grasp the handle firmly, placing the fingers of one hand near the cutting edge to ensure the tool rides solidly on the stone, and move the tool the length of the stone at the same angle. The leading finger of the hand grasping the handle is against the block, which presents

a uniform distance of the cutting edge from the block as the tool is being moved along the length of the stone. Otherwise, any deviation of distance between the block and the cutting edge will alter portions of the degree in the bevel. This will result in a waving effect, which often happens when a block or guide is not used. I've not personally tried a guide block, as my gouges have square shanks and would not ride evenly during the twisting motion. Some carvers might find that this method works for them, however.

The next step in honing a gouge is to form and polish the inner bevel. For this a special stone known as a slip-stone is used. A slip-stone is a wedge-shaped stone with two different rounded edges to enable you to hone gouges of different curves and sizes. To use a slip-stone, apply oil to the stone and rub the stone back and forth along the inside portion of the gouge (fig. 13). Hold the stone at an angle to the gouge as near as possible to that which was done to the outer bevel. A tool that has both an inner and outer bevel can be used with the hollow side up or down. In either instance the opposing bevel gives a lift to the handle that prevents the need to hold the tool nearly flat with the wood, which could result in the handle causing damage to surrounding or previously carved areas. The lift created by the opposing bevel also helps prevent the cutting edge from digging in or skipping.

Many professional carvers hone the inner bevel from a quarter to half the length of the outer bevel (fig. 14). The actual sharpening of

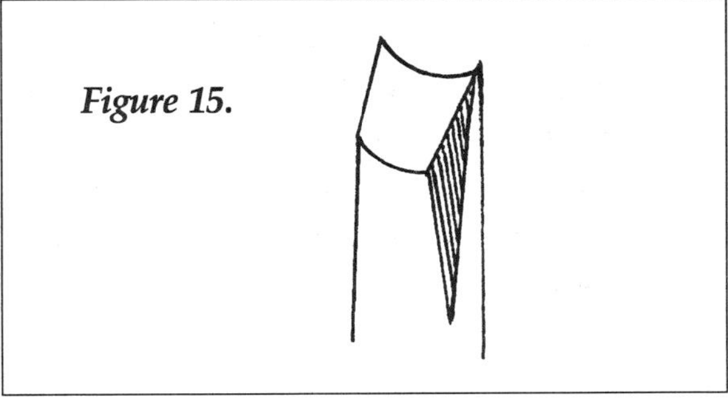

Figure 15.

the gouge is accomplished by honing the inner bevel after the outer bevel has been honed. Some carvers customize a gouge by removing the corner of the heel as shown in figure 15. Some even round over the heel of the bevel. I feel that these refinements are unnecessary. Experience will teach a carver which bevels and tools work best. I suggest that novice carvers keep the preset bevels until they become more expert at handling the tool.

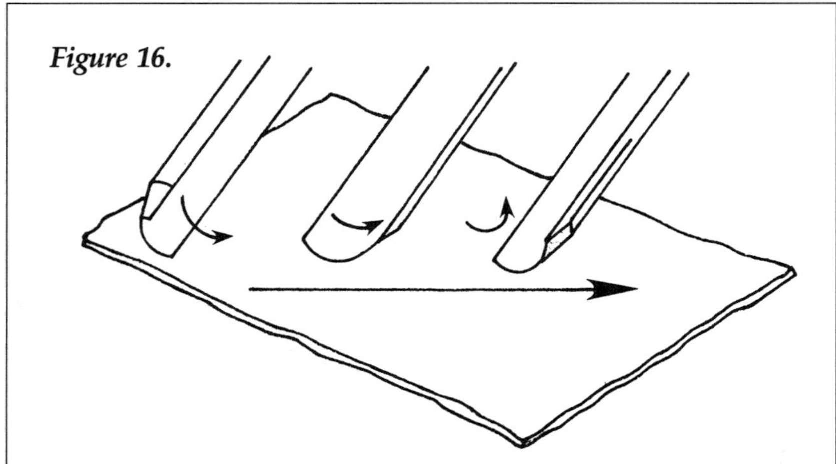

Figure 16.

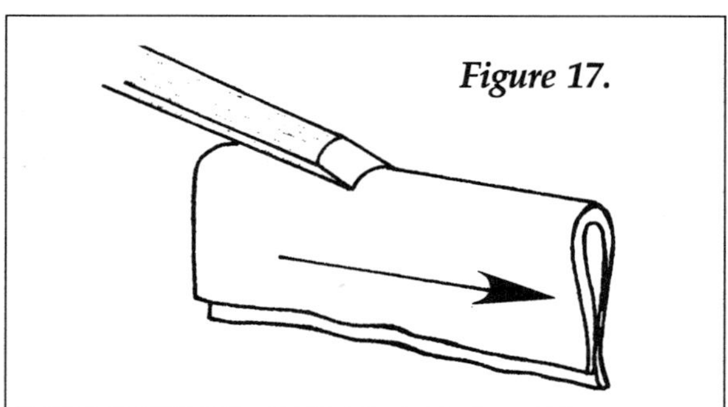

Figure 17.

Honing any cutting tool will produce burrs or a thin ribbon of metal along the cutting edge that must be removed by stropping. To do this, I use leather dressed with a commercially sold abrasive wax produced specifically for polishing and bringing a fine edge to cutting tools, the same wax used by barbers to sharpen razors.

To strop a tool, draw the gouge across the strop-slip as shown in figure 16 (see arrows). As you draw the gouge, twist it, too. Strop the entire outer edge in this manner. The inner bevel is stropped using a piece of treated soft leather folded to meet the shape of the gouge and drawn across the cutting edge as shown in figure 17. Some prefer to draw the gouge along a firmly held strop-slip instead of drawing the strop-slip along the tool. It's usually only necessary to strop both the inner and outer bevels a few times each to remove any burrs or excess metal caused by the honing. If the tool becomes dull during use, restore the cutting edge by stropping both edges several times. Eventually, during the course of usage, stropping alone will not be enough to restore the edge and the gouge will have to be honed and stropped again to ensure peak performance. When this is necessary, you don't have to rehone the entire bevel. Lightly honing the outer bevel by holding the handle just slightly higher than the previous honing will create a slight additional bevel along the cutting edge. This can be done several times before it has any significant effect on the overall degree of the outer bevel.

To correct an edge that has become seriously out of shape (fig. 18), hold the tool at a right angle to the stone and rub it until the edge

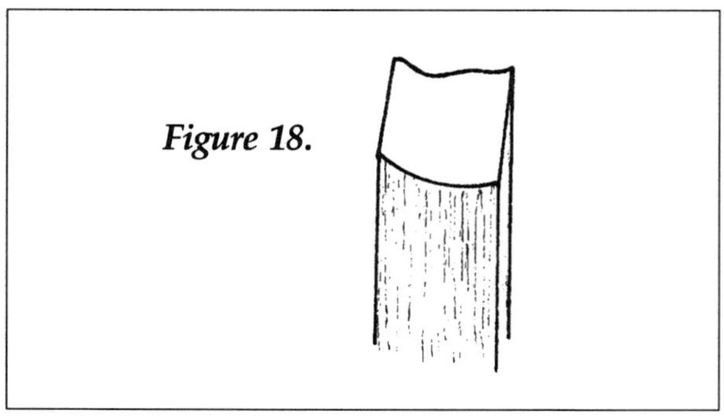

Figure 18.

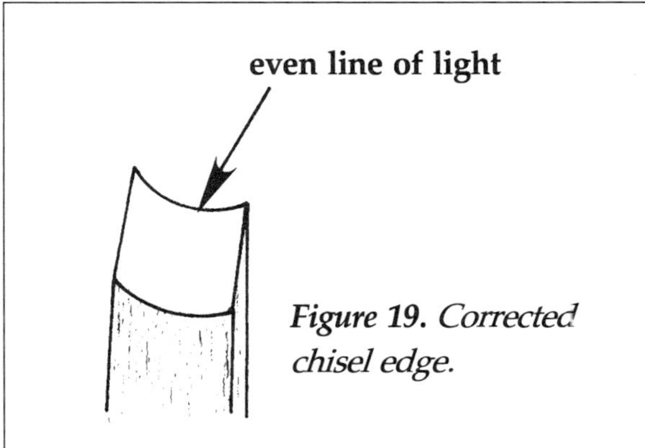

Figure 19. Corrected chisel edge.

once again becomes uniform across its entire length. For this type of operation a coarse stone is necessary. Both the outer and inner bevels will then have to be honed to eliminate the flat edge and establish the newly shaped and sharpened cutting edge. A well-sharpened carving tool will leave a burnished look to the wood as it cuts.

CHISELS

Chisels fall into two categories: ones with a straight cutting edge and ones with a skewed

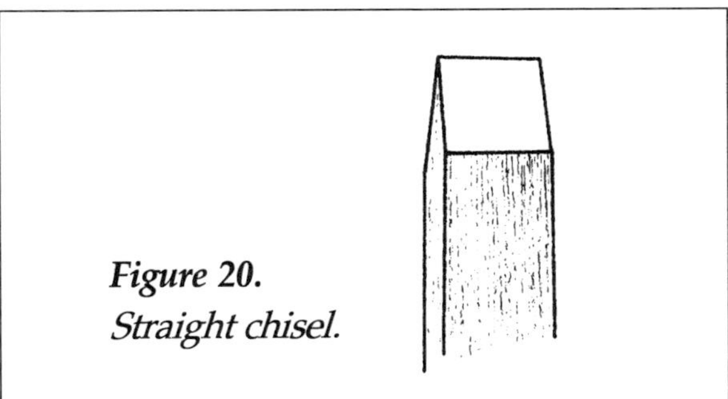

Figure 20. Straight chisel.

Figure 21. Skewed chisel.

cutting edge. While either might have a variation in the shank, each is distinguished more by the line of the cutting edge. Both the straight and skewed chisel have an equally angled bevel on each side to form the cutting edge. As with the gouge, burrs and possibly a thin line of excess metal will be created by honing. These can be removed by lightly drawing the cutting

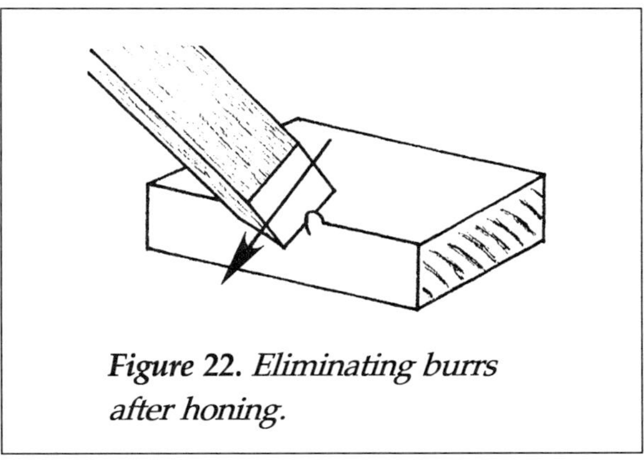

Figure 22. Eliminating burrs after honing.

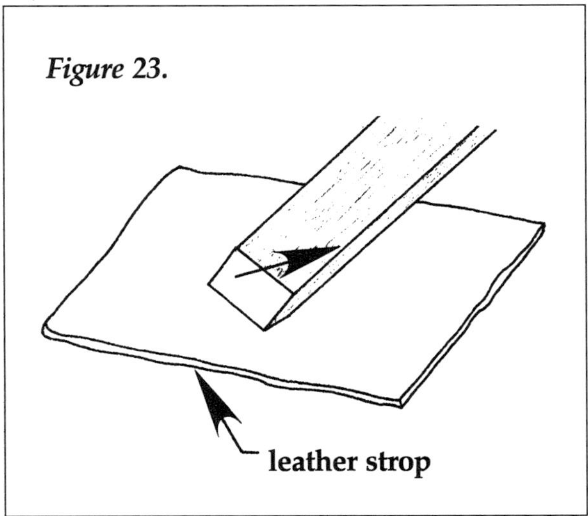

Figure 23.

edge across a block of wood. This may dull the cutting edge just a bit, but the dulling is so minimal that peak sharpness can be brought back during the stropping procedure. Both bevels of the chisel should be shaped identically and stropped in the manner shown in figure 23. As with the gouge, the chisel can be restored several times to peak sharpness during use by honing each side at a slightly higher angle.

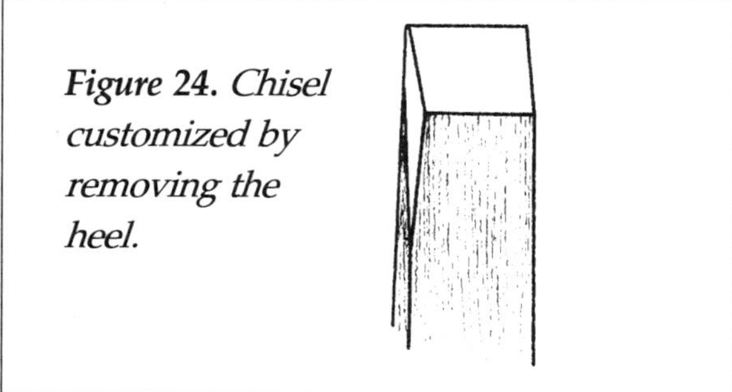

Figure 24. Chisel customized by removing the heel.

Eventually, both sides will have to be honed to restore the original set bevel.

If desired, the chisel can be customized by removing the thickness of the heel. Some carvers believe this modification allows the tool to work corners and curves more easily. Both corners of one side are generally removed.

PARTING TOOL

This tool is really just two straight chisels joined together to form a V-chisel. The parting tool seems to be the most difficult to sharpen, yet it, more so than any other tool, must be sharpened correctly to avoid serious damage to a carving during its use. The problem that occurs during sharpening is the formation of a hook at the point of the intersecting sides (fig. 25 *A*). This condition generally becomes worse when a slip-stone that has become rounded is used; this prevents the proper honing of the inner bevel. Instead, it produces a slight rounding that creates a blunt area at the point of the intersecting sides (*B* top). To correct this, remove the hook by honing the outer bevel in a manner that will create a rounding of the intersecting outer bevels (*B* bottom). This will restore the cutting edge to full sharpness by eliminating the blunt area (*C*). To help prevent this problem, use an Arkansas slip-stone, as it is a hard stone lest apt to wear as quickly. It is also hard enough to be shaped to have a sharp edge that will fit this type of tool.

With a small parting tool, which is used widely in gunstock carving, another undesirable condition often occurs during honing: one side of the tool is honed more so than the other. This causes a deep depression to one side near the intersecting point (*D*). To correct this condition you must form a new edge with the gouge. The entire cutting edge must be uniformly honed by holding the tool straight into the stone and rubbing back and forth until the depression is eliminated. This will leave a considerably large flat area along the entire range of the cutting edge. Once the uniform edge is accomplished, both

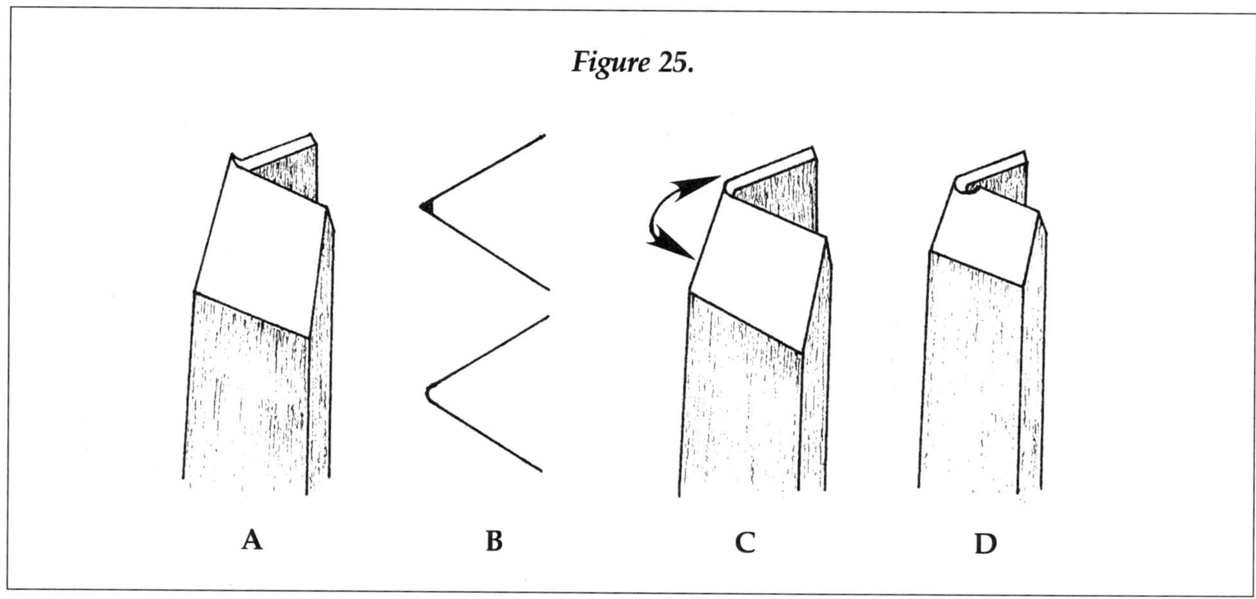

Figure 25.

the outer and inner bevels must be rehoned until the sharp cutting edge is reestablished.

The cutting edge of gouges and chisels must never be allowed to become concave (recessed in the center with the outer edges more forward) or convex (forward in the center with the outer edges more to the rear). Either condition must be corrected at the very first sign.

GUNSTOCK WOOD

A relatively small number of hardwoods meet the standards and have the characteristics necessary for gunstock wood. Unfortunately, since the mid-1960s, there has been a steady decline in the quality of wood used in the making of gunstocks. So pronounced is this decline that for a number of years those involved in or connected with the firearms trade have been referring to the majority of stocks now produced as being made of "Early American orange-crate." There is simply no comparison between stock wood before the sixties and today. Because of the prohibitive cost and unavailability of quality wood, even most premier firearms manufacturers are forced to use stock woods that just a few years ago barely would have qualified for use on their less expensive production model. This becomes evident if you remove the finish from a stock of recent vintage. Most European stocks are of walnut imported from the United States, as most of the suitable wood from their respective areas has neared depletion. The better-grade woods still available are primarily used for furniture veneer, as it brings a higher price this way than when sold as a solid block for gunstock use. Quality stock wood can still be obtained, but the cost is fast becoming out of reach for most of us.

It could safely be estimated that as much as 85 percent of the wood you will carve will be American walnut, more popularly known as black walnut. This estimate may be conservative, especially if carvings are limited to stock

woods of medium- to low-cost firearms. This is by no means to imply that all American black walnut is of inferior grade. Without question, the better grades can be considered some of the finest stock wood available. Nowadays, better wood of any type is usually found only when dealing with stocks made before the mid-sixties, custom stocks, or stocks found on extremely expensive firearms. Otherwise, poorer grades of wood are that which you encounter.

Several conditions determine the quality of black walnut, and other woods as well. Of prime consideration is where the tree grew. There is a marked difference between the trees of the same species grown in tropical, arid, or balanced climates. An equally important factor is soil. The same species of tree grown in sandy marshlands, or rich, humus soil will be affected by the medium in which it grew. The combination of climate and soil condition has an effect on the porosity, grain, color, and weight of the wood, which is gauged by cubic foot.

Profit considerations determine what the better grades of wood will be used for. The wood that is most suitable for gunstocks—that which is most porous, flatter in color, and has less grain—is often earmarked for that purpose. When comparing raw stock woods of modern-day rifles and shotguns that haven't been prettied up with fillers and a nice, shiny finish, you will find that shotgun woods are generally of a better quality than rifle woods. This is because shotguns do not require nearly as large a block of wood. The relatively shorter one or two blocks needed for shotguns are often the leftovers from the better grades that are used for veneer.

The carver does not need to know the details about all woods used in the making of gunstocks. You will be carving whatever your or a client's firearm is made from, and regardless of the grade of wood, carving procedures remain basically the same, except that some require more care during certain steps than others. Some woods are much preferred over others even in the average class range, as they have a lesser degree of fuzzing and less risk of splitting or chipping.

Obviously, I prefer using the better grade of walnut, which is rich in color and devoid of deep pores. English walnut is such a wood, but it has become a rarity. Top-grade English walnut will allow a clean cut from any direction with little fear of splitting or chipping out critical detailed areas. Using a properly sharpened tool leaves a shine to this wood with nearly every cut.

The characteristics of bird's eye maple makes it my least favored to carve. The eyes, which are predominant throughout the wood, are often areas that need to be carved. This wood presents a high potential for chipping should cuts run through the eyes.

With luck, the gunstock wood you encounter will be of the better grades, but don't count on it. If not, you will still use the same procedures, the same common sense, but increased caution.

3

Design Selection and Preparation

The information in this chapter is directed at both those who intend to carve for themselves only and those who wish to carve on a professional level.

Quality designs and the ability to execute them as carvings will determine a carver's success as a professional. Designs are unquestionably the lifeblood of a carver, and their importance cannot be overstated. Some carvers develop a recognizable style or degree of perfection in their work. Their craftsmanship is a testimony of their creativity and ability to perform.

The major obstacle for those who would like to carve but feel they cannot seems to be the lack of a schooled or natural ability to draw. There is no question that drawings are important in gunstock carving and that either trained or natural ability is a strong advantage, but there are alternatives. Near ready-made designs are available at the library in the form of photographs or drawings. There you have access to every species of wildlife in the world, as well as floral and border design patterns, all available at no cost. Other sources of designs are magazines, advertisements, and greeting cards. Clients will sometimes bring their own designs to be carved as well as some they think you may be interested in having. The supply is unlimited.

Once you have found an interesting subject or border matter, you need to consider the image's degree of clarity and in some cases the degree of alteration that will be necessary. Do not be concerned with the size of the original to be copied. It can be reduced or enlarged mechanically to the appropriate size.

To make duplications from photographs or drawings, you can use tracing paper, a photocopier, a pantograph, or a Magna-Jector. Which method you should use at any given time depends largely on the situation. When using tracing paper, I always use the magni-viewer (discussed in chapter 2) as it helps me to pick up lines that I might otherwise miss.

If the source of your material is the library, make use of the photocopier that is usually available at a small cost. It will save a great deal of time and effort. The type of copier that has enlarging and reducing capabilities is ideal but is generally not available at libraries. A photocopy is preferable for library material so that you will not damage the resources that are there for others to use. Tracing a photo or drawing will leave an indentation on the material.

For enlarging and reducing, I generally prefer to use a mechanical device known as a pantograph. With this instrument, consisting of adjustable jointed rods in a roughly parallelogram form, you can reproduce a drawing on the same or a different scale. The end of one rod remains at a fixed position while rod attachment screws allow the rest of the unit to swivel. One rod end has a needlelike pin with which you trace over the lines of the image being copied, while another rod end holds a lead point that draws the image on a separate piece of paper. With the pantograph, you can make accurate copies on all scales with only minor touchup necessary afterward.

The first step in design reduction is to trace the outline of the configuration of the area to be carved on tracing paper. The reduced carving must fit within this outline. Place the tracing needle in the outermost setting and the lead in the innermost setting of the respective pantograph arms. Using the adjustment screws, adjust the scale marked on the arms to about the ¾-size marks. Stretch the arm holding the needle outward so there is an area of 12 inches between needle and lead to allow ample room to pivot the arms. Place the assembly onto the anchored guide post. Raise the arm holding the tracing pin slightly and slip the design under so it is at center with the needle, then lower the arm. Do the same with the outline sketch under the lead housing assembly. Secure the design that is being reduced with masking tape to prevent shifting. Tape or use a finger to hold the outline paper in place. Pick up the arm that holds the needle housing and move it so the needle can come to rest when the arm is lowered on the highest point of the design, the lowest point, and the width at each side. With each movement check to see where the tracing lead is in relation to the traced outline. It generally takes one or two times to adjust the arms with the adjustment screws to reduce the design to a size that will fit into the outlined area. With each arm adjustment either the design or the outline paper will have to be repositioned. Make enlargements in the same manner, but with the lead and needle housings, design, and outline paper reversed, and the scale adjustments on the pantograph arms raised instead of lowered.

Before you show a complete design or individual component to a client, it will need to be as near as possible to the appropriate size. Since stock shape and size vary, you generally will have to alter the size of the design, even if it is one you have used before. Not only is the pantograph capable of copying at the same scale, enlarging, and reducing, it also is a tremendous aid in determining the correct size of a design for a specific area in just two steps.

A Magna-Jector is easy to work with, but your tracings will not have the same accuracy as with a pantograph. This device uses a light bulb, mirror, and adjustable lens to project an image from one source to another. When the image is projected onto white paper, a reasonable accurate outline and heavier interior detail lines can be reproduced, but finer interior lines of the projected image are not easily traced and often are missed altogether. The copies thus produced generally are nowhere near the quality of those made with the pantograph, and the finished product will need considerable touching up. It is much easier to enlarge a copy with the Magna-Jector than to obtain a good-quality reduced copy. In either case, clarity suffers a great deal. There are times, though, when a Magna-Jector is very helpful for its enlarging ability, and therefore I consider it a useful tool. I often use a Magna-Jector to project an image onto a tracing of the configuration of a specific area of the stock in order to assess the exact size the subject matter should be for that area, and how it would look. The cost of this tool is reasonable for the less fancy models, and these serve as well as the more expensive models.

When selecting components for designs, do not limit yourself to only those that appeal to you. Everyone does not have the same tastes, and the carver who restricts himself to only what he likes not only may lose business but also will close the door to personal growth.

Hunters will constitute the majority of a stock carver's trade. This being so, pay particular attention to native foliage and wildlife. Most clients will choose the game they hunt. If the white-tailed deer is the predominant big-game animal in your area, you should have an abundant supply of white-tailed deer designs to show prospective clients. This does not mean that you should ignore other species of animals, but that you should have more designs in certain categories. Where I live, near the Chesapeake Bay, the white-tailed deer is the predominant big-game animal, but waterfowl and upland game bird hunting are equally popular, and I have found it necessary to have a sizable number of bird designs in addition to whitetail. Once you have a respectable amount of designs representative of the local area, add designs of animals and foliage of other states and even other countries, such as those in Africa.

A carver can never have enough designs and should see to it that their number increases as time goes by. In this way, you will continue to offer new things for steady clients to view and you will prevent stagnation, which would cause you to lose clients. Regardless of how many designs you may have available, you will come across clients who feel you do not have exactly what they are looking for. This is the time to create good will by going the extra mile to satisfy the client. Discuss what he or she is seeking, and set a time that the client may return to view the designs you will come up with. The effort is well worth it, and you will be surprised at how many clients feel you are their personal carver. Friendships and loyal clients develop from your willingness to put forth a little effort on their behalf. Such times should be welcomed, as they stimulate your creativity.

When putting together a collection of designs to show to clients, give considerable thought to individual components and completed designs before deciding with certainty that each will be included. You need to know with certainty that you have the ability to carve what is depicted in the drawing. This also applies to a design you are considering for your own use. If you have the slightest doubt about any aspect of the overall design, yet the design itself is of great appeal, try it out on a practice piece before you present it for client viewing or begin carving your own firearm. You can do this on a piece of walnut from a lumberyard, but if possible, obtain a damaged stock from a gunsmith or gun store that does restocking. Once the carving is completed, if it does not live up to its original appeal or is found to be too difficult to execute, nothing is lost. The time spent on the practice piece gives you an awareness of your ability while providing practice that over the long run will increase that ability. If the design is too difficult at this time, it need not be discarded. Instead, place it in a file under a heading for such designs and use it at a later date when your carving ability has improved. If, on the other hand, the carving turns out to meet all expectations, again, you have gained knowledge of your ability, have another exhibition stock to add to your display, and can justifiably place the design with others that you will show. In addition, you now know the amount of time required to complete the carving and can place a fair price on the work. Thus there are many advantages to doing practice pieces, and all top-notch carvers do them.

You can present selected components either separately or as a completed design. It's good to do both to a certain extent, presenting a fair number of completed designs and a large number of individual patterns for the main subject matter, along with an assortment of border designs. From these individual components, a client can more easily choose a border to be used with a particular subject. With both the subject matter and border design on tracing paper, it's a simple task to lay one over the other to get a general idea of how the final design will appear. At this time, you can explain to the client that changes can be made to the design to suit him.

Designs for client viewing can be presented in two ways. One way is to trace individual designs onto a sheet of heavy bond white paper and then trace over the lines in black ink. This will present an uncluttered, highly visible design. The other way is to present designs on tracing paper that is backed with white paper. Either is appropriate. In both cases, should the design incorporate a border and you wish to show how the feature of the design would look with another style of border, just block off a portion of the existing border with white paper and overlay that area with a different border design. Samples of all border designs should be on tracing paper for this purpose.

The manner in which components are assembled to form a completed design is a judgmental process that, although allowing a large degree of flexibility, is founded on sound principles that cannot be ignored. There are five considerations: choice of subject matter, border design (if any), proportion, harmony, and balance. Having a collection of compatible subject matter and border patterns increases the total number of possible completed designs and eliminates the need for a large quantity of completed designs. For example, four different views of a white-tailed deer and four different border patterns yield an overall total of sixteen different completed designs. With individual components, each new pattern for the main subject matter increases the number of possible designs by the total number of border patterns, and vice versa.

Thought and planning are necessary in order to assemble a harmonious design. It is essential to ensure the compatibility of the components that are in harmony with each other.

You would not want to use a deer as the subject matter on a goose gun or cactus as a border with a duck design.

When a form of wildlife is to be part of the design, you need to consider the things that are part of the animal's natural surroundings. Your design can feature wildlife engaged in some part of its daily routine, such as a whitetail drinking water from a stream or leaping a fallen log or fence. Action carvings are always received more favorably than those where an animal appears to be posing. Designs that show ducks or geese in flight with wings fully spread are far more appealing than those depicting them floating on water or roosting.

When one is used, the border is every bit as important as the main subject matter. Unless the border is a straight cut line, it should be appropriate to the main subject. For example, with a form of wildlife, the border might represent flora from the animal's natural environment. Also consider placement and the overall form of the design as appropriate to the shape of the gunstock. Subject matter and border design should appear to flow with the lines of the stock's configuration.

Generally, it will be necessary to alter only the placement of portions of the border pattern to ensure that the overall design is in proportion and that it fits into the configuration of the area. On occasion a featured subject will have to be reduced to fit into the intended area and to leave room for a border. It is a mistake not to alter a design to fit the stock's configuration, no matter how little the design overruns into an adjoining area.

Balance of design is another way of expressing the harmonious arrangement of a design's components with relation to each other and the configuration of the area with relation to the design. Harmony must be maintained between a single featured subject and the border, between two (or more) featured subjects, between a group of subjects and the border. Embellishments are discussed in chapter 10.

Any feature subject that is off center within an overall layout will probably detract from the balance of the design. Sometimes other objects must be placed within the border to achieve balance between a single subject and the border. For example, with a deer as the featured subject, the animal's natural surroundings of deep woods or farmland or a tree, stream, large rock, or fence can be added to the design to offset the imbalance of the lone deer and the border. Consider using additional portions of the border pattern in the form of a cluster if it is floral. Study the complete designs in chapter 10 to see the advantages and the method.

When carving two or more animal subjects of the same size, allowing the size of a male and female of the species, make sure the hooves are at the same level. If there is only one full leg showing on one animal due to the flow of the border and the size of the subjects, the smaller of the animals must be presented at its natural height with relation to the larger animal. There is some latitude with bird layouts in this instance, but very little with animal layouts. A good rule of thumb is that if two or more figures are in the same design and are to be presented at their relative natural sizes, then put the feet at the same level. To suggest distance with one or more animal or bird beyond a main subject, reduce the size and raise the background subject above the plane of the lowest part of the main subject. The greater the distance, the smaller and higher the background subject. When detailing an all-animal design with a distant bird in flight, the placement of the bird is judged from the height of the animal's back, not the lowest part of the main subject.

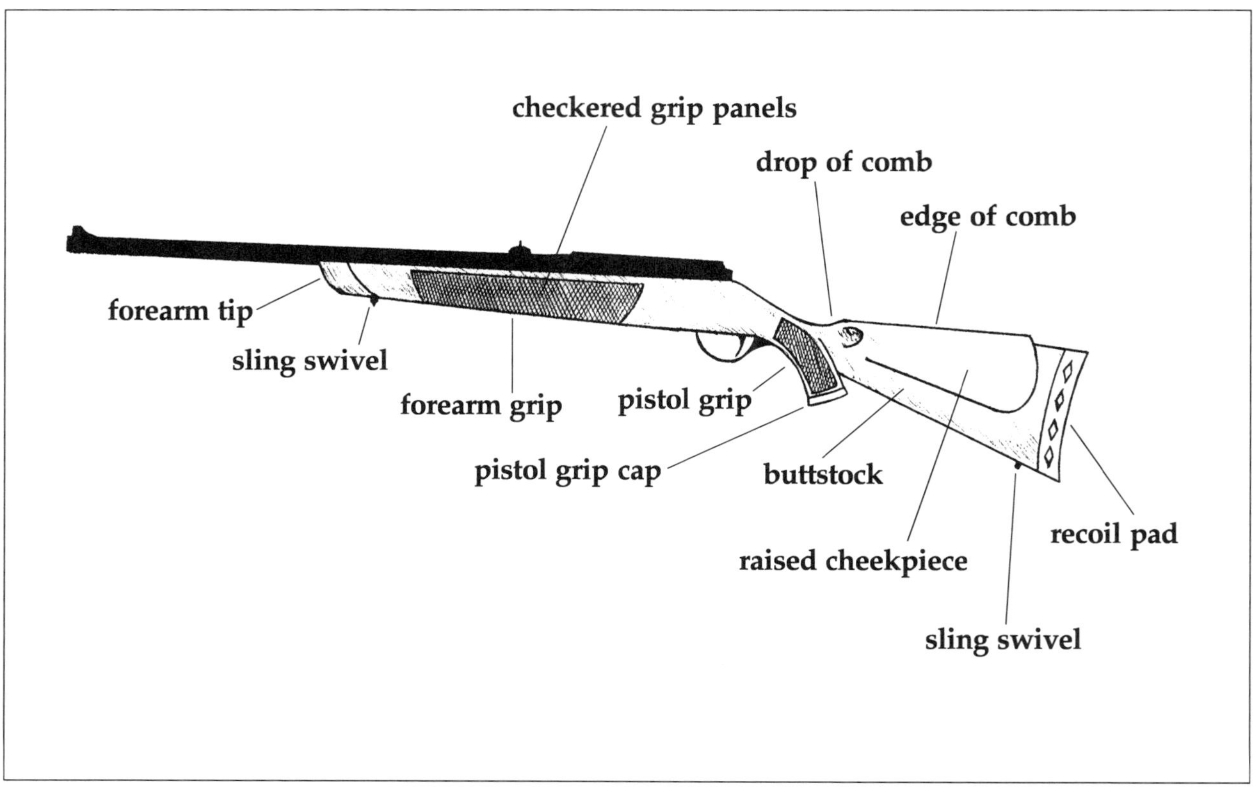

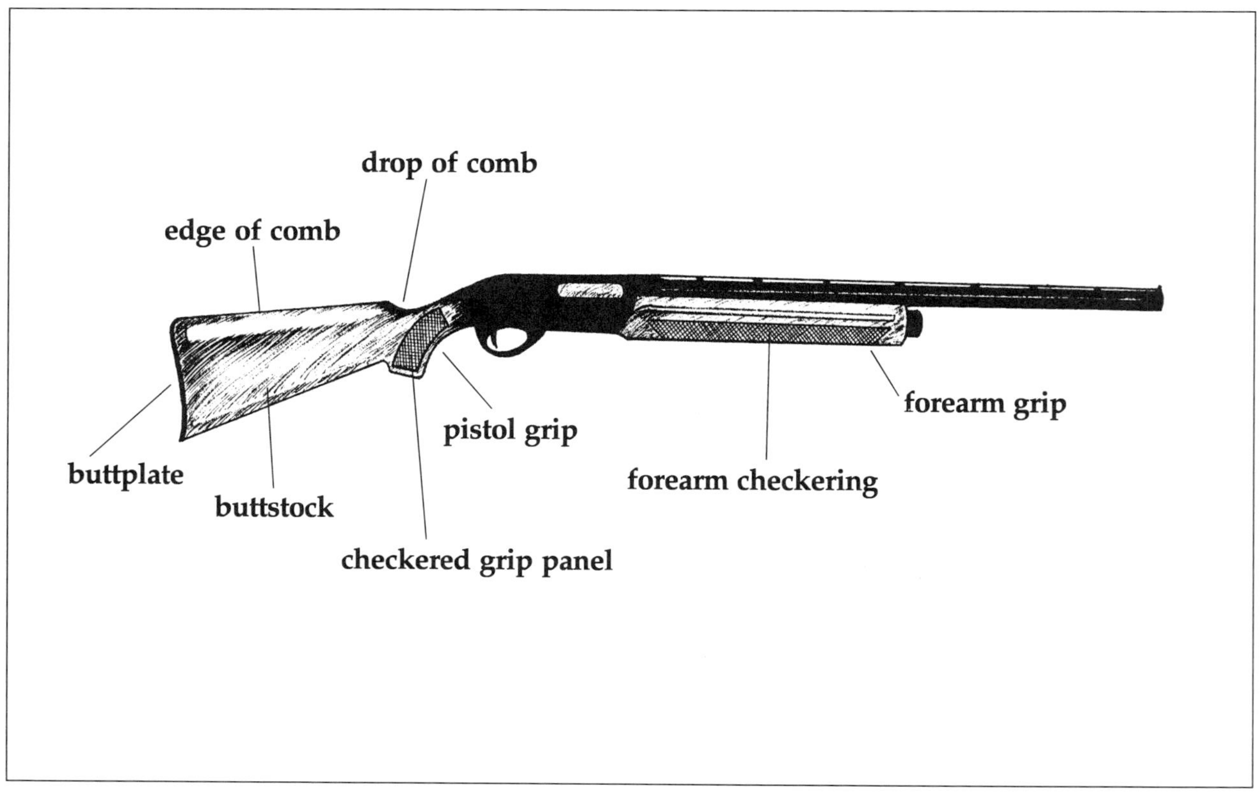

Figure 26. *Parts of a rifle (top) and a semiautomatic shotgun (bottom).*

4

Pattern Forming and Design Application

HIS CHAPTER EXAMINES THE PLACEMENT OF DE-
signs on the different areas of the gunstock.
There are seven basic areas for carving on a
gunstock: the forearm tip, forearm grip, side
receiver area, pistol grip, buttstock, pistol grip
cap, and buttplate. The last two are not often
called to be carved upon, and whether they can
be carved depends on the material they are
made from.

BUTTSTOCK

The buttstock is the part of the gunstock most
often carved. It is usually carved on the off side,
which is the side that faces away from the
shooter when the gun is held in firing position.

Depending on how elaborate a client wishes
the stock to be, it can also be carved on the
cheekpiece side. When carving on the cheekpiece side it is best to follow the basic guidelines set forth in the section covering cheekpiece
patterns.

To determine the size of the area that can
be carved, and to maintain the exact positioning of the design once it has been determined,
you need to be able to tape the design pattern
sheet to the stock, remove it, and place it back
in precisely the same position. For this purpose
you will need to use locator tapes, such as pieces
of 1-inch-wide masking tape.

On a straight stock (fig. 27), place a 1-inch
to 2-inch piece of tape lengthwise across the top

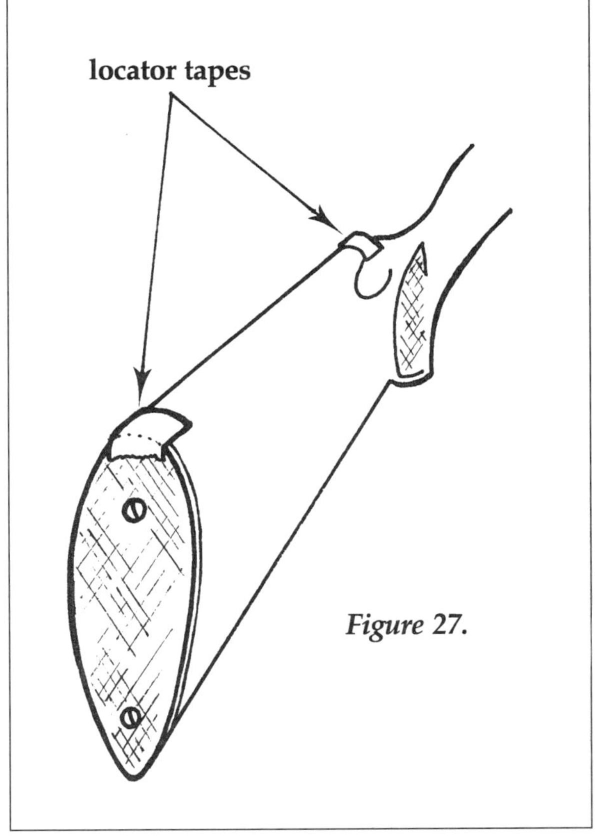

Figure 27.

of the stock with at least half its width on wood
and the remainder overlapping the buttplate or
recoil pad. Approximately half the length of the
tape should be on each side of the stock. Place
a second piece of tape in a similar manner across
the top of the stock at the drop of the comb just
above the grip. These are the top-of-stock forward and rear locator tapes.

Now, using a pad as protection against

damage, lay the stock on its cheekpiece side with the off side facing up. Place a full sheet of tracing paper onto the stock, carefully aligning one of the short edges of the paper with the inside edge of the buttplate or recoil pad. Keep the approximate center of the paper running lengthwise at the center of the side area of the buttstock from front to rear. This doesn't need to be exact; there's ample paper to compensate for any deviation. What's important is that the paper follows the contour of the inside edge of the buttplate where it meets the wood of the buttstock and that a nearly equal amount of paper running along that edge falls on each side of the buttstock. Be sure the positioning of the paper from front to rear enables the outline marking of the ball of thumb recess and rear border line of the checkered grip panel, which is the maximum forward area of a buttstock carving. Use a small piece of masking tape to secure the paper at each end at the center of the stock's side area. The paper should be lying flat against the wood and pulled reasonably taut

between the securing tapes but not so taut as to cause a pull line or ripple. The rear securing tape should overlap no more than ¼ inch onto the paper.

Once the paper is securely attached at each end, fold the upper half across the top of the stock, then bring it downward to lie flat on the opposite side (fig. 28). Check to make sure the forward locator tape at the top of the stock is only half covered by the paper. You may have to move this tape or trim the paper to allow half coverage. Then pull the paper lightly taut, and place a securing tape at the center of the paper along its edge on the cheekrest side. Working outward from this piece of tape, space additional securing tapes in spots along the entire edge. Fold the bottom half of the paper around the underside of the stock, and secure this edge in the same manner. When you are certain the paper is in the proper position with no pulls or ripples, place additional securing tapes on the buttplate and checkered area edges on the off side above and below the tapes at the center.

Make certain there are no ripples, folds, or creases anywhere in the paper on the side where the design will go.

Now turn the stock upright and look straight down at the locator tapes. Determine the center point of thickness of the stock, and draw a pencil mark running off the paper from the center onto each of the tapes (fig. 29). These marks should be about ½ inch in length, with about ¼ inch each on the paper and the tape. These marks will enable you to

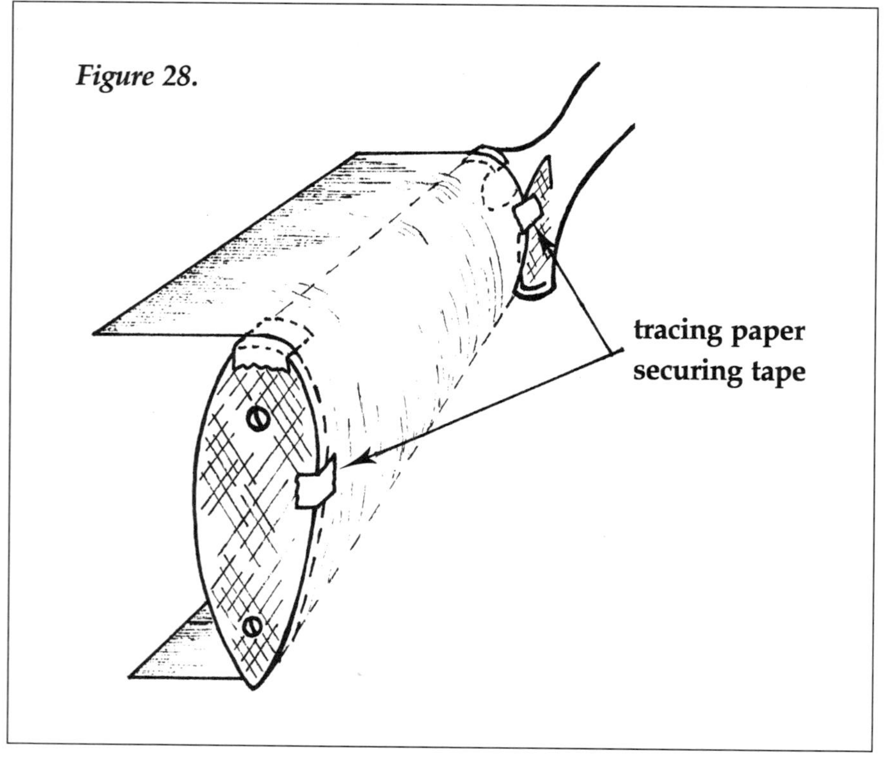

Figure 28.

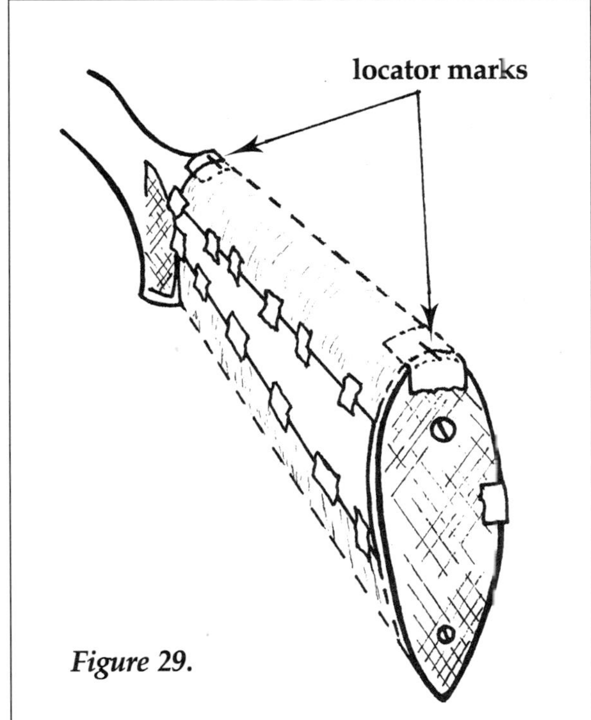

Figure 29.

At the grip end, draw a line showing the location of the upper edge of the ball-of-thumb recess and rear borderline of the checkering. When connected (fig. 30), these marks (fig. 31) will show the overall area available for carving. Do not connect the marks with the longer area-defining lines while the paper is on the stock. Remove the paper from the stock, place it on a

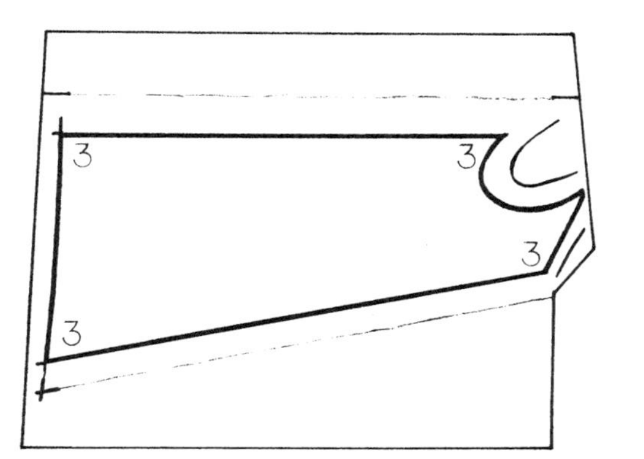

Figure 30. Area marks are connected with straight lines after the paper is removed from the stock. The line around the ball of thumb recess is sketched freehand.

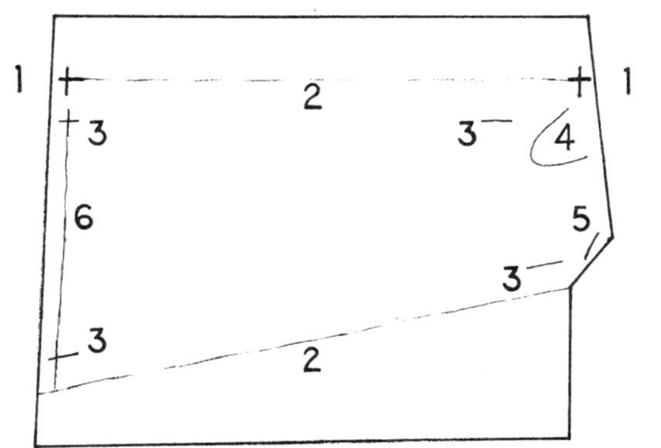

Figure 31. Design transfer marks: 1, locator mark tapes; 2, bottom and top centerline of stock; 3, area marks; 4, ball of thumb recess edge; 5, rear edge of grip; 6, area line ³/₈ inch to ½ inch off the inside edge of the buttplate or recoil pad.

place the pattern back onto the stock in this exact position after you have traced the design. Recheck the pencil centerline marks to make certain they are at center of the thickness of the stock. Make any needed correction, then darken the locator marks on both paper and tape with a dark, fine-point felt-tip pen. Next, using the side of the lead of a pencil, draw a full-length line connecting the inked locator marks. Do not draw this line with the point of the pencil; doing so is likely to cause an indentation in the finish of the stock. Keep the line as near straight as possible, but don't be overly concerned with minor irregularities. Make a similar full-length mark on the paper down the center of the bottom portion of the buttstock. Again using the side of the lead, lightly draw a line following the contour of the inner edge of the buttplate but about ³/₈ inch in on the paper. At both buttplate and grip ends, place a short, lightly drawn horizontal pencil mark 1 inch inward toward the center of the side of the stock from the top and bottom centerline-of-stock marks.

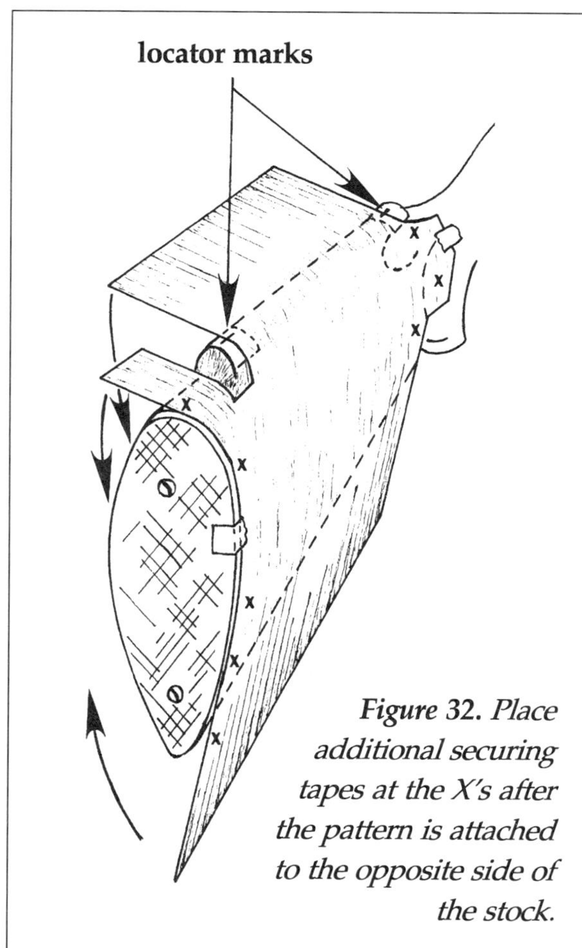

Figure 32. Place additional securing tapes at the X's after the pattern is attached to the opposite side of the stock.

for the shape of the stock (fig. 32). The area marks can be clearly defined following the same procedure as with the straight stock (fig. 33).

Only on rare occasions is the entire area of the off side of the buttstock ever carved. Most times the focal point of a carving is located at the area nearest the buttplate end of the stock (fig. 34).

Carving on the cheekpiece side of the buttstock is not often requested, but I encourage the carving of this area. When it is carved in harmony with other carved areas, it adds a dimension that is both unusual and very appealing.

A raised cheekpiece begins at the same plane as the lower portion of the buttstock at the area of the grip. As it progresses to the rear it gradually rises until it reaches its full height at its rearmost position. This rise is usually ¾ inch, but it can vary with individual stocks. Stocks vary in design, and a raised cheekpiece will end either very near the buttplace or as much as 2 inches from the buttplate. This rise creates a two-level configuration to the cheekpiece side of the stock with the lower portion maintaining

flat surface, and connect the lines with a straightedge. This line is referred to as the maximum-area-of-coverage line.

The process of determining the area on a stock with a high cheekpiece at the top, known as a Monte Carlo type stock, is similar, but there are differences in the placement of the rear locator tape and the positioning of the paper to allow

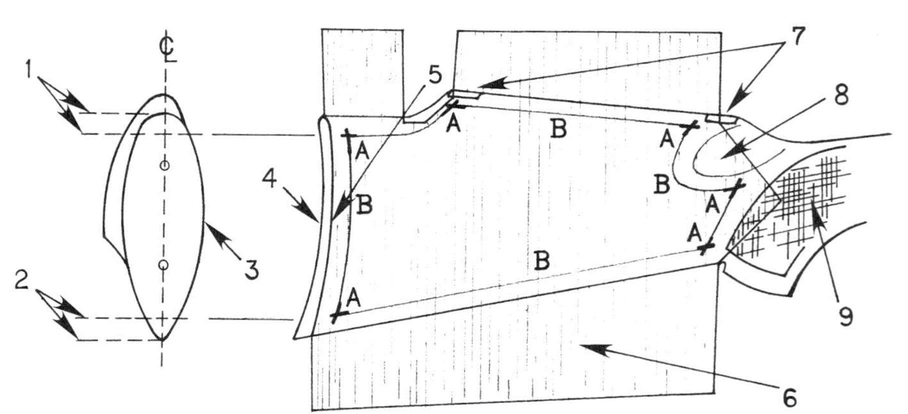

Figure 33. Design transfer marks for a Monte Carlo type stock: 1 and 2, 1-inch width; 3, carving side; 4, buttplate; 5, rear edge of stock; 6, tracing paper; 7, locator mark tapes; 8, ball of thumb recess; 9, checkering; A, area marks; B, area connecting lines placed after paper is removed from stock.

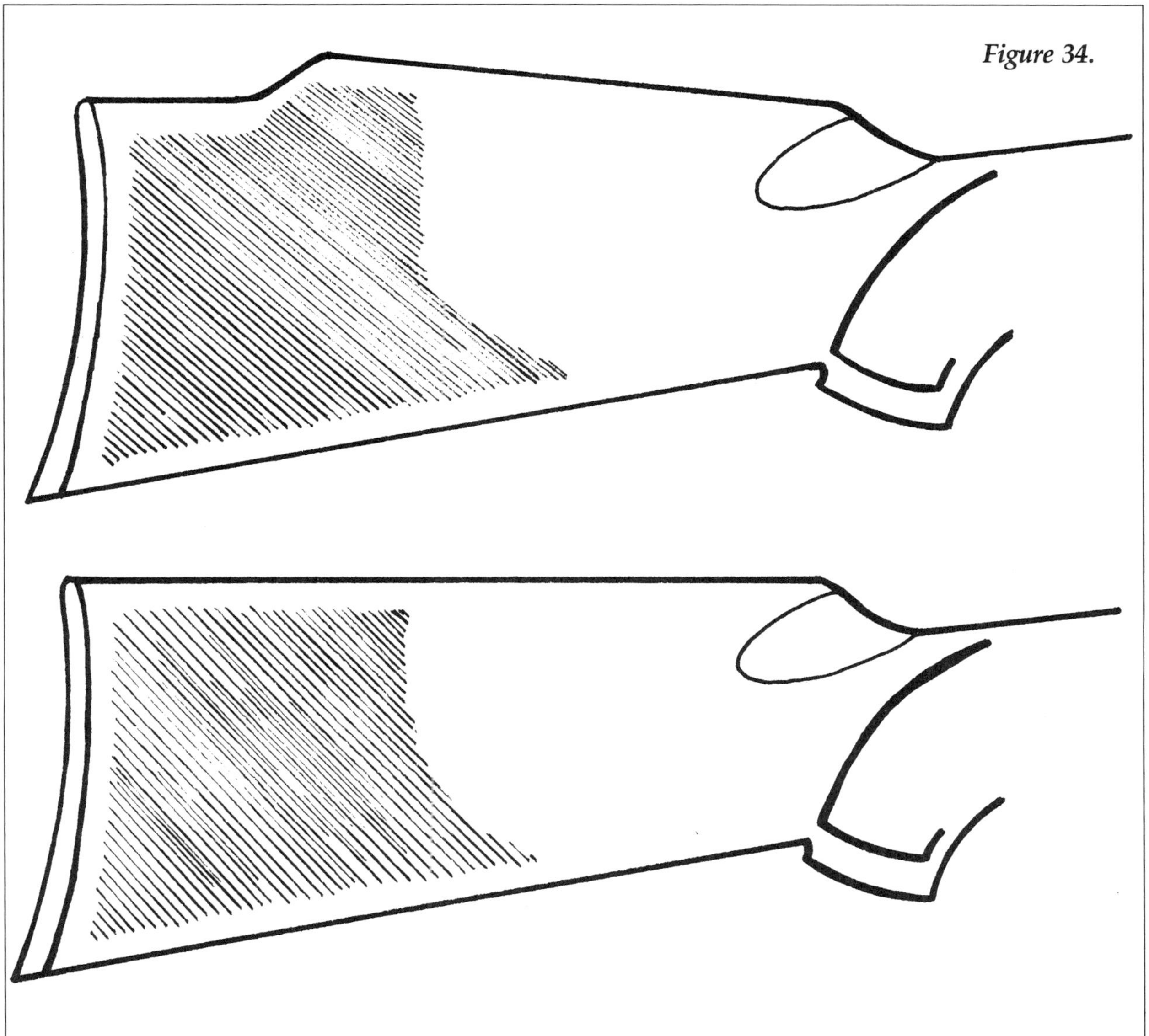

Figure 34.

a uniform configuration with the opposite side of the stock. As the cheekpiece rises, the area of wood from the line of the upper edge of the cheekpiece to the lower area of the buttstock becomes more pronounced. The extreme upper edge of the cheekpiece begins as little more than a scratch at the grip area where both the upper and lower areas are on the same plane but with the rise of the cheekpiece the area between levels increases. As stock configurations do vary, the connecting area of wood is sometimes cut straight from one level to the other, or it might have a slight curve downward and outward from the upper edge of the cheekpiece to the lower area. This connecting area of wood is considered part of the cheekpiece, not part of the lower portion of the buttstock. When laying out a design on the pattern sheet, mark the entire length of the line that meets the lower configuration of the buttstock. This line and the centerline-of-stock mark along the bottom of the stock predetermine the vertical limits of the carving area. You need only lay out tracing paper to suit the curve of the cheekpiece at its underside. Unless you are quite skilled and can execute a very shallow carving, I do not recom-

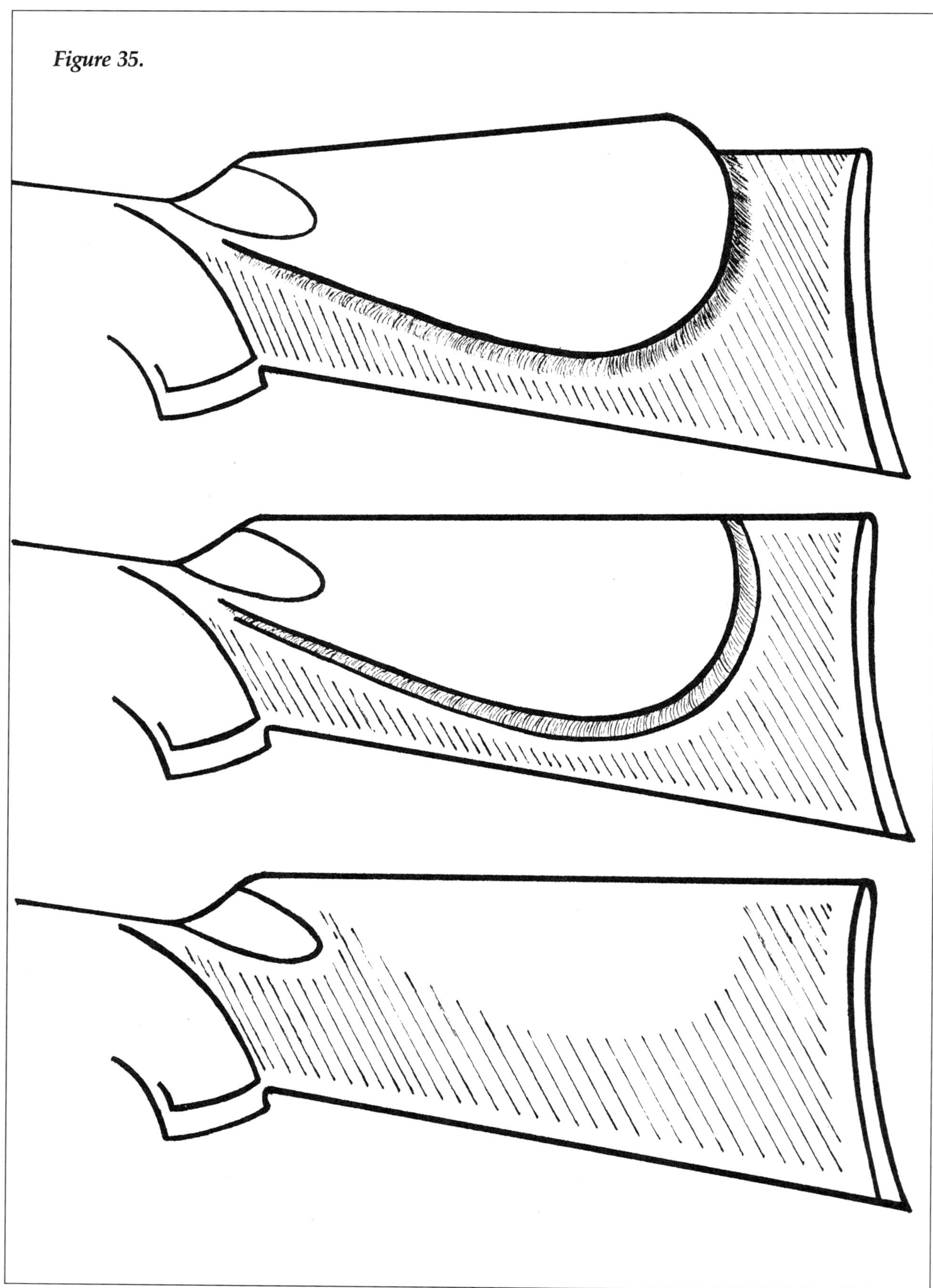

Figure 35.

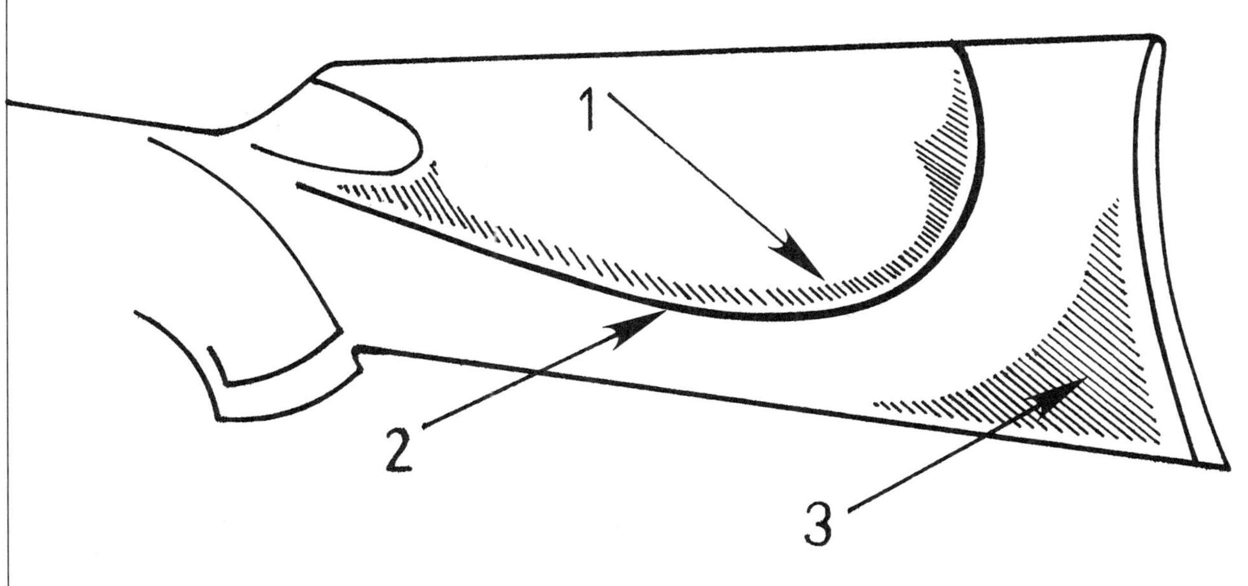

Figure 36. *Carving around a raised cheekpiece: 1, area open for carving on raised portion of cheekpiece; 2, upper edge of raised cheekpiece; 3, toe area open for carving.*

mend carving the area where the shooter rests his or her cheek, as it could very well be a source of discomfort to the shooter. Carving of this area (fig. 36) should only be done by those who have gained ample experience through numerous carvings, and then only after a test piece has been successfully completed. Otherwise, confine all carving to the shaded areas shown in figure 35.

With a straight stock that has no defined raised cheekpiece, you can judge and lay out the carving area freehand, as shown by the shaded areas in figure 35, leaving approximately the same amount of smooth area for the shooter's cheek as would be found on stocks with a raised cheekpiece.

If you do decide to carve on the raised portion of the cheekpiece, keep it confined to a thin portion following the contour of the cheekpiece just above its edge. To avoid an overworked appearance, there should be no other carving on that side of the buttstock running below the cheekpiece, except possibly at the toe of the

stock. Should you carve the toe area as well, both areas must be in harmony with each other and with any carving on the pistol grip and forearm.

To lay out a pattern for the area below a raised cheekpiece of either straight or Monte Carlo type stock, first place as a locator a small piece of masking tape on the buttplate, overlapping about ¼ inch onto the stock in line with the bottom curve of the cheekpiece (fig. 37). Place the stock on a pad with the cheekpiece facing down. Tape a full sheet of tracing paper securely on the off side of the stock, lengthwise from front to rear, positioning one of the longer edges of the paper near the center of the buttstock side. Then, turn the stock over and fold the paper under the bottom of the stock to cover the area below the cheekpiece (fig. 38). Position the rear short edge of the paper to match the line of the buttplate or project slightly beyond the butt end of the stock, ensuring that all of the wood along the line of the buttplate is covered. With the paper extending beyond the

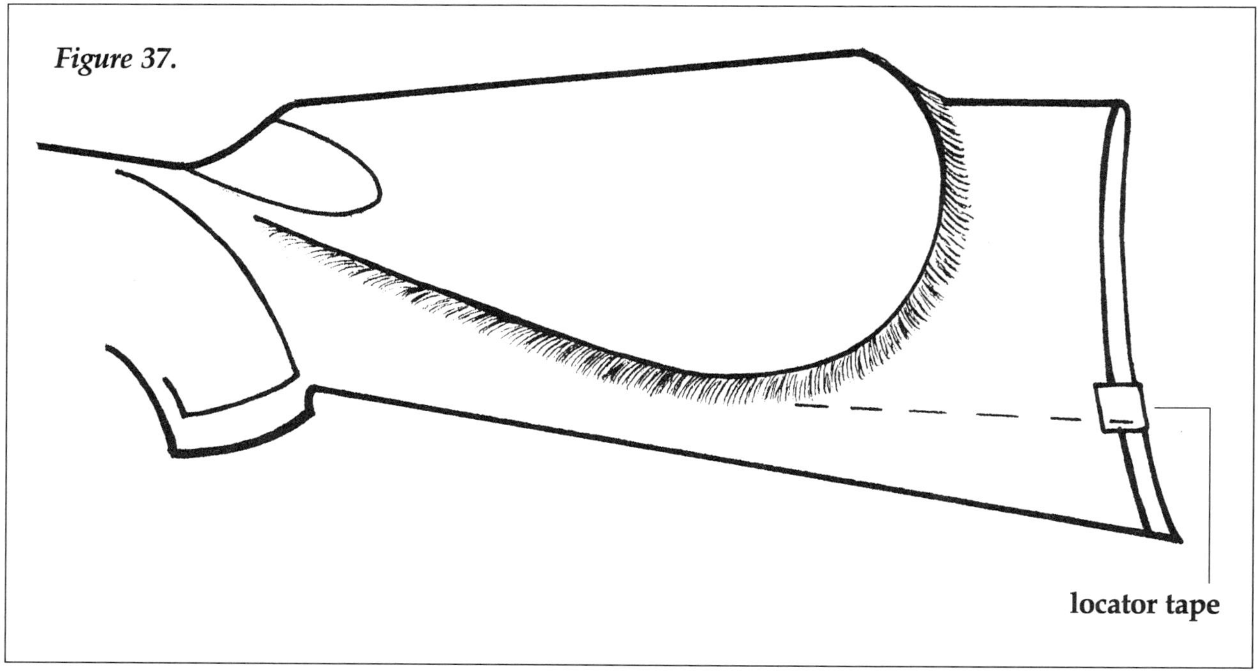

Figure 37.

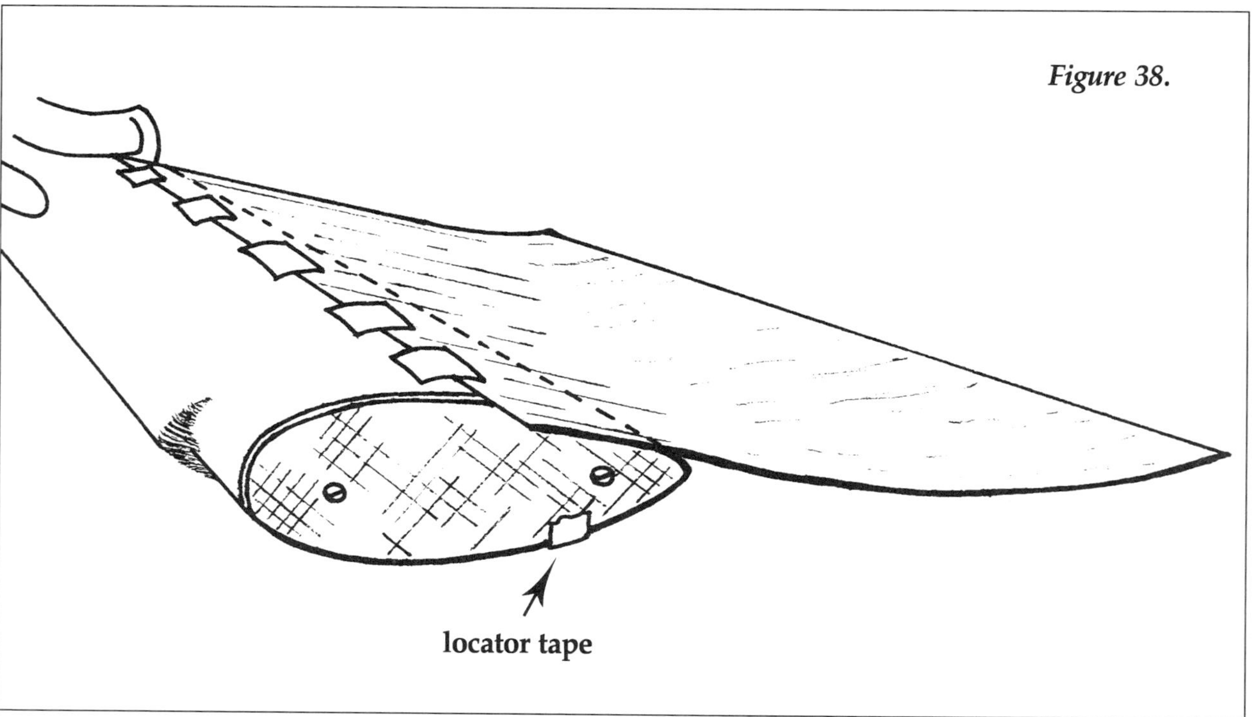

Figure 38.

buttplate, you can mark the inside edge of the buttplate where it meets wood. Place another mark at ³/₈ to ½ inch from the buttplate; this will serve as the rear boundary line for the carving. All marks on this side of the stock pattern sheet are to be made after the paper is securely taped.

To achieve a correct fit of the paper on the cheekpiece side after you've secured it to the off side, adjust the stock so that it's lying on the off side with the paper flat, extending well beyond the bottom edge of the stock. Pull the paper upward and lay it over the cheekpiece. With the tip of a fingernail, lightly press the paper flat to the stock below the raised cheekpiece, moving the finger upward from the bottom of the stock to the lowest part of the curve of the cheekpiece at the stock's flat lower surface (fig. 39). Use a felt-tip pen to place a small dot on the paper at the point of the fingernail where it meets the beginning of the rise of the cheekpiece. Repeat this procedure at ½-inch intervals from the lowest point of the curve of the cheekpiece to its ending point near the pistol grip. At this time, do not attempt to place marks along the portion

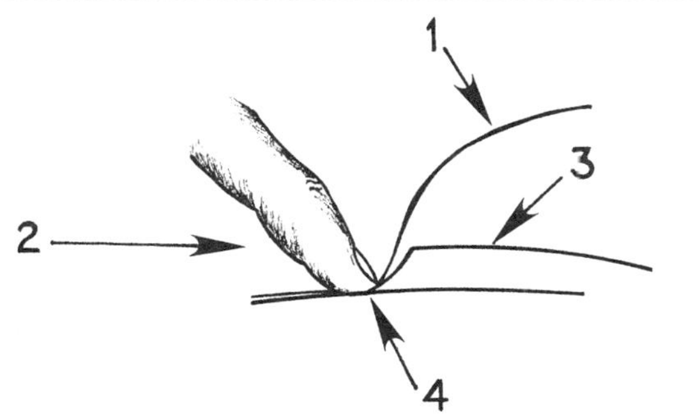

Figure 39. Placing paper on a cheekpiece: 1, tracing paper; 2, direction paper is pushed and held taut; 3, cheekpiece; 4, point at which mark is made at 1/2-inch intervals along the lower length of the cheekpiece.

of the curve rounding upward toward the top of the stock nearest the butt end.

After you have made the marks on the grip area, turn the stock to lie on the cheekpiece side, allowing the paper to be straightened. Then cut with scissors along the line of dots until you reach the first mark made at the lowest point of the curve. Trim off the trailing excess paper that overlays the raised cheekpiece. Then turn the stock to lie on the off side once again, and position the paper on the cheekpiece side as before. Place a holding tape at the forward portion of the line just cut and another just shy of the ending point of the cut by the dot first made.

Now place marks along the base of the rear rounded portion of the curve that runs upward nearest the butt end of the stock, beginning at the center area of the stock and ending at its upper edge. Then remove the holding tapes from the forward portion, lift the paper, and cut it along the line of dots as before, trimming away the remaining excess from the top portion of the paper. Your pattern sheet should now be able to lie flat against the stock, with a long rear portion that you can roll over the top of the stock and secure to the opposite side. Once it is secured, make a light pencil mark along the inside edge of the buttplace and a parallel line $^3/_8$ to ½ inch forward of the buttplate edge. If your paper reaches or extends beyond the pistol grip portion, you should also mark the upper line of curve of the ball-of-thumb, the recess, and the rear borderline of the checkering. Mark a full-length line on the paper along the center of the buttstock underside from buttplate to grip area, then make a light ¼-inch-long line on the cheekpiece side at each end of the pattern sheet at 1 inch from, and parallel with, the centerline-of-stock mark. Place two such marks $^3/_8$ to ½ inch rearward of the border of the checkering, one at the top and one at the bottom (fig. 40, 1). You will use these ¼-inch lines, in conjunction with the marks at the grip and butt areas, to outline the exact area open for carving (fig. 40, 8). Slip an inch-long piece of masking tape half under the forward edge of the paper, and press it securely to the stock. Draw a ½-inch-long line half on the paper and half on the tape.

If your paper extends beyond the buttplate and fully covers the locator tape, trim the paper in place so that its edge only partially overlaps the tape, exposing enough tape on which to draw a locator mark but leaving sufficient paper to cover all of the stock where it meets the buttplate. This sometimes means trimming a half-round circle in the paper at the area of the tape. If for some reason this should not be possible, you will have to lift the paper, draw a locator mark in ink on the tape, and then trace

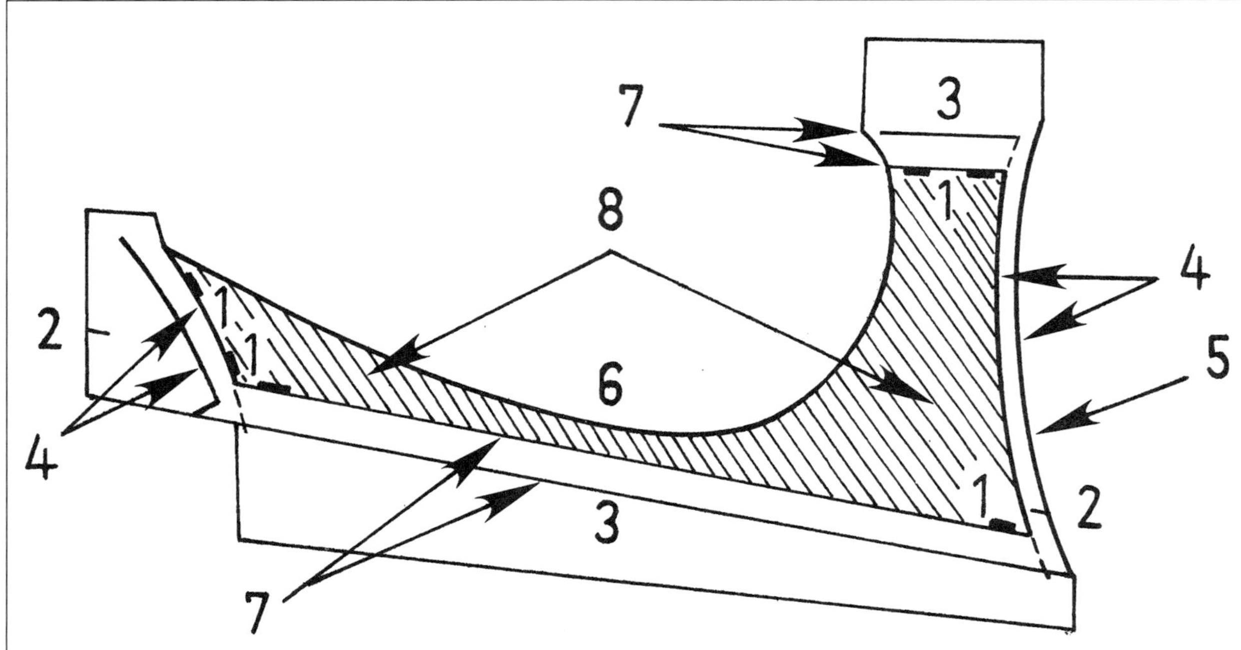

Figure 40. *Outline of area open for carving: 1, area line mark; 2, locator marks; 3, centerline; 4, ³/₈-inch to ¹/₂-inch spacing; 5, trimming at inside edge of buttplate; 6, lower edge of cheekpiece; 7, 1-inch space between centerline and area mark; 8, area open for carving.*

this mark on the pattern sheet. This latter procedure is standard on several pattern layouts described later in the book.

After marking the locator tapes, place a full-length line along the rear edge of the buttstock at its meeting point with the buttplate. Then remove the pattern and connect the area lines using a pen and a straightedge. Trim away any excess paper beyond the extreme rear of the buttplate. The pattern sheet is trimmed along the rear edge of the buttplate in order to provide a more suitable edge for securing tapes during subsequent procedures.

A somewhat different procedure is used to mark the extreme raised edge of a cheekpiece that has a high rear portion with a lower short space between the cheekpiece and buttplate, such as that of the Monte Carlo type stock.

To determine the upper edge of a raised cheekpiece (fig. 41), attach the tracing paper to the off side in a manner that will allow you to

bring the paper over the top of the stock rather than underneath. Place locator tapes on the top of the stock at the drop of the comb and the rearmost upper portion of the cheekpiece. The paper will completely cover the locator tape at the butt end. To mark the tape, you will have to trim the paper or draw a mark in ink on the tape and then trace it onto the paper, as previously described.

After folding the paper over the top of the stock, bring it to the lower edge of the buttstock and beyond to the opposite side; temporarily secure it with tape at the center of the paper's edge. Be sure there is no slack in the paper anywhere around the stock in line with the securing tape. Starting at the forward portion near the grip, gently pull the paper taut downward across the cheekpiece, pulling it at a 90-degree angle to the edge of the cheekpiece, and hold it angled to the wood at the bottom of the buttstock near the centerline-of-stock mark.

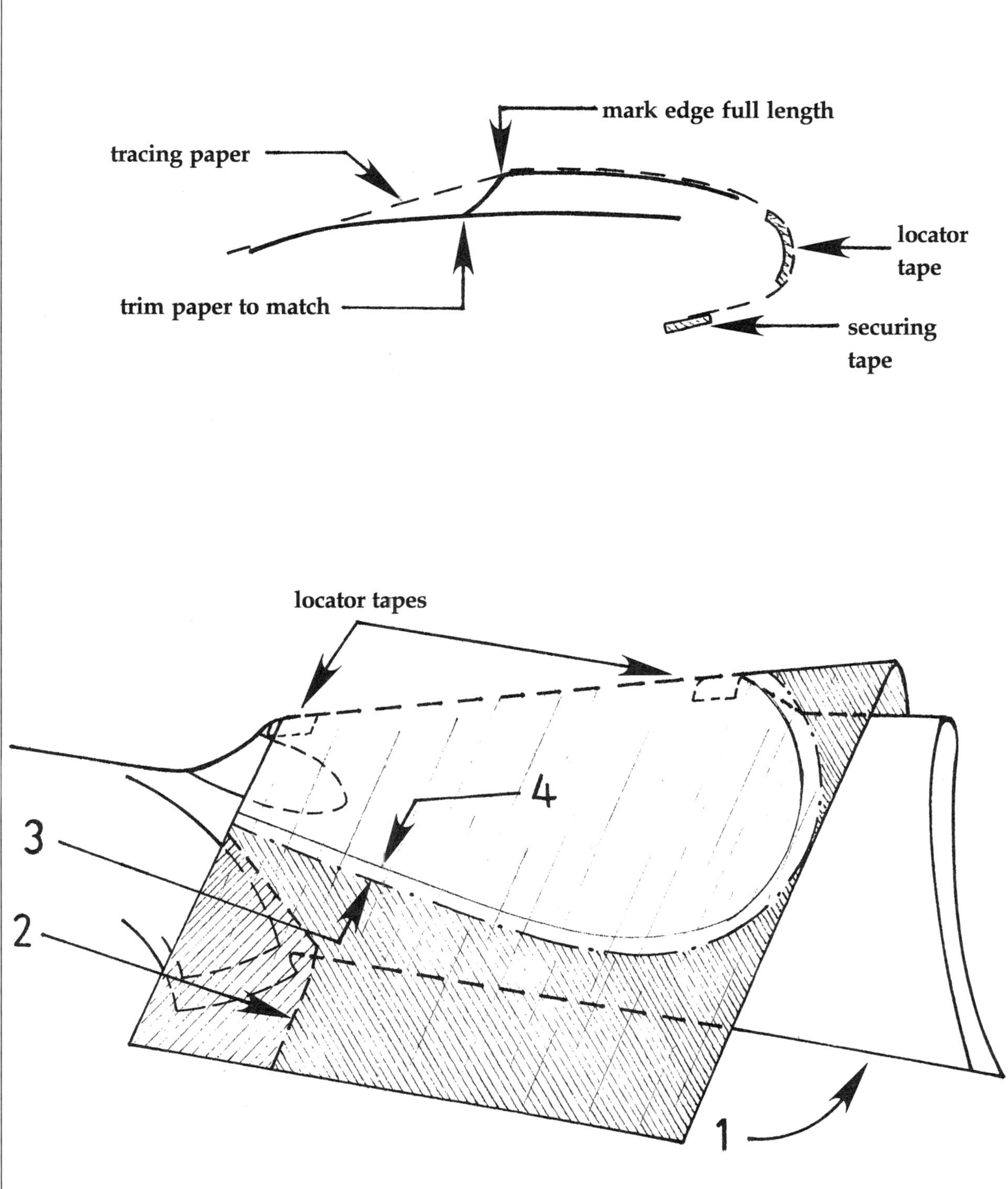

Figure 41. *Determining the upper edge of a raised cheekpiece: 1, fold and secure paper to opposite side of the stock; 2, trim to allow folding; 3, trim line at lower edge of cheekpiece; 4, make full-length mark at upper edge of cheekpiece.*

There will be a clearly defined crease in the paper at the edge of the cheekpiece. Use the side of the lead of a pencil to make a continuous line along the upper edge of the cheekpiece. Take care not to draw on the paper that extends beyond the wood, as it will easily tear.

After you have marked the portion forward of the securing tape, repeat the process to mark the rear edge of the cheekpiece on the butt side of the tape. When complete, there should be a full-length line along the extreme upper edge of the cheekpiece, beginning between the ball-of-thumb recess and the rear border of the checkered panel, and ending at the rear centerline marked tape on the top of the cheekpiece. In this instance it is not necessary to mark the rear border of the checkering onto the pattern sheet, but you do need to mark the upper edge of the ball-of-thumb recess.

Remove the pattern sheet from the stock and trim the paper ³/₈ to ½ inch below the line of the cheekpiece edge. This excess will enable you to place securing tapes to hold the pattern to the stock during future procedures. After you trace the design onto the pattern sheet, you have merely to align the locator marks of the paper with those of the tape and the edge mark of the paper with the edge of the cheekpiece to ensure a proper alignment.

STRAIGHT GRIP

Straight grips are found mostly on custom-grade and European style side-by-side double-barrel shotguns. Those encountered on rifles are generally found on the Winchester or Marlin lever-action types. The straight grip is also known as the wrist grip and is often mistakenly referred to as the pistol grip. Pattern forming is relatively simple for the straight grip, as tracing paper will easily conform to its configuration. The straight type grip will lend itself to almost any design layout, including those that completely encircle the grip.

You begin pattern forming for a straight-grip configuration at the underside of the stock. The first step is to place a length of tape on the bottom of the stock on which the centerline of the stock will be marked. Depending on the length of the design, this piece of tape will range anywhere from 4 to 12 inches. On stocks with inletting, place the tape immediately behind the inletting and extending beyond the rearmost point of your intended design. On those with no inletting, place the tape at the forward edge of the stock, again extending as described. Place a second piece of tape at the forward edge of the stock about midway. This tape will serve as the forward locator. Both pieces of tape will remain on the stock until the entire wrist design

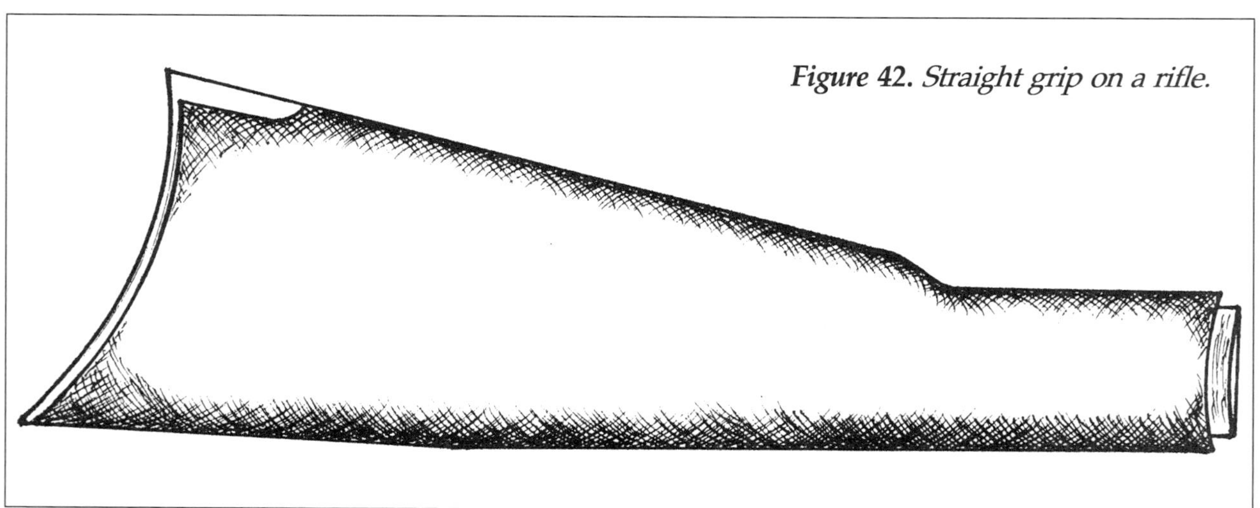

Figure 42. Straight grip on a rifle.

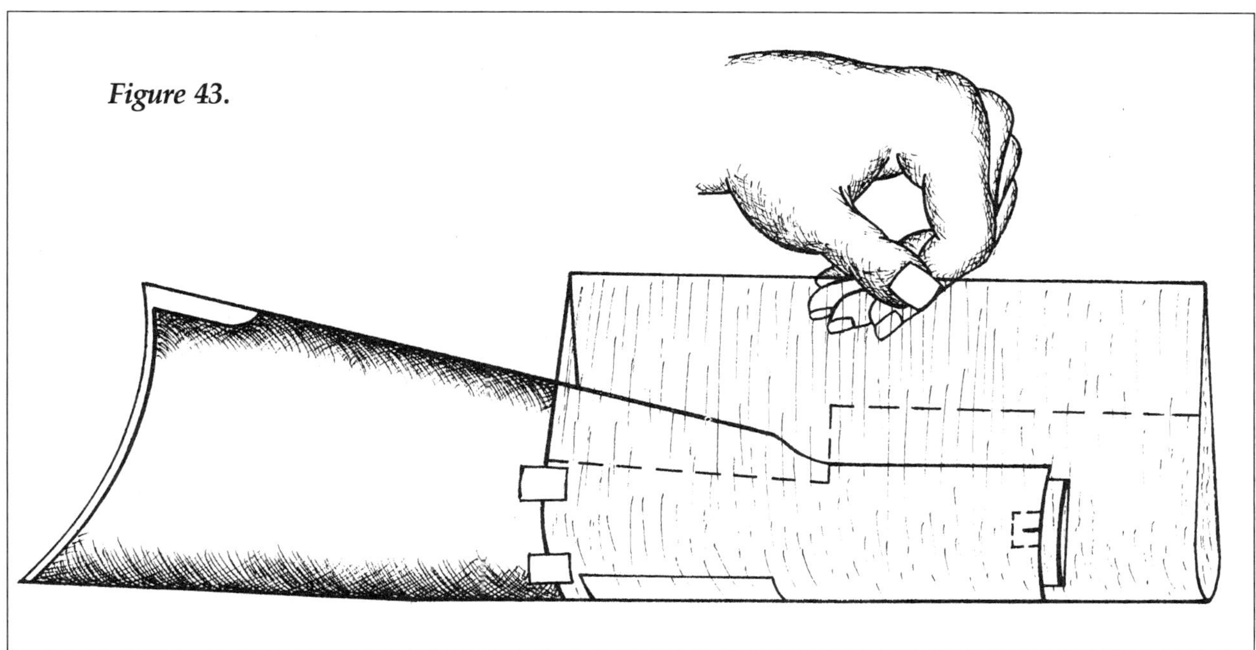

Figure 43.

is transferred to the wood. The transfer of the design will take place through the tape.

The next step is to cradle the wrist with a full sheet of tracing paper running lengthwise from front to rear, with equal amounts of paper on each side of the stock (fig. 43). Keep the paper centered along the bottom of the stock. Some stocks will allow full coverage of the forward portion around the circumference without the need to compensate for individual features; others will require excess paper extending beyond the forward portion to ensure total coverage. The paper's length is sufficient to cover the area of the wrist and still allow a considerable overhang. How much the paper extends beyond the forward edge of the stock depends on the rearmost point of your intended design. Position the rear edge of the paper with 1 to 2 inches of excess length beyond the rear line of the design. This will determine how much excess extends beyond the forward portion of the stock.

While holding the paper in this cradled position around the wrist, place two holding tapes along the rear edge to keep the pattern from shifting. If necessary, lay the stock on its side and hold the upper portion of the paper as shown in figure 43. Place one tape near the center of the side of the stock and the other at the curve to the underside. While pulling upward to ensure that the paper sheet remains flush to the underside of the stock, use a felt-tip pen to lightly mark a line on the pattern sheet from the rear to the forward edge of the paper (fig. 44). The beginning point of line *A* at the rear edge of the paper can be positioned anywhere, depending on the intended design. Part *B* of the line designates where and how the paper is trimmed to allow a flush fit of part *C* as it rolls over the top of the wrist. Part *C* is the extended portion that after trimming will roll over the top of the grip and be secured to the opposite side. After marking the complete line, turn the stock over and mark the opposite side in the same manner. Parts *A* and *C* of this line do not have to exactly match the first marked line but should be reasonably close. Part *B*, however, must curve around the base of the comb in the same manner as on the first side to allow a flush fit of part *C* after you roll it over to the opposite side.

With the paper still secured by the holding

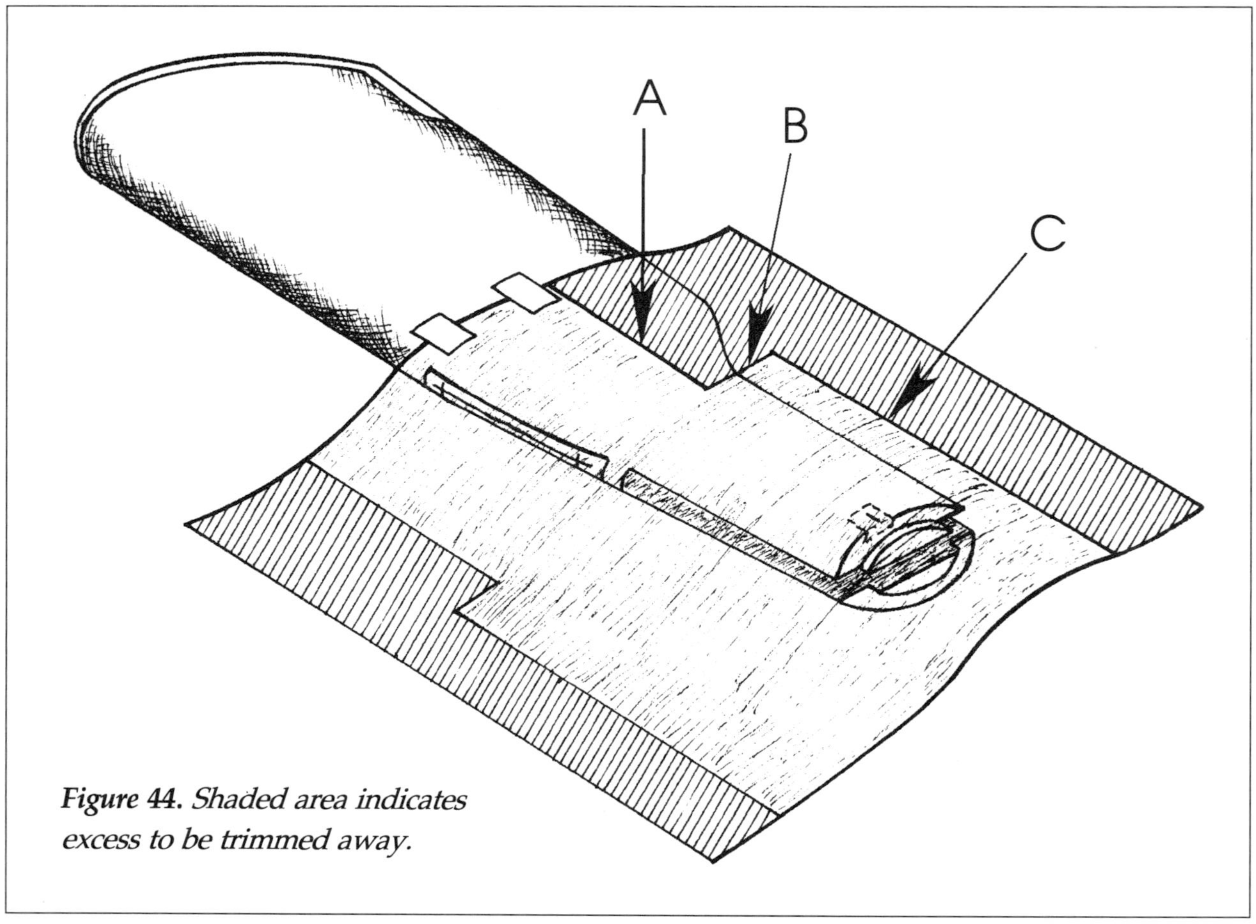

Figure 44. *Shaded area indicates excess to be trimmed away.*

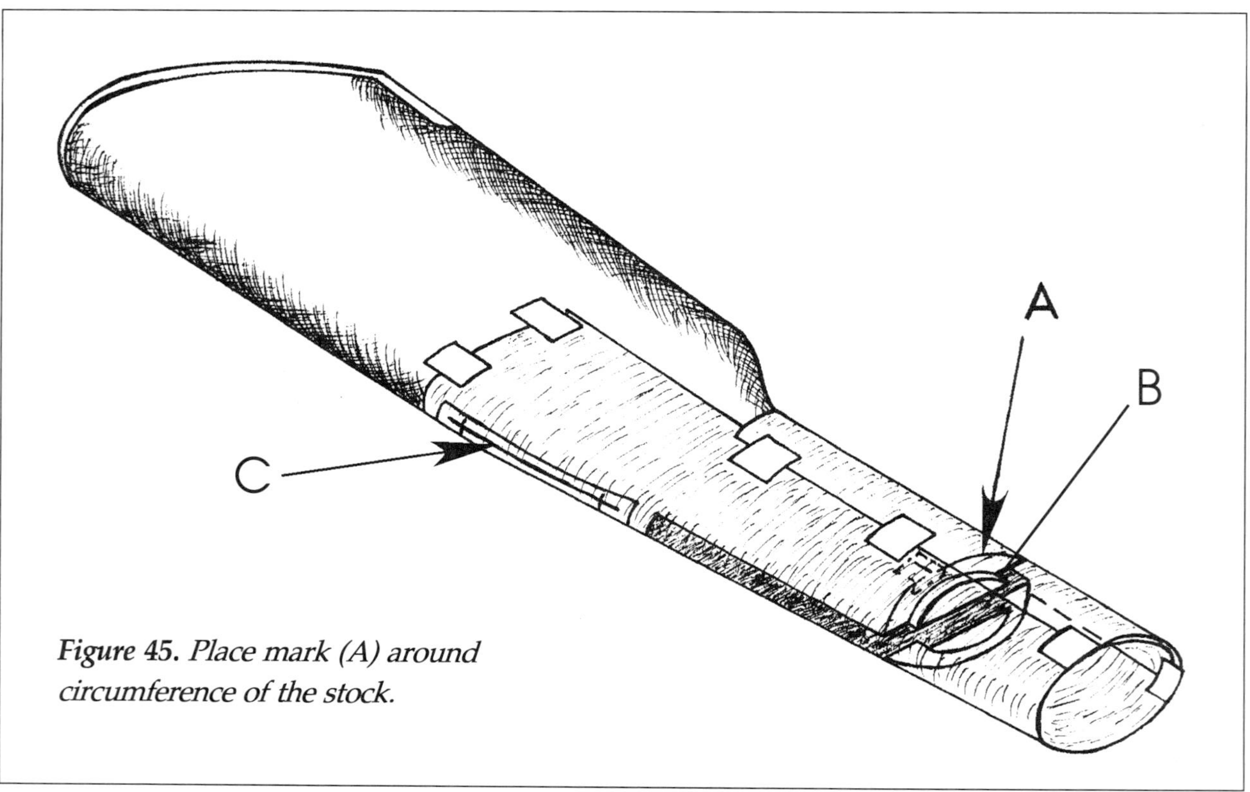

Figure 45. *Place mark (A) around circumference of the stock.*

tapes along its rear edge, lay the stock flat on its side and unfold the pattern sheet to expose the lines drawn on both sides (fig. 44). Then cut along the lines of both sides with scissors.

After trimming, reposition the paper as before. With one hand, turn and hold the stock upward in a lengthwise position so that you can roll the first side portion of line *C* over the top of the grip and secure it to the opposite side. Make a centerline mark on this portion of the paper along the top of the grip from the drop of the comb forward to the end of the stock at the area of the action. Then secure the second side in the same manner (fig. 45), and trace the centerline mark from the other side. You may need to adjust the holding tapes to eliminate ripples and to ensure a flush fit of the paper at all points of the wrist area. If you make any adjustment to the pattern sheet, recheck the centerline marks. After you have obtained a flush fit and secured the pattern, place an additional securing tape along the forward edge of the excess on each side.

To complete the marking of the wrist area pattern sheet you need only to trace the centerline of stock from the bottom of the stock locator-marked tape (fig. 45 *C*), the forward locator mark, and the area around the higher circumference of the wrist at the action (fig. 45 *A*) and to make a stock length mark around the circumference of the forward edge of the recessed wood at the action (fig. 45 *B*). The mark around the higher circumference will serve as a guide for the forward placement of the design. The mark around the forward edge of the recessed portion is the stock length mark and is where the pattern sheet is to be trimmed. This bit of paper beyond the higher circumference design area mark will be enough to place pattern-securing tapes without their overlapping the design area. Remove the pattern sheet after marking and trim away the excess paper beyond the stock length mark.

For a wrist pattern sheet, you need only one centerline-of-stock-marked tape with two crossing marks (fig. 45 *C*). These marks are essential so that you will be able to correctly reposition the pattern later. The centerline marks made at the top of the wrist are strictly to ensure a match of overlapping side portions. The centerline marks on each side must match each other exactly when you reposition the pattern sheet. If they do not, this indicates that the initial positioning along the bottom centerline likely is incorrect. If you correctly match the bottom centerline-of-stock and forward locator marks, an error in pattern placement is very unlikely.

After you have trimmed the pattern to fit, lay it flat on a white surface. A large sheet of white poster board is ideal, but any clean, flat white surface will do. The white background will make all the lines on the pattern sheet more visible and tracing easier. The area available for carving is that portion that falls between the top and bottom centerline, the forward edge mark, and wherever the rear edge of the design will be. Of course, it is not necessary for the design to fill all of the area between these lines. A typical wrist pattern layout is shown in figure 46.

When laying out a design on the pattern sheet, remember that the forward portion of the design's border must never extend to the forward marked edge of the wood, or the design would run up to the metal when the stock is joined to the action. This also would create a weak area of wood susceptible to chipping and expose areas of metal meant to be hidden when the buttstock and action are joined. A good rule of thumb to follow when laying out a design for this type of grip is to mark a parallel line following the contour of the forward edge at a constant $^3/_{16}$ to ¼ inch. This line will serve as the forward boundary not to be exceeded by any portion of the design.

After you have drawn a design on one side of the pattern sheet, you can easily make an

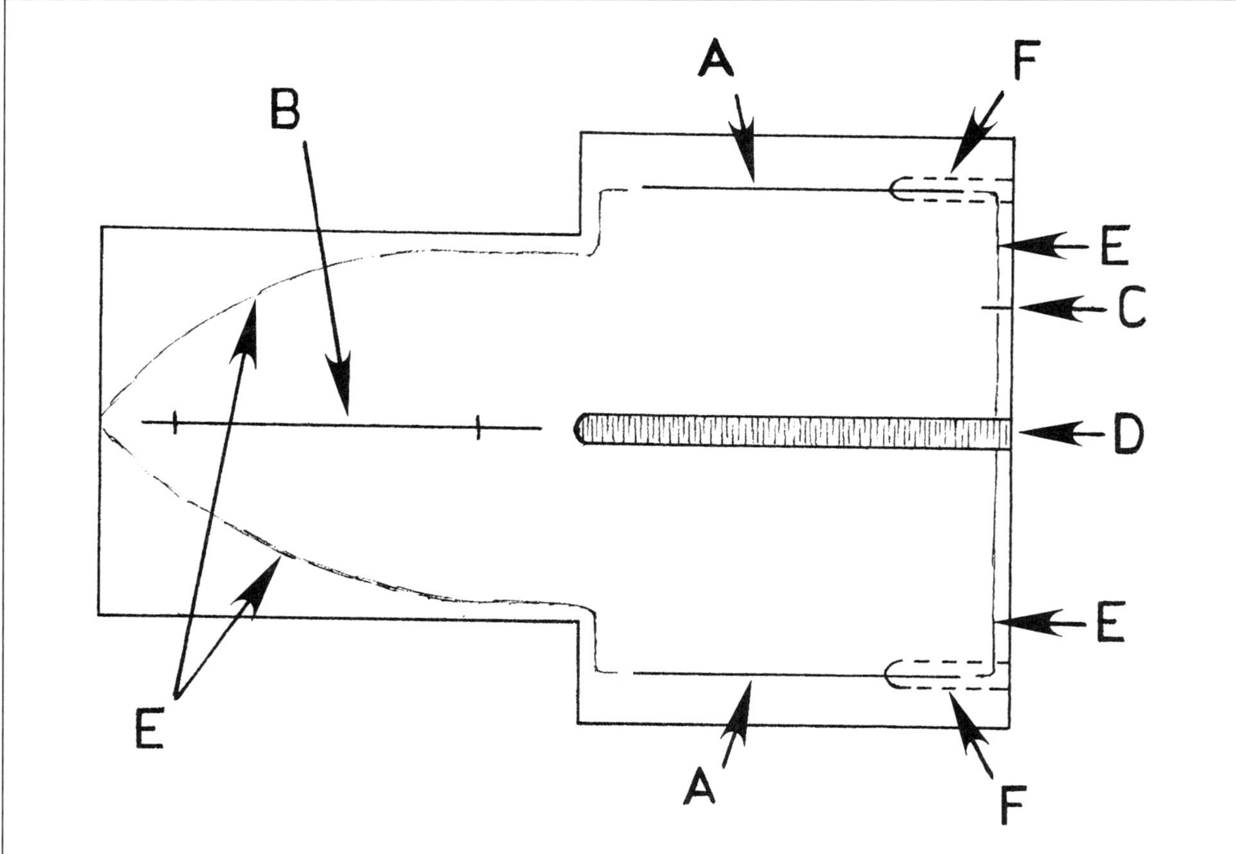

Figure 46. *Typical wrist layout: A, top centerline-of-stock mark; B, bottom centerline-of-stock mark; C, forward locator mark; D, outline of inletting; E, line sketched to indicate area available for carving; F, outline of inletting needed for some stocks.*

exact reproduction for the opposite side of the grip by folding the paper along the bottom centerline-of-stock mark and tracing the design on the second side. Make certain to fold the paper exactly on the line. Any deviation will cause the second side panel to be out of balance. When you match up the centerline marks later, the design will automatically be in the correct position with both sides balanced. When tracing a design for the second side in this manner, the second tracing will be drawn on the side of the pattern sheet that will lie against the wood. Retrace the design through the tracing paper so that when the pattern sheet is repositioned on the stock, the designs on both sides will be fac-

ing outward. Otherwise, it can be very difficult to pick up important detail lines through the paper and you may miss some altogether.

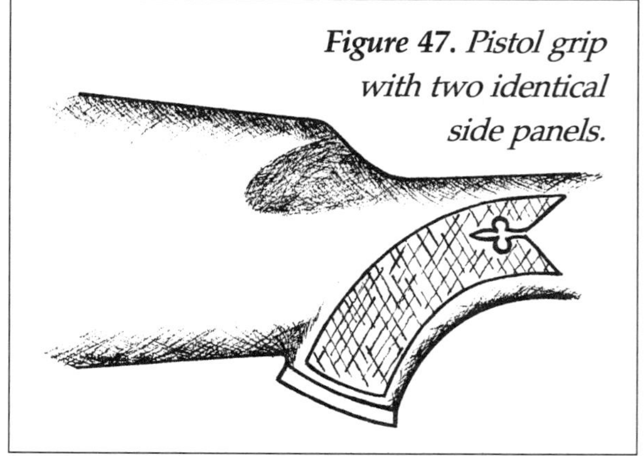

Figure 47. *Pistol grip with two identical side panels.*

PISTOL GRIP

This section covers procedures for laying out a pattern for a pistol grip that consists of two standard single side panels of identical size and shape, placed one on each side of the grip.

Though certain aspects of opposite side panels must be identical in shape, placement, or main subject matter, some features need not be. Variations in border and feature designs can be used, and some are presented in chapter 10. This section will first address standard-type opposite side grip panels of identical size and shape. To obtain the exact size and area place-ment of existing side panels so that the carvings will match in both size and placement, all you need to do is take a rub of the area.

Rubs

A rub is a simple means of making a rough tracing of an existing design or an area layout. Rubs are made with a pencil having more lead exposed than usual, and using the side of the lead rather than the point. Use of the point would likely tear the tracing paper. The more an area is rubbed, backed by wood or not, the darker it will become. Be careful not to rub too much so

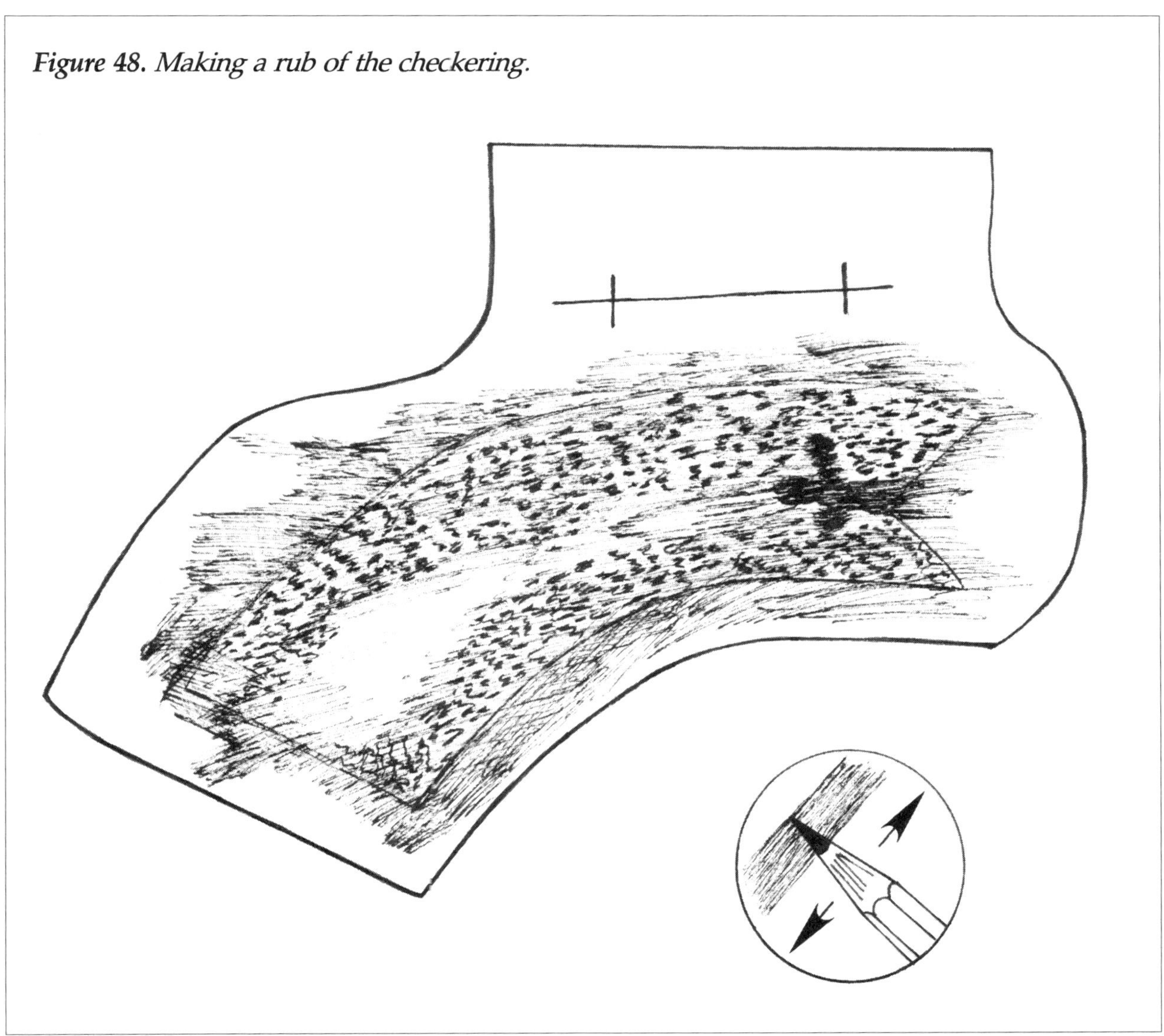

Figure 48. *Making a rub of the checkering.*

that you do not darken areas that should remain light or lose clear definable lines. Should this happen, the paper is best discarded and the process begun over. The trick to taking a good rub is to cover a small area at a time, pressing lightly. Strokes of ½ to 1 inch are best for taking rubs; don't try to do it all in a couple of strokes. As soon as the lines in one area become clearly defined, move on to the next section. It isn't necessary to rub the entire checkered area unless you wish to preserve a pattern of the checkering for some reason. Note that the paper above the lower cut portions forming the grooves will not have as pronounced marks as the higher portions. The purpose of the rub in this case is simply to provide you with a pattern layout for the location, size, and shape of the border.

Rubs also can be used to copy patterns from other gunstocks. Carry along a notebook and a pencil with which to take rubs whenever you think you might run across an interesting design. Always get the owner's permission before you take a rub.

Stocks with Checkering

Though many stocks have no checkering, most will have checkering on at least the pistol grip area. Generally, when checkering is present, it will be on both the pistol grip and the forearm grip. When areas of opposing single side panels are to be carved, you will need to make two side panel patterns. The design on each side must be positioned in exact balance in relation to each other when viewed from any angle where like sections can be seen at the same time. If a stock has checkered side panels and you wish to replace them with a carved design, first take a rub of the border of the panel to determine its size, shape, and placement. Before taking the rub and removing the checkering, you need to establish markings so that you will be able to position the new pattern in the exact location of the checkering.

Place the first locator tape at the top of the grip running lengthwise from the lower portion of the buttstock comb to just short of the inletting at the forward portion behind the action. Press the tape securely in place, then sight straight down the stock and make a light pencil dot on the tape at each end along the centerline of the stock. Connect the dots with a light pencil line. Remember, never make a heavy mark using the point of the pencil; this could leave an indentation in the stock's finish.

To ensure that the line runs down the centerline of the stock, turn the stock so that you can view the line from the butt end straight down its length, then turn to view from the

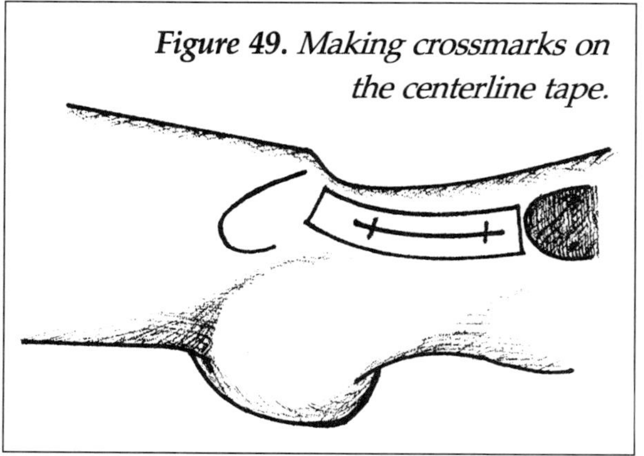

Figure 49. Making crossmarks on the centerline tape.

forearm end. Make any needed adjustments. When you are sure that line is correctly positioned, trace over it with a black, fine-point, felt-tip pen. Next, make two short pencil marks 1 to 2 inches apart at a 90-degree angle crossing over the centerline. The placement of these marks is not critical; they will serve as additional helps in placing the design laterally. Trace over them with the pen. Make all marks on the tapes and those copied onto the rub paper as thin as possible to allow for a more precise alignment.

All final markings should be done in ink so that the lines will not fade and will be seen more clearly through the tracing paper.

This marked tape along the top of the grip

is all you need to take a rub. You will add other locator tapes and marks afterward that will aid you in the correct placement of the opposite side panel. Your next step at this point is to secure a sheet of tracing paper over the existing checkered side panel. Trim the paper, allowing a ¼- to ½-inch excess beyond the border of the checkering at both the longer forward and rear segments. Trim the top portion of the paper to a width equal to or slightly less than the length of the top centerline tape. Leave excess length so that the paper extends beyond the tape onto the wood area of the opposite side in order to tape the paper directly over the stock. Do not place pattern holding tapes over the centerline marked tape; this would risk lifting the centerline tape when you remove the pattern. Trim the rear upper portion of the paper at the comb end of the centerline well enough away from the curve of the stock at the base of the comb to allow the paper to lie completely flat to the wood as it runs over the top of the grip.

As an alternative, you can use the inletting as an additional reference mark. In this case, the forward portion of the paper should be left wider than previously stated to allow marking of the metal inletting. Remember that the overall pattern must lie flat to the stock without any ripples in the paper. If including any portion of the inletting causes ripples, do not use this option.

The length from top to bottom of the rub will vary with individual gunstocks depending on the shape and placement of the checkered areas. A checkering layout pattern sheet must allow enough space between the bottom border of the checkering and the bottom edge of the grip so that pattern securing tapes can be attached beyond the line of the border. It's important that the paper is trimmed along the bottom edge of the grip and secured at that point. This edge of the paper should never be long enough that it can be folded around the grip's under-

side; the curve of the lower grip edge would create a number of large ripples along the entire lower edge.

Once you have trimmed the sheet along the bottom edge of the grip, press a small piece of securing tape partway onto the paper short of the edge of the checkering and partway onto the underside of the grip. Thus it is the tape that folds under the grip, not the pattern sheet.

If there is a grip cap, trim the paper along the edge of the cap where it meets the wood or extending to, but not exceeding, the lower edge of the grip cap. With the second option, you will have to mark the edge of the wood on the pattern sheet where it meets the cap. Mark its entire length when doing so. Place a securing tape partway onto the underside of the grip and partway onto the paper along the thin excess, clear of the border that extends onto the side of the cap, or to the edge of the grip if no cap is present.

After the paper is secured along the lower edge of the grip and to the off side of the stock at the top, place additional securing tapes at the center of both the front and rear edges (fig. 50). Adjust the tapes to eliminate any ripples, but be sure to maintain the correct positioning of the paper. Trace the centerline and crossing locator marks onto the pattern paper in ink. If you wish to incorporate the inletted area, trace its outline also.

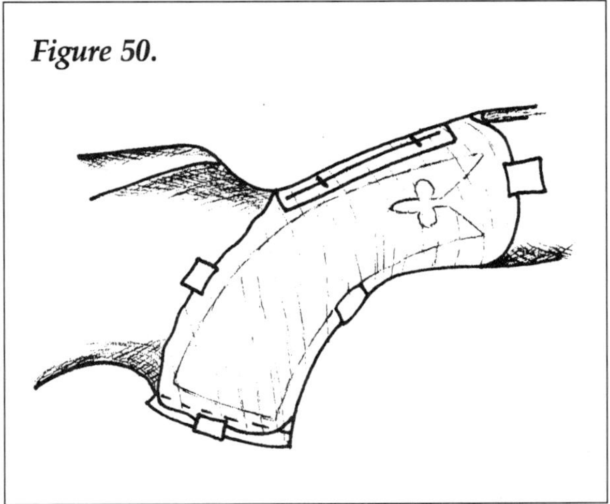

Figure 50.

To take a rub of the side panel, use firm but light pressure to rub the side of the lead back and forth over the area around the perimeter for about ¼ inch onto the checkered area to about ¼ inch onto the surrounding stock surface.

Before removing a rub sheet, make certain you have traced all locator marks. Then remove all pattern holding tapes by peeling them outward from the center to lessen the chance of tearing the paper. When all holding tapes have been removed, lift the paper from the stock and place it on a clean white background paper. This paper should be larger than the rub sheet so that you can tape the rub sheet in place.

Use the felt-tip pen to carefully trace over the borderline of the checkering; on the rub sheet, this line will appear light because it is a groove on the gunstock. Trace over all the other pencil-drawn locator markings in ink. Then place a larger fresh sheet of tracing paper over the rub sheet, and tape its corners to the white paper to prevent its shifting. Trim if necessary. Once the paper is secure, trace the complete outline of the rub sheet, the panel border, and all other pertinent lines from the rub sheet onto this new sheet. When you have finished, remove the paper and trim along the line that marks the outline of the rub sheet. This paper is your final pattern sheet for a single side panel, and on it, within the marked border area, you should now trace a design. Once you have done so, you need to trace an exact copy onto yet another sheet of tracing paper for the opposite side panel pattern. As before, you need to trace this second panel sheet on both sides of the paper so that you will have a mirror image of the first panel design, and when you place it onto the stock, the side of the paper on which the design is drawn will be facing outward.

You cannot use a single design sheet for both sides by simply flipping the sheet over. The process used to transfer the design to the stock will make the pattern unusable a second time.

Having used an overlay to trace the second pattern and then flipping it to match directions on the opposite side of the stock, the tracing will be on the stock side of the paper. Though the tracing can be seen, it will appear as cloudy and indistinct, which increases the risk of missing smaller detail lines when transferring the design to wood. To avoid this it's necessary to trace the lines to the outward side. During this process, view each side to ensure that you haven't missed smaller lines. To view smaller detail lines from the reverse side of the paper, place the paper on clear glass or plastic with a light source behind it.

Remove any existing checkering from the stock by sanding. The entire stock will then need refinishing. Some prefer to refinish after all carving has been completed; others, like me, prefer refinishing before carving, because bare wood is extremely susceptible to damage and moisture absorption. Also, the design transfer process works best with a finished surface. Refinishing procedures both for the entire stock and for carved areas when total refinishing isn't necessary are covered in chapter 6.

To place the first completed side panel pattern, match both centerline and crossing locator marks on the pattern paper exactly with those on the tape. Secure the pattern sheet at each end of the upper grip centerline and to the off side of the stock, then place securing tapes at the bottom edge of the grip, using at least two on both the forward and rear side edges. The pattern is now sufficiently secure.

After you have carved one side panel, you will need to place an additional centerline-of-stock tape to aid in positioning the opposite side panel pattern. When placing the second pattern, take care to maintain equal distances from all inletting and balance opposing side stock configurations, matching their positions to those on the first side panel. As an aid, place a strip of tape on the finger rest area of the grip running

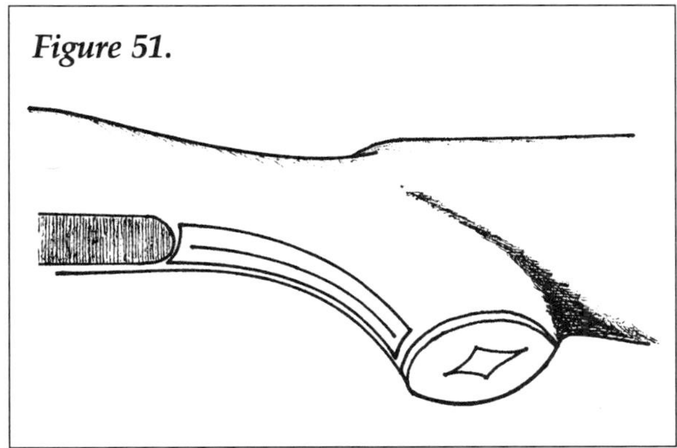

Figure 51.

from behind the trigger guard inletting to the bottom edge of the grip. On it, draw a full-length mark at the centerline of the stock (fig. 51). The centerline and crossing locator marks on the tape at the top of the grip will usually be enough to place the second panel pattern in its correct position in balance with the first panel. In the event you made a slight miscalculation during the initial marking of the top-of-grip tape, this tape will make you aware of it and will provide a measuring point from which to make adjustments in the placement of the second pattern. To do this, compare the distance between the carved panel and the centerline-marked tape with that between the centerline and the pattern sheet. After you have placed and marked the second tape, take a measurement from its centerline mark to the forward lower corner of the carved panel. Compare that measurement with the layout of the pattern sheet of the second panel's forward lower corner, and if necessary, make adjustments to ensure equal placement.

Stocks without Checkering

With stocks that have no checkering to begin with, you need to freehand sketch the border of a side panel. Before attempting to do so, a beginning carver should make a trip to the local gun store and closely observe various styles, shapes, and sizes of single side panel layouts on a number of firearms. You can gain a great deal

of knowledge with just a little effort. When observing panels, pay particular attention to features of various border sections on other areas, such as the grip cap area, the width of the panel at various points, and the overall position in relation to curves and recesses.

When freehand sketching a pattern, be sure to allow excess paper for holding tapes so that the tape will not interfere with intended border or design lines. After trimming to fit the area, secure the paper to the stock using the procedure outlined above for stocks with checkering, including the layout of locator marked tapes at the top and finger rest areas. Then lightly sketch the line of the panel border onto the paper with a soft lead pencil. After you have sketched the basic overall shape, make corrections where needed to produce the desired final shape. Remove the pattern from the stock, then straighten any irregularities in the line and retrace the entire border and locator marks in ink. The opposite side panel is made in the manner described above for stocks with checkering.

FOREARM GRIP

The forearm grip is generally the largest area to be carved. The usual boundaries for a design on this part of a rifle are from the forward trigger guard inletting to the sling-swivel inletting near the forearm tip (fig. 52), and no less than $3/16$ inch from the outer edge of the flat upper portion of the stock where the barrel channel is located (the finger rail), ranging along the underside to no less than $3/16$ from the opposite outer edge of the barrel channel flat (fig. 53). The opposing distances should be equal.

To create a pattern, lay the stock on a flat surface with the bottom side up. Place a full-length sheet of tracing paper lengthwise from the front to the rear of the stock within the grip area. Secure the forward and rear edges of the paper while keeping the approximate center of the paper at the approximate center of the stock.

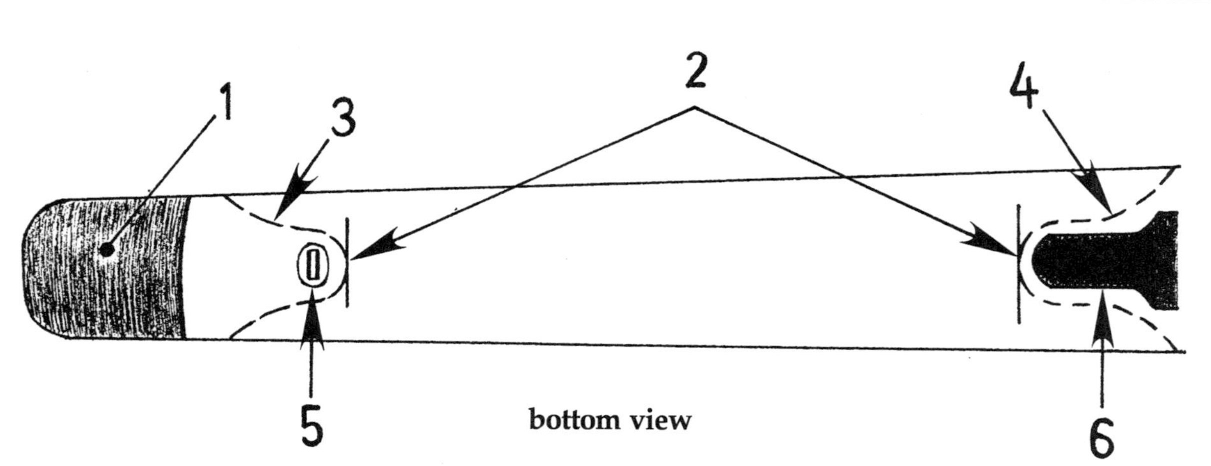

Figure 52. *Boundaries of forearm grip carving: 1, forearm tip (if present); 2, maximum length of carving; 3, optional forward length; 4, optional rear length; 5, sling swivel attachment; 6, floor plate or trigger guard inletting.*

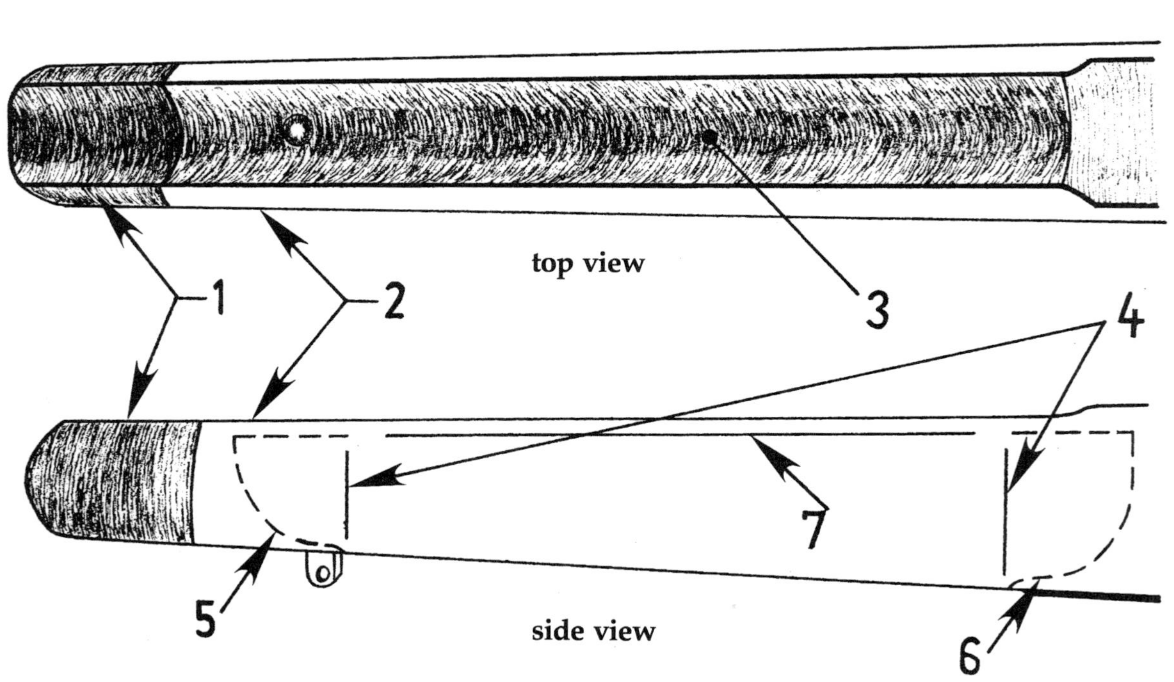

Figure 53. *Boundaries of forearm grip carving: 1, forearm tip; 2, barrel channel flat, outer edge; 3, barrel channel; 4, maximum length of carving; 5, optional forward length; 6, optional rear length; 7, area boundary line, ¼-inch minimum from barrel channel flat outer edge.*

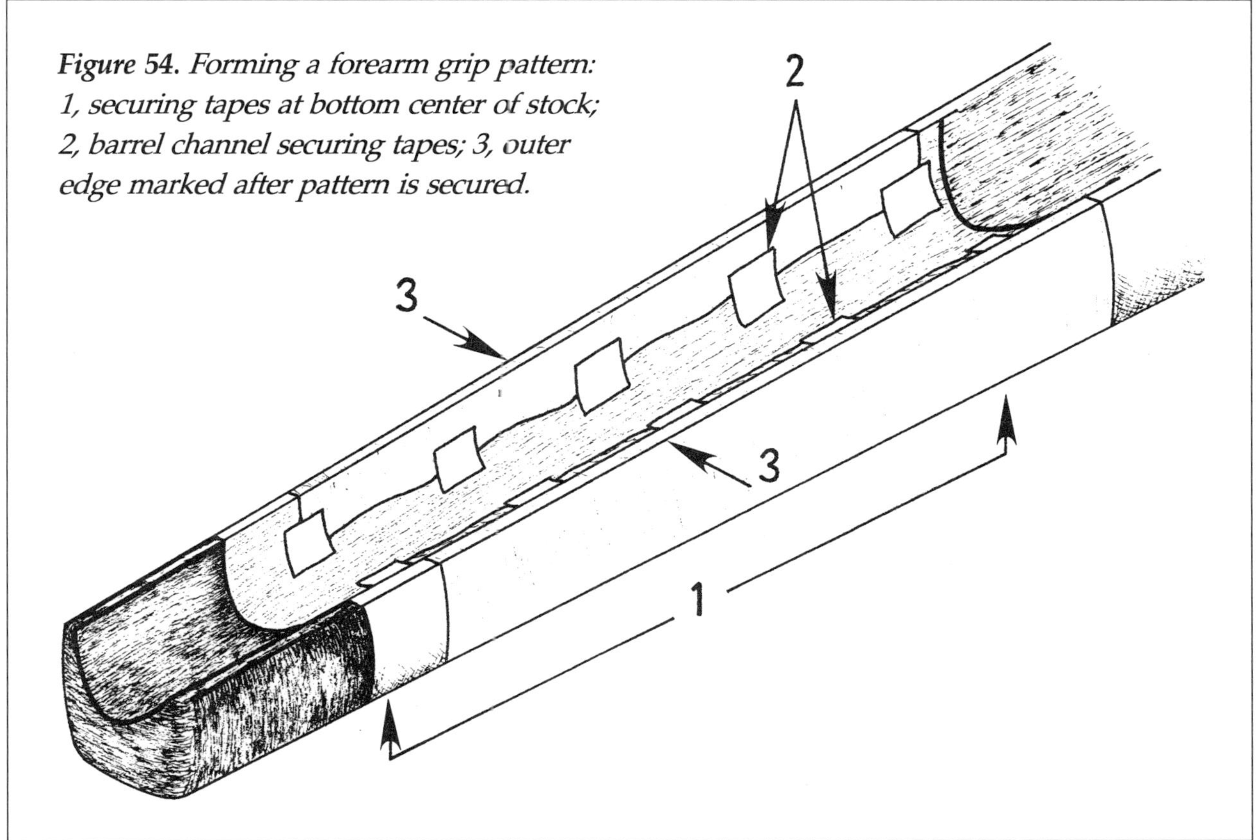

Figure 54. Forming a forearm grip pattern: 1, securing tapes at bottom center of stock; 2, barrel channel securing tapes; 3, outer edge marked after pattern is secured.

Place the stock on the flat surface with the top facing upward and the paper extending outward from both sides. Roll the paper from one side completely over the top of the stock and hold it snugly in this position. Cut the paper down the center of the barrel channel its full length and discard the excess. Secure the trimmed paper at several points in the barrel channel. Repeat this procedure for the opposite side. So as not to mark the stock, after the paper is secured use the side of a pencil lead to trace a line along both outer edges of the barrel flat (fig. 54). If there is no sling swivel or the swivel attaches to the barrel, you must use your best judgment as to the placement of the forward boundary. Proper placement can range from 2 to 4 inches from the end of the stock. As a variation, the design can be extended on the sides of a rifle beyond the foremost point of the trigger inletting on the underside of the stock

(fig. 53 5 & 6). To determine the true center of the pattern sheet, after the paper is removed from the stock, match the two barrel-flat edge lines and press the paper together to form a crease. Flatten the paper and use a straightedge to draw a line down the full length of the crease. Use a fine-point ink pen to make this line.

Forearm pattern shaping procedures are basically the same for both shotgun and rifle, although design layouts for shotguns will require a somewhat different approach, as there is generally a forearm release tang within the area to be carved. Most are located at the center of the firearm, but some are placed more to the rear, and a few run nearly full-length. Other shotguns have none at all, as the forearm is retained by the shell holding tube and screw-on cap at the tip.

The finished pattern sheet will cover almost all of the wood of the forearm. First, set the

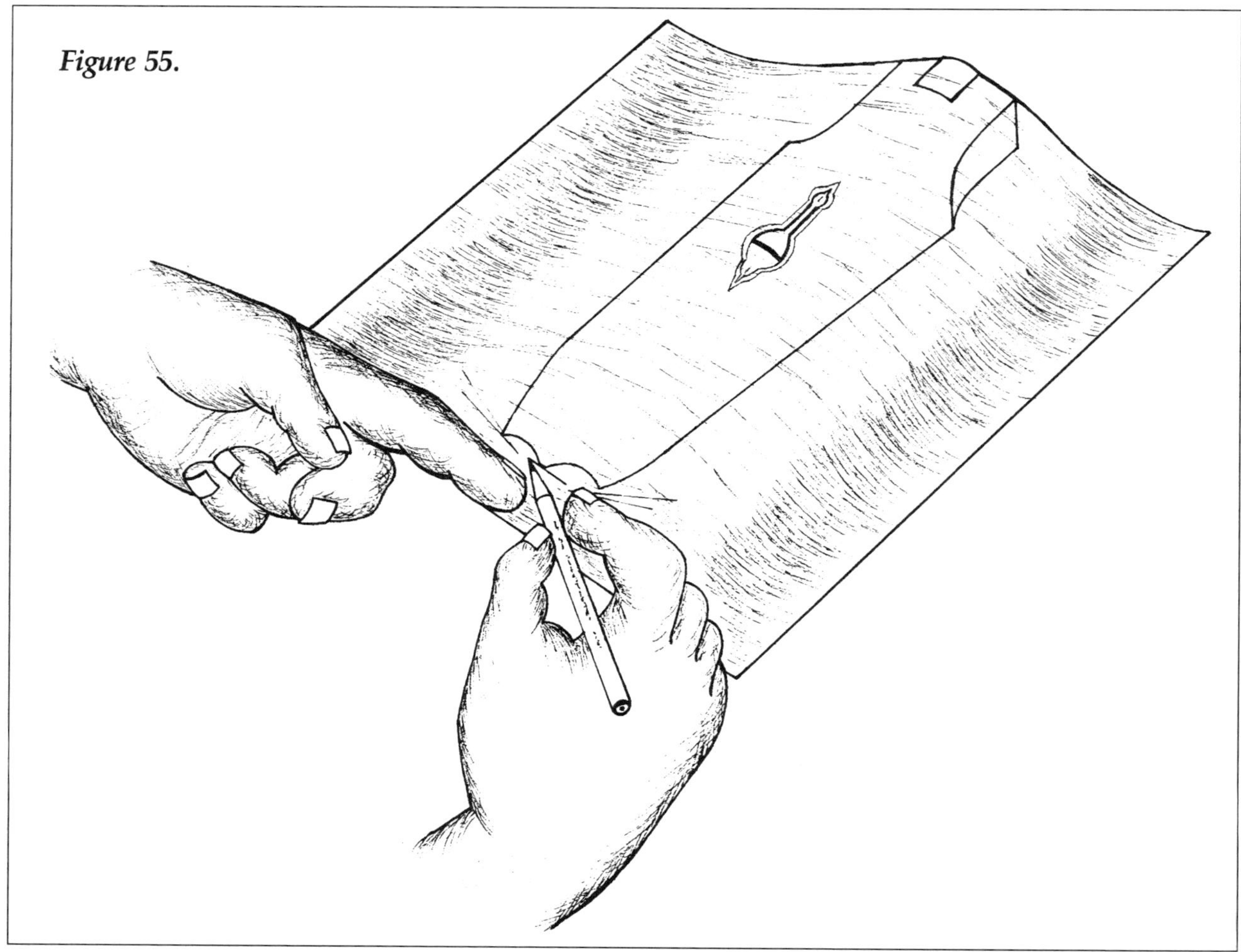

Figure 55.

forearm grip on a padded surface with its underside facing up. Place a full-length sheet of tracing paper lengthwise from front to rear, with the paper centered along the center of the forearm. Align the rear edge of the paper with the rear edge of the grip and secure with a piece of tape at the center of the stock along the edge (fig. 55). Then gently pull the paper forward by its leading edge, and while holding it flush to the wood, place a mark at the center of the extreme forward edge (fig. 55). Lift the paper and trim away the excess beyond this mark to leave the overall length of the pattern sheet to match the length of the forearm grip. Secure the paper at its center along the forward edge, then turn over the grip so that the gripping portion faces downward and the paper extends outward. Pull the side portion of paper gently

upward, and extend it over the top of the stock across the barrel inletting. Draw a full-length pencil line down the center of the barrel channel, then remove the paper and make a scissor cut along this line. Now secure the paper inside the barrel channel at various points along its entire edge as shown in figure 54, first securing the paper at its center side length and then working outward to each corner. Repeat this process with the opposite side paper.

After both sides are secured in the barrel channel, lightly draw a pencil mark along the full length of the upper outside edge of the grip, on both sides where the configuration of the wood begins to turn toward the barrel, not at the edge of the barrel channel itself. Should there be a release tang, outline the perimeter of the related hardware on the pattern sheet.

Remove the paper, and retrace all pencil marks in ink. Fold the paper in half lengthwise, matching the full-length upper edge marks of both sides, then crease it down the center. Open the paper and lay it flat, then, using a pen and a straightedge, draw a line along the crease on the side that will face outward when the pattern is replaced on the stock.

Shotgun forearm pattern forming varies depending on the type of shotgun: side-by-side double-barrel, over-under, pump action, semiautomatic, or single-barrel bolt action. The bolt action shotgun generally has a stock configuration similar to that of a rifle, and thus pattern forming is done as for a rifle. This type is of a lesser grade and rather inexpensive, however, so the owner is not likely to have it professionally hand carved, as the cost would far exceed the value of the shotgun.

Semiautomatic, over-under, and pump action shotguns may have a finger groove on each side of the grip. As this area is gripped by the fingertips, carving here could cause discomfort to the shooter and is not recommended.

The semiautomatic, over-under, and pump action types lend themselves easily to the fitting of a pattern sheet if you wish also to carve the area of the forearm tip. When fitting the pattern sheet to the main body of the forearm grip, usually the tip will also be covered. Conform-

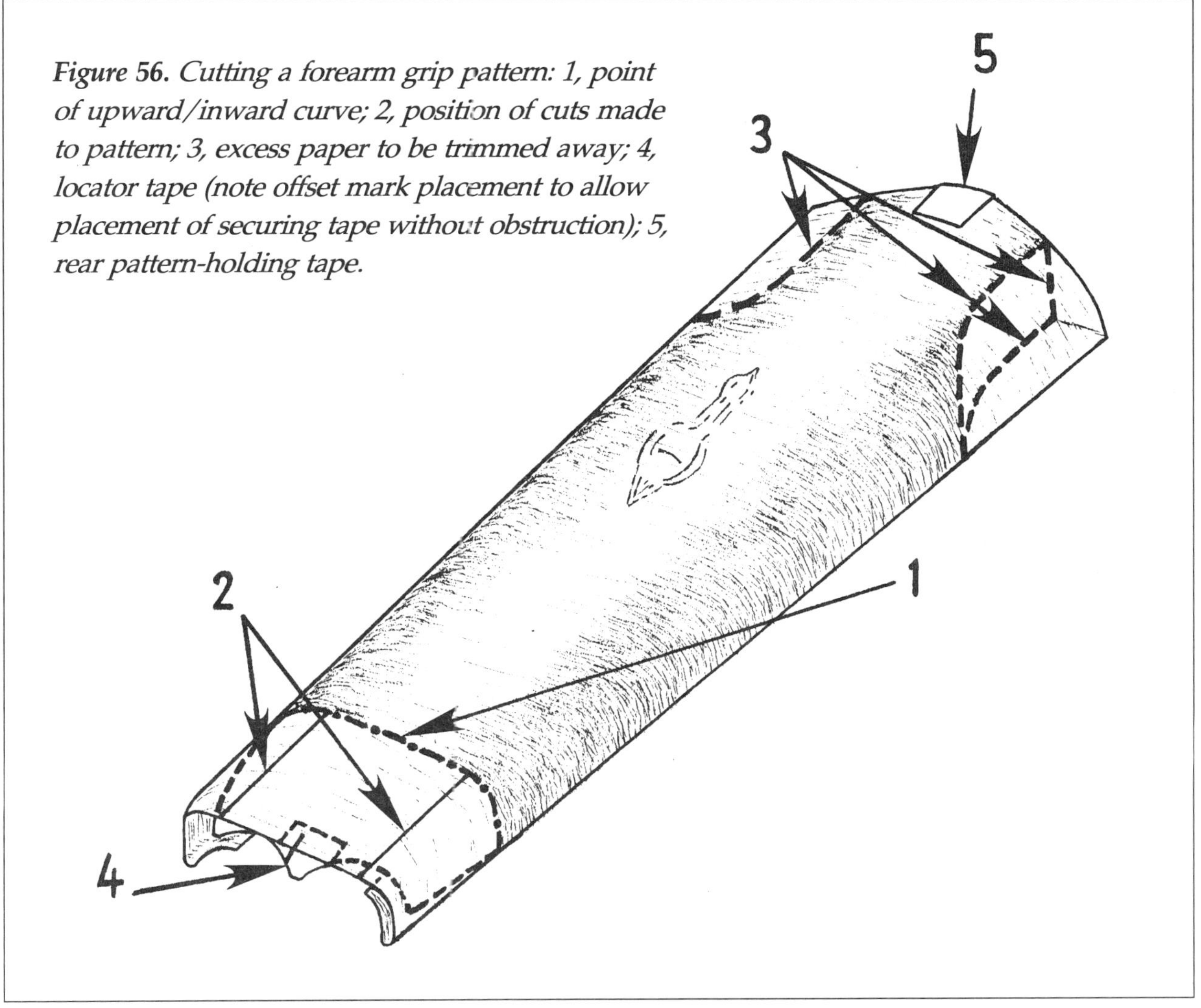

Figure 56. Cutting a forearm grip pattern: 1, point of upward/inward curve; 2, position of cuts made to pattern; 3, excess paper to be trimmed away; 4, locator tape (note offset mark placement to allow placement of securing tape without obstruction); 5, rear pattern-holding tape.

ing a pattern sheet to the shape of a side-by-side double-barrel forearm grip will generally require a bit more work. The following instructions are for the pattern forming of this shape of shotgun forearm grip. The tip on this type usually curves inward and upward from a point farther from the leading edge than on most other types of shotguns. Because of this, after you secure the pattern sheet at the forward, rear, and side edges to the inside of the barrel channel, you will notice that the paper along the forward edge has a large buckle on each side of the securing tape. To make this paper lie flush, remove the securing tape at the center of the forward edge. This will allow the entire forward edge of the paper to rise above the surface level of the wood. Then place a small piece of tape at the spot from which you removed the first pattern-securing tape, but this time place the tape only on the wood. Draw a line in ink on this tape from front to rear of the forearm grip. This new tape will serve as a pattern locator tape. Next, make two scissor cuts

from the forward edge of the paper straight toward the rear, each at an equal distance between the center of the grip and the extreme outer side edge and stopping at the point where the paper is lying flush with the wood of the grip (fig. 56). After you have made these cuts, bring the center portion of the paper between the cuts up to the forward edge, and place a securing tape just off center to allow the locator mark to remain visible so that it can be traced onto the paper.

To make the side sections of the forearm tip pattern conform to the stock, cut two slits (fig. 57 6). You might need to remove a securing tape from the barrel channel to do this. After the paper is cut, grasp the side section at its center at the forward edge and conform the paper to the outside curve of the tip. As you hold the pattern in position, fold the bottom portion across the forearm tip and secure it in place with a temporary holding tape. Secure the leading edge in the same manner. This generally will mean placing the leading side holding tape di-

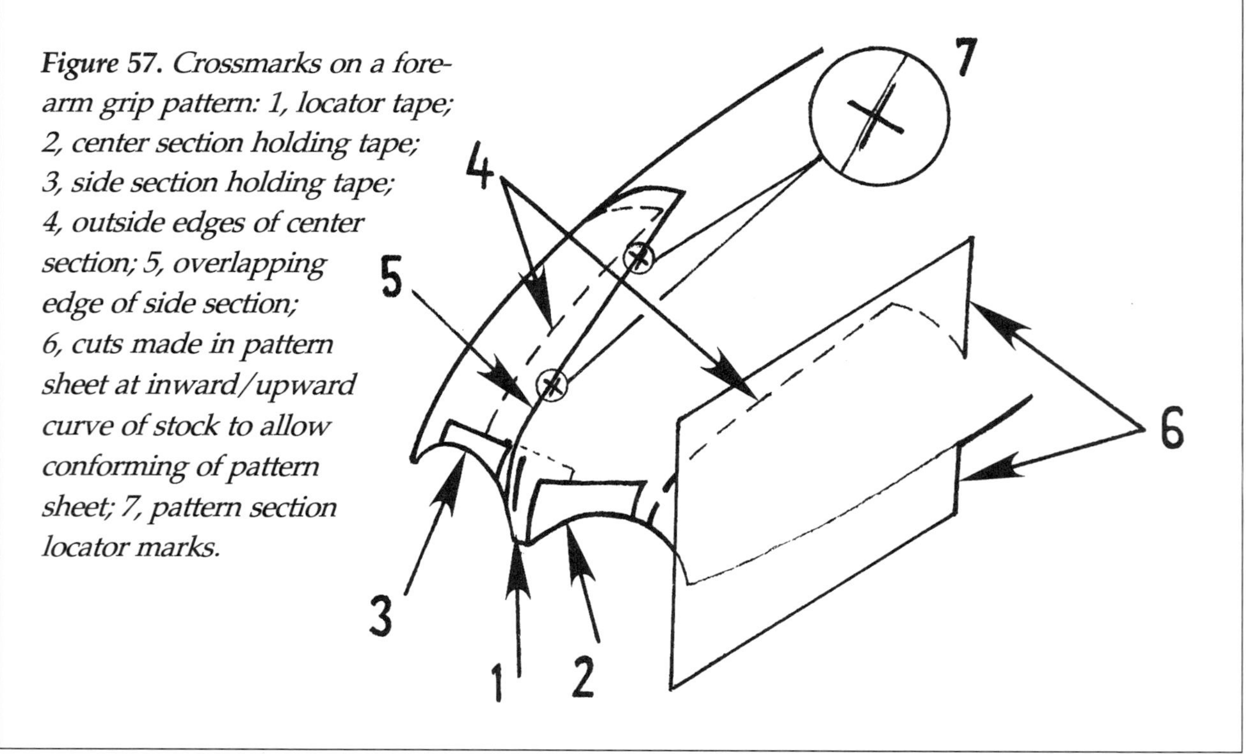

Figure 57. Crossmarks on a forearm grip pattern: 1, locator tape; 2, center section holding tape; 3, side section holding tape; 4, outside edges of center section; 5, overlapping edge of side section; 6, cuts made in pattern sheet at inward/upward curve of stock to allow conforming of pattern sheet; 7, pattern section locator marks.

rectly on top of the center section holding tape. A small crease may form at the tip, but it generally will not be within the area of the intended design and thus is of no consequence. On occasion, depending on the degree of the curve, the overlapping of the side sections onto the center section may be excessive. If so, before placing a securing tape, mark the side section and make a scissor cut along its length to allow only $1/8$ to $3/16$ inch of overlap. After trimming and securing the upper portion, fold the top portion into the barrel channel and secure it at several places along its length. Here, depending on the degree of the curve, there may be a few small creases or ripples along the edge of the stock, but these too are of no consequence. Use as many temporary holding tapes as necessary to ensure that the area on which the design is to be traced is flush with the wood of the stock.

After both side sections have been fitted and secured, you need to place additional locator marks, in the form of crossmarks, on the pattern sheet itself. Use a pencil to make a light line the full length of the edge of the overlapped sections onto the lower center section of the pattern. These marks will enable you to correctly position the side sections when the pattern is placed back onto the grip after you trace the appropriate portion of the design onto each section. The marks are especially helpful in maintaining the design's correct proportion should it include extensive detailing in the area of the sloped tip. Draw the crossmarks with a horizontal line beginning on the side section and continuing onto the center section, and a vertical line entirely on the center section along the very edge of the side section. When you trace the appropriate portions of the design onto the individual strips, these lines will indicate where the design lines end on one strip and pick up on the next. Always begin design tracing on the center strip and match the side strips to it afterward. Tracing of the overall design is best done by using a soft lead pencil to first retrace the side section edge line marks on the side of the pattern sheet that will be in direct contact with the surface of the design. When tracing the design that is to be on the center strip, these edge line marks are traced over and imprinted on the surface of the design itself. When tracing the portions of the design continuing on the adjoining strip, you need only to match the edge of the paper to the imprinted line that was left on the design.

If you have a complete design you plan to use for the forearm of either shotgun or rifle, place the pattern sheet over the design to determine whether you need to make any alterations. The pattern sheet will also help you in creating a design to fit within the marked maximum area of coverage. If your design will cover most of the available area, be sure to leave a minimum of $1/8$ inch around the design from all edges.

5

PATTERNS FOR TROUBLESOME PISTOL GRIP CONFIGURATIONS

SINCE THE ADVENT OF MACHINE-PRESSED CHECKER-ing, which became prevalent during the 1960s, it's not uncommon for grips to have an added area of checkering on each of the standard side panels. These areas are independent of the main panel, generally placed to the lower rear edge, and vary in shape and size. Such additions are solely for decoration and in no way serve to aid in the gripping of the stock.

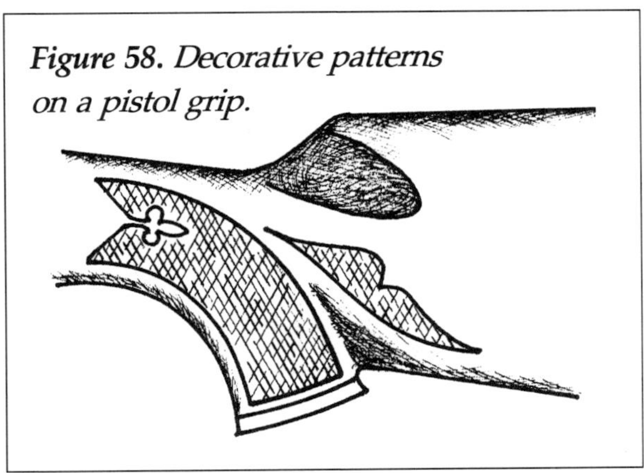

Figure 58. Decorative patterns on a pistol grip.

If you intend to incorporate such a section along with the grip panel into the overall area of a carving, you need to take a rub of the side panel plus the addition in the manner outlined previously. Be aware that the boundaries of a carving need not be held to those of the original checkered areas; in fact, carvings usually exceed the original area of checkering. This area generally needs no alteration for an appealing shape. If you decide to retain the overall shape, you need only to connect the upper and lower borderlines of the panel and the added section, thus forming a single area for carving. A beginning carver should study various sizes and shapes of such grip sections. You may wish to take advantage of borderline layouts that have already been done. If you find one you like but it is not the type you wish to use at this time, take a rub and store if for future reference. Also consider mixing parts of different layouts.

The pistol grip area of a stock is often the most difficult to lay out. Except for use on standard single side panels and those with the added extension, a sheet of tracing paper usually cannot be trimmed such that it will cover the entire area to be carved yet lie flush with the surface of the stock. An individual stock's characteristics will dictate which of the following methods is best for laying out a pattern.

It is relatively easy to create a pattern for a single-sheet side panel with extension for a stock surface that remains at virtually the same level from the forward portion to the buttplate or recoil pad compared with stock surfaces that have excessive curves, recesses, and high spots. With this type, there is but one minor recess to be dealt with. This is directly behind the lower rear portion of the grip and is the transition point between the grip and the rounded bottom edge of the buttstock (fig. 59). Some variations

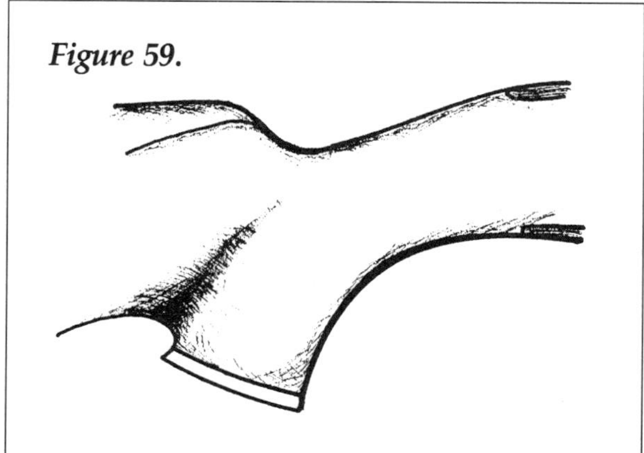

Figure 59.

are found in the degree of recess and shape of the transition area, but in most cases the recess and shape are generally similar.

Figure 60 illustrates a completed typical border layout showing joining, with options, of a panel and added section. Dotted line *A* represents the eliminated rear portion of the grip label; the forward portion was left as is. Dotted line *B* represents the eliminated bottom borderline of the added checkered area, and *C* represents a small portion of the upper border that has been altered from the location of line *D*. By connecting line *D* of the smaller checkered section to the upper and lower points of line *A* of the larger grip panel, the area between the grip panel and the checkered section connects to form a single large area. Note the manner in which the grip panel's upper portion of border at the connection of lines *A* and *D* has been extended beyond its original placement to match the curve of the smaller section. It's best to present the connection of the two sections with a curve rather than a straight line; it looks better. A curved line can be adjusted somewhat to compensate for the size of a design if necessary. Note the curve of line *D* at the transition point: The extended length to the rear is lower than the lowest point of the added panel. In this instance, it was determined that a more visually appealing border would be created by following the angle of the stock's lower edge than having the border rise to meet the lower point of the smaller added panel.

To correctly position the lower border, you

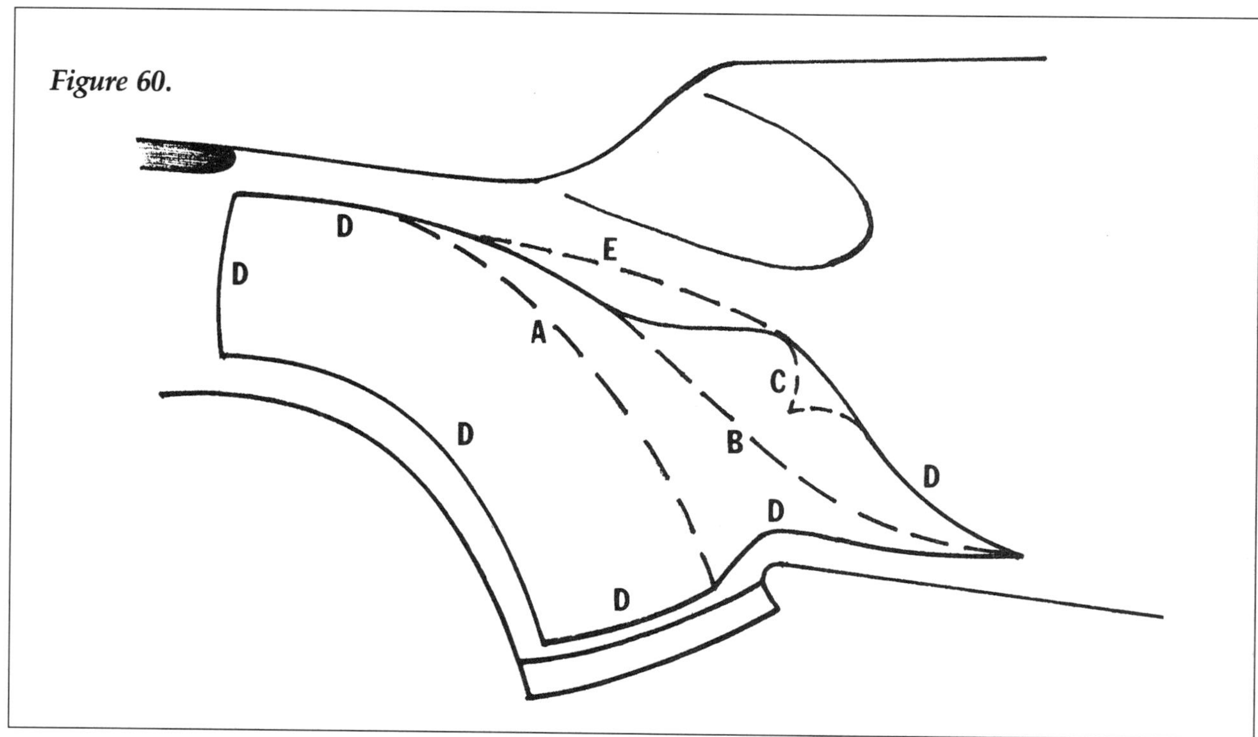

Figure 60.

need to place guide marks on the pattern sheet. While the pattern is secured to the stock, lightly draw small reference marks at two points along the beginning of the curve of the buttstock bottom. Make the first mark just beyond the rearmost portion of where you intend to position the completed design. Place the second at the rear of the transition. Now view the stock from the side with these marks held at eye level. Place another set of marks at what appears to be an equal distance between the first set of marks and the bottom edge of the buttstock. If you took an actual measurement between the centerline-of-stock mark on the tape and the first set of marks by following the contour of the stock, you would discover that the second set of marks is not centered exactly between the stock centerline mark and the first set of marks; it is slightly higher. The small difference between actual center and what appears to be center is enough to achieve a balanced appearance with relation to the configuration of the stock. Placing the design at the exact center between the stock centerline mark and the upper mark will make the design appear just a bit too much on the curved underside of the stock. The complete grip pattern layout and marks necessary for correct positioning of the extended design's lower border is shown in figure 61.

When contemplating the position of this portion of the border, keep in mind that when the border is placed deeper into the bottom curve of the buttstock, the rearmost vertical border of the smaller panel will have to be extended in length to meet the position of the lower placed border. One option is to curve the

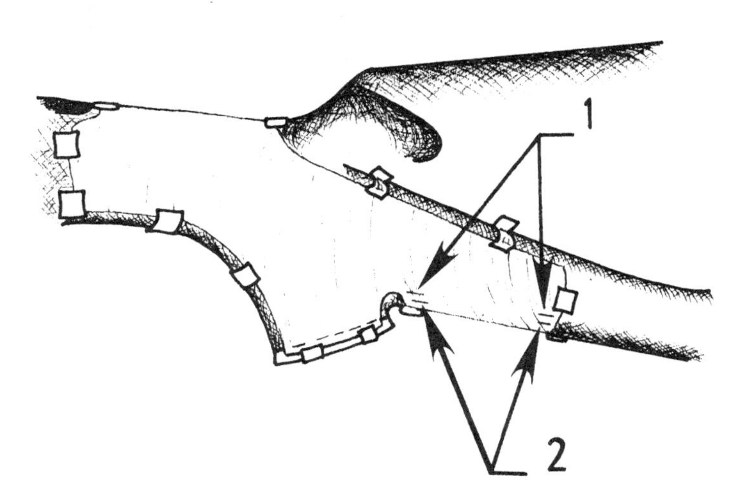

Figure 61. *Complete grip pattern layout with marks: 1, beginning of curve; 2, marks half the distance between the bottom centerline of stock and the beginning of curve.*

bottom borderline upward near its end, as shown in figure 60. This rearmost portion of the extended design could be held to its original overall length even with the lowered bottom borderline, but this would mean either a more abrupt rising of the lower border or a sharper downward curve of the upper border so that the two will meet. This to some degree would diminish the graceful flowing appearance that is sought. At the transition area, the border curves upward and follows the upper edge of the recess rather than running through the area, until it meets the lower border of the grip panel at line *A*.

After you have marked all the lines of the newly shaped border and applied all locator marks, make any necessary adjustments to the layout before removing the pattern sheet from the stock. Remove the sheet, touch up as needed, and retrace all lines in dark ink, then proceed to make the final pattern and opposite side pattern using techniques outlined in chapter 4.

When you have finished carving the first

side of the grip, place a piece of tape with a centerline-of-stock mark on the underside of the buttstock, running from the transition area and extending to, or beyond, the rearmost length of the design. You can later measure from the centerline mark of this tape to ensure that you are placing the opposite side design at the same distance.

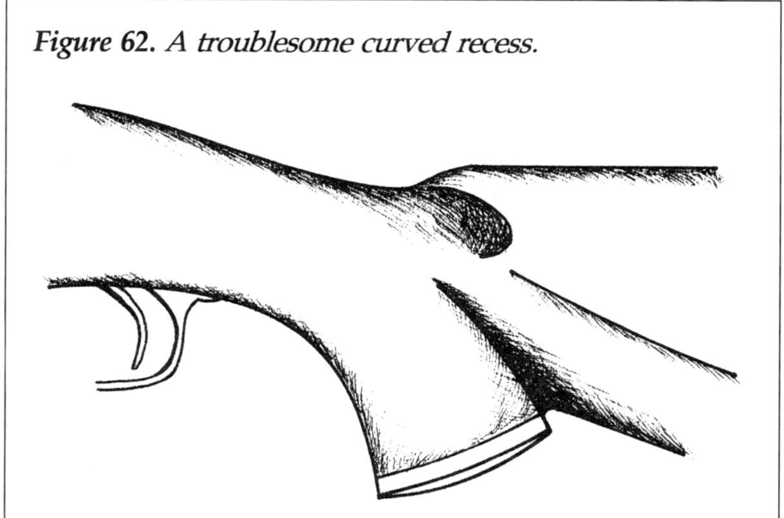

Figure 62. A troublesome curved recess.

You have many options when forming a borderline incorporating a side panel plus added area. With the pattern depicted in figure 60, the area between lines *B* and *D* can be eliminated altogether by using line *B* as the rearmost border of the design. Another option would be to leave the solid line intact but to extend it as far as line *E*. In this case, the connecting point will likely need to be forward of line *A* to present a uniform curve. The fleur-de-lis shown in the original layout has been eliminated. This too is optional. Before deciding on an option, be sure to consider its compatibility with the configuration of the grip and the featured design. If working on a client's firearm, discuss options with him or her before executing them. In my experience, most clients respect and appreciate advice and suggestions.

SECTIONAL PATTERNS

Sectional patterns are composed of two or more segments joined to form a single complete pattern. They are principally used when a gunstock's configuration makes it impossible to correctly fit a single sheet. This section gives instructions on pattern forming for stocks that have a curved recess at the rear of the grip that would fall within the limits of an extended design. This recess begins at the transition area between the rear edge of the grip and the buttstock, and gradually curves upward and forward while decreasing in width and depth until ending at stock surface level. This ending is usually at a point that is nearly in line with the bottom portion of the comb at the rear of the top rollover area of the grip. The overall length of such a curved recess is about 2 inches. This is the most difficult configuration for pattern shaping that you may encounter.

Errors in a completed carving can largely be attributed to improper pattern layout. Layout and placement of a pattern can at times be tedious, but these steps are always critical and should never be rushed or taken lightly.

Except on custom or California style stocks, grip configurations are generally one of two types (figs. 63 and 64). Each of these may at times require a sectional pattern but usually will not. The style shown in figure 63 is the more common of the two. Its recess behind the grip is wider, with softer edges at all points. This gives a flowing roll to its upper portion and a more rounded shape to the lower portion of the grip at the transition area. The degree of difficulty of pattern and design layout for either type depends more on the length and position-

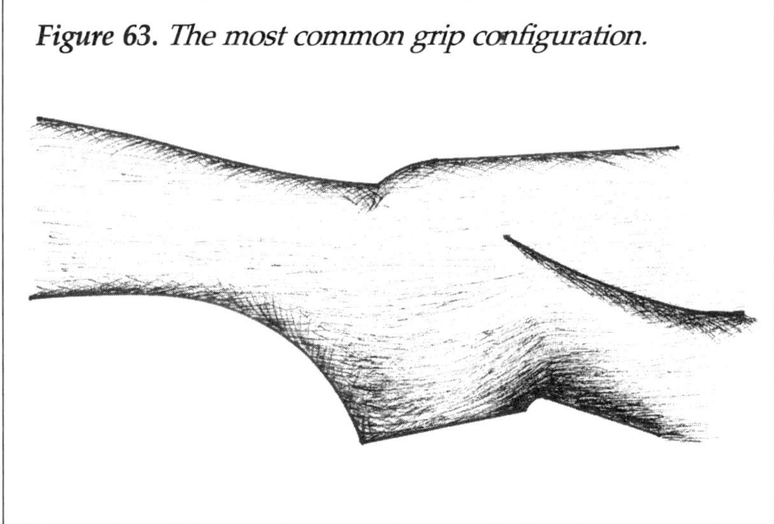

Figure 63. The most common grip configuration.

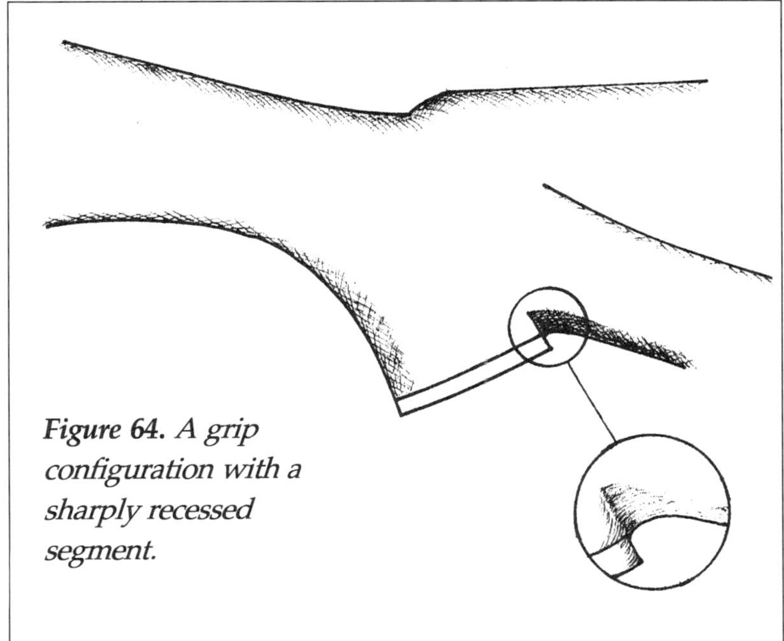

Figure 64. A grip configuration with a sharply recessed segment.

procedure to apply to all. The following are general guidelines with alternatives that you can apply to meet specific situations. You can follow the basic steps given here for the first and third segments of the overall pattern, which are the grip panel and buttstock segments. The procedure for the center segment, however, that of the curved recess, will vary from one stock to another.

The initial step is the placement of marked centerline and locator tapes. Position and mark these tapes as described previously for grip and rub segments. In this case, however, all are placed from the very beginning.

Curved Recess Segment

The curved recess segment is the first section to be formed. For a particular stock, use whichever method produces the fewest ripples in the pattern sheet while at the same time allows matching of continuing detail lines with adjoining segments. Some light rippling will be unavoidable, as tracing paper

ing of the curve than on the depth of the recess, although deeper-than-normal recesses will also increase difficulty.

The first sectional pattern we will look at is used only on excessively rounded stocks that have been altered. You will not encounter this type of grip on a standard production model.

This procedure will have to be modified for the particular stock you are working on, as there are far too many variables to allow an identical

cannot be made to uniformly match the contour of a curved recess. A minor high spot on a pattern sheet that will lie flat with a light touch presents no problem as long as no shifting or rolling of the paper occurs. Any ripple that will fold or form a sharp crease when touched from the side, however, will cause some degree of distortion within the design during design transfer. Any fragment of a detail line that falls on a gathered or raised portion of a ripple cannot be transferred to the wood, in which case you will lose some detail lines.

Method 1. This first method is the most desirable; use it if possible.

The first pattern segment is made for just the curve and forward side surface area of the recess. You generally will need only an inch-wide strip of tracing paper, although in some cases the paper may need to be wider for recesses that are wider at the transition area. This is one of the variables found among individual stocks, and you must be the judge. In all cases, the length is cut to extend from the bottom edge of the stock at the transition to the extreme top edge of the stock. Cut this strip straight, not on a radius to follow the full line of the curve. Begin shaping the paper from the bottom right rear of the grip. From this point, curve the paper upward to extend beyond the ending point of the curved recess.

Begin by securing the strip at the transition area below the intended range of the design. The paper, in addition to covering the transition area, should cover as much of the curved recess as possible above the transition area. Position the paper so that nearly half falls on each side of the lower groove of the curve. The paper's center should not deviate from the line of the curve more than $1/8$ inch in either direction. Then, holding the paper lightly taut at its top with thumb and index finger of your left hand, run the thumbnail of your right hand along the bottom groove of the recess upward from the transition area. Stop when the paper moves off center.

Because the paper will not lie flat around the curve, you need to make a series of scissor cuts along the rear edge of the strip to ease tension

and prevent the paper from tearing when being configured to match the curve. These cuts will allow a degree of flex near the center of the paper, where it's most important. The scissor cuts along this edge can usually be made half to three-quarters the distance from the rear edge of the paper to the groove. If necessary, these cuts can be longer, but keep them shy of the groove itself.

Make the first scissor cut slightly below where the line of the curve begins to exceed $1/8$ inch from the center of the paper. Before you make the next cut, keeping a thumbnail in the groove, tape the paper to the stock on the low side of the cut on the buttstock portion only. Reposition your thumbnail in the groove at the area of the securing tape. While guiding the paper with your left hand, continue to run your thumbnail in the groove until you can no longer

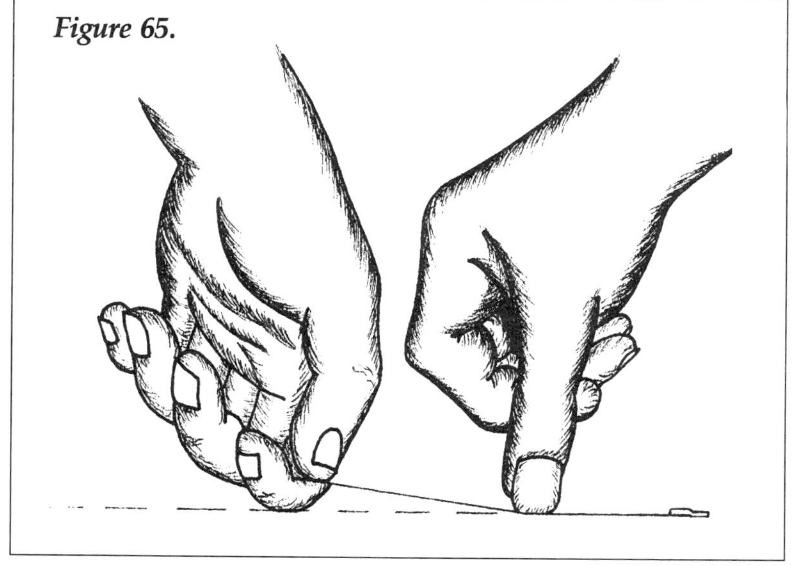

Figure 65.

hold the groove within the allowed center range of the paper (fig. 65). At this point, the paper is at risk of tearing if forced. Make another scissor cut at this point, and tape the paper to the stock as before while maintaining the crease in the paper with the curve of the groove. Make the cuts closer together around curves with a sharper radius. Continue this process until you have followed the line of the groove to its end. Tape the paper's rear edge from bottom to top while maintaining the indention made to match the lower half of the curve. From the end of the recess the strip continues, unmarked, until slightly beyond the area of the intended design. Place another securing tape there, on the rear edge of the paper at the end of the strip, not on the very end itself (fig. 66).

Because the paper was pressed to the wood at the bottom of the groove along the curve, the forward half of the pattern segment will be somewhat raised from the level of the wood. To deal with this raised portion, begin by position-

ing the thumbnail of your right hand in the groove at the lowest point nearest the transition area. While holding the paper in place with your thumbnail to avoid shifting or lifting of the rear portion, use a finger of the left hand to press the paper to the wood by moving away from the line of the curve at a 90-degree angle from the portion of the curve being worked. Hold the paper flush to the stock at the end of the stroke, remove your thumbnail from the groove, and secure the edge of the paper with tape. This procedure is somewhat awkward but doable.

Repeat this shaping and securing process throughout the entire length of the curve. There will be a number of ripples because of the in-

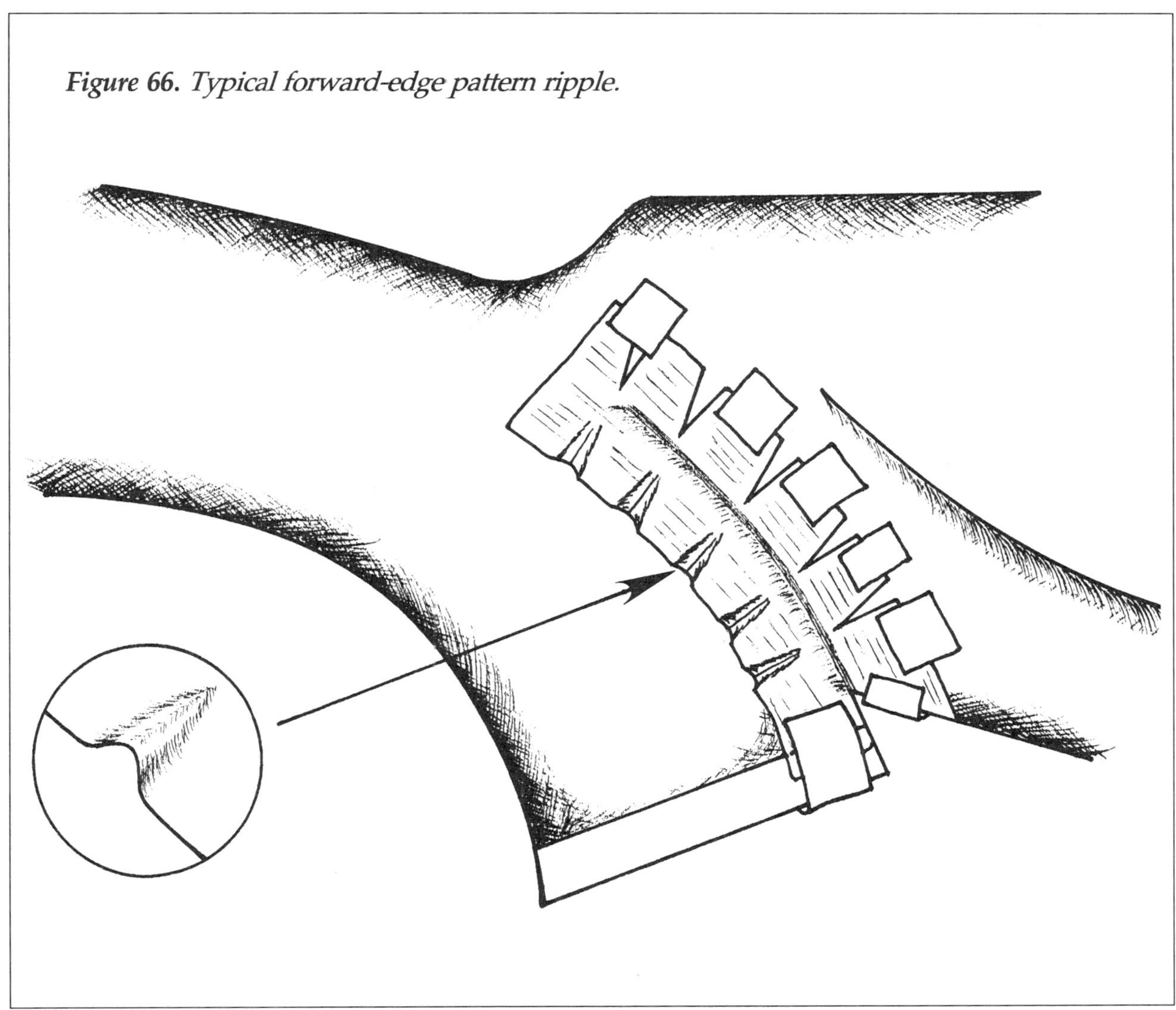

Figure 66. Typical forward-edge pattern ripple.

ward curving of the forward portion of the pattern sheet. How many and how severe the ripples will depend on the depth and degree of the curve. Severe ripples must be eliminated. Do so after the entire forward edge of the paper has been pressed and secured to the stock. Begin by using a pencil to lightly mark each ripple along its center from about $1/8$ inch from the groove to the forward edge of the paper. Then remove the tapes holding the forward edge to the stock, and scissor-cut each line the exact length of the mark. Do not cut beyond the beginning of the downward curve of the wood that leads into the groove. Leave at least $1/8$ inch of the paper from the upper edge of the curve uncut.

Once you have made the cuts, replace the forward portion of the paper onto the stock. The paper on each side of the scissor cut will now overlap (fig. 67). Retape the forward edge to the stock, maintaining the position of the recess. To ensure that this segment holds its shape when you remove it to trace design lines, place thin strips of masking tape lengthwise over the overlapping parts of the forward half of the pattern and cut segments of the rear portion. If there is excessive overlapping on the forward half and open slits on the rear half, an option is to cut and place a single long, thin strip of tape on each half that will cover all of the overlapping and open portions of the segment (fig. 68). This is done prior to removing the pattern from the stock. Should you do so, be sure to maintain at

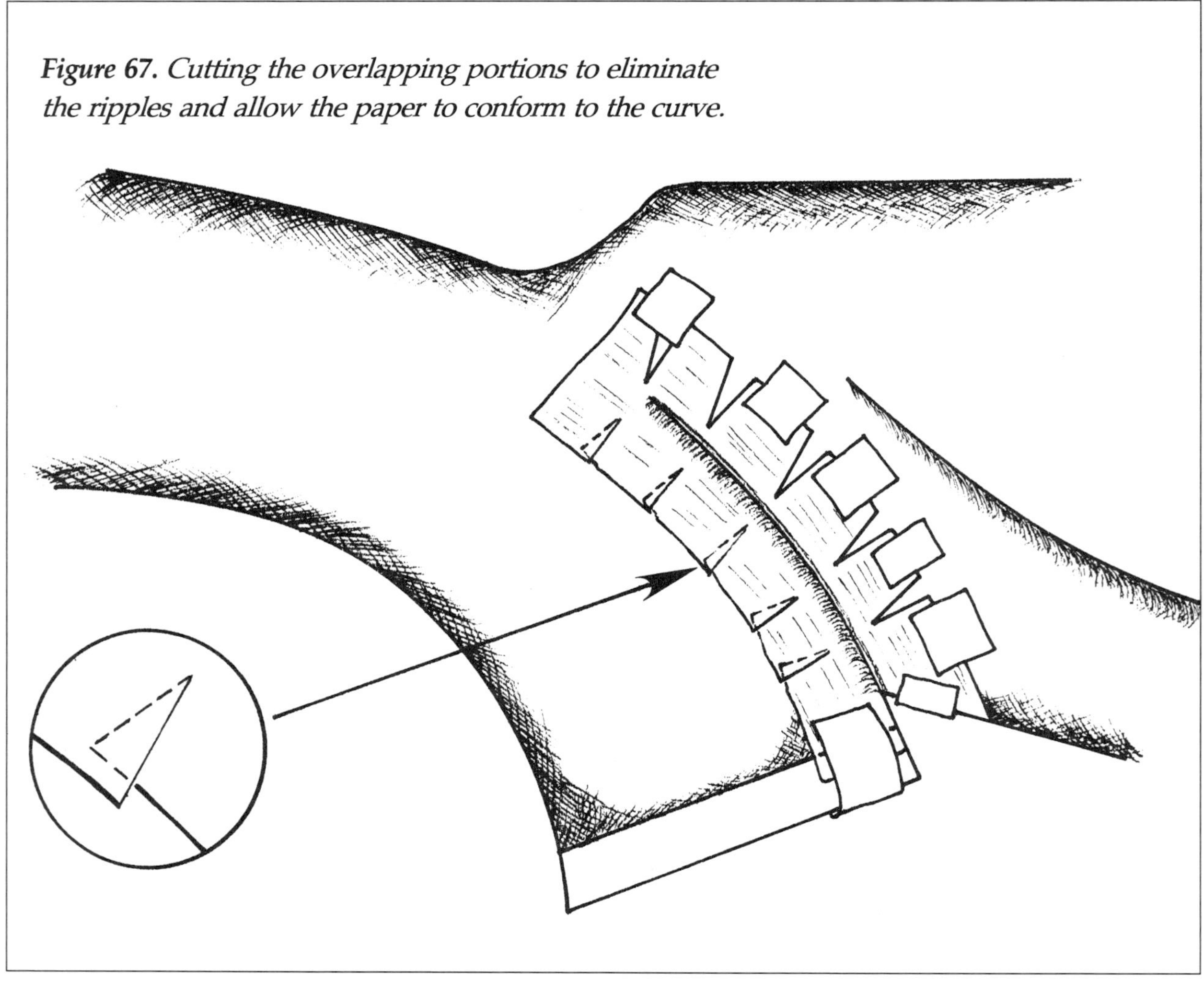

Figure 67. Cutting the overlapping portions to eliminate the ripples and allow the paper to conform to the curve.

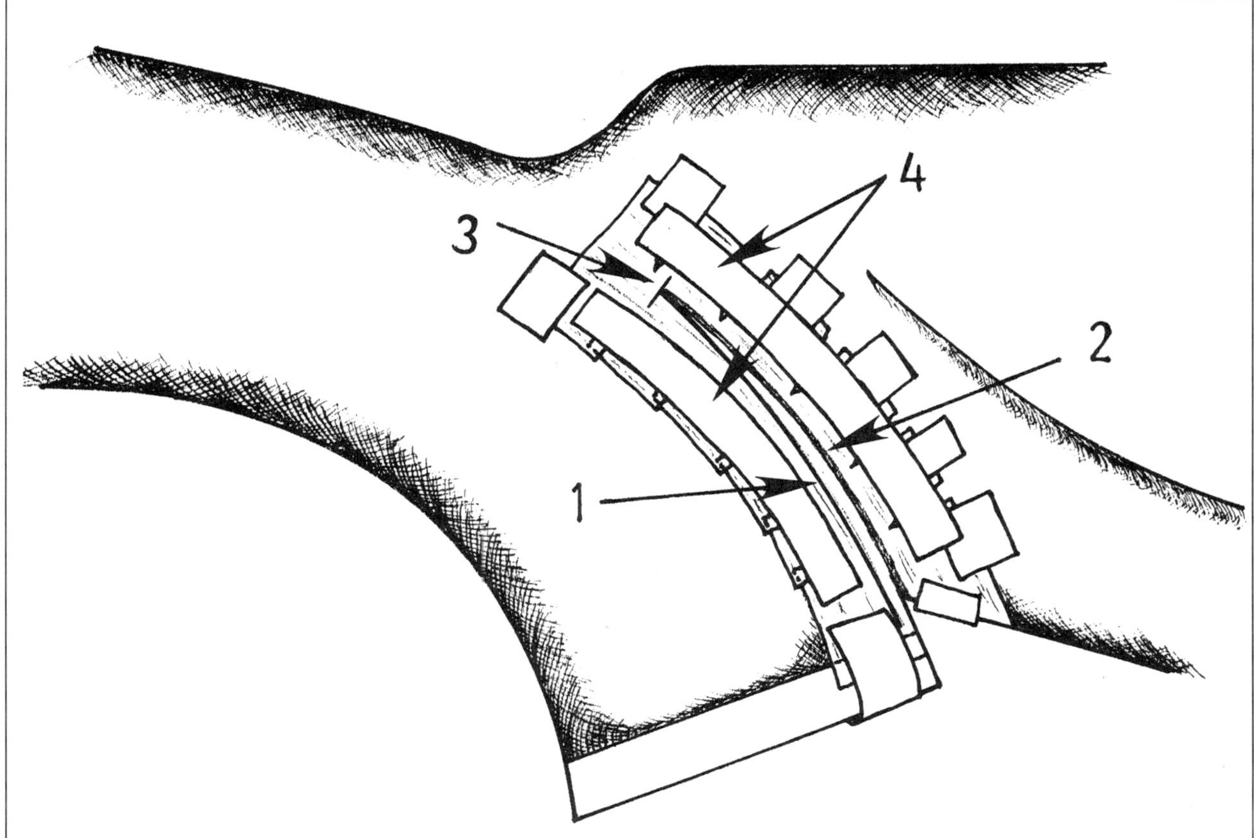

Figure 68. *Taping over many slits: 1, upper edge of grip; 2, lower groove; 3, end of groove mark; 4, pattern-holding strips.*

least $^1/_8$ inch of exposed paper along the entire upper edge of the curve, and equally as much rearward from the lower portion of the recess. Afterward, when you remove the segment for design tracing, you will trim away the initially placed securing tapes to remove the bulk. Now, mark the entire upper edge of the curve in ink from the transition area to its end. This segment is now complete. Keep it secured to the stock until you have finished the remaining segments.

The second pattern segment, the forward-most, is laid out and shaped as described for a standard single side panel, with one exception: Allow a greater excess of paper toward the rear so that it extends beyond the ink-marked edge of the curved recess of the first segment. After this segment is fitted and securely taped in place, trace the curving upper edge of the first segment onto it exactly as seen through the paper. Scissor-cut the paper along this line on the forward segment to remove all excess beyond. You may need to loosen a holding tape at the top of the grip to do this. With ink, make two pattern locator marks running from this segment onto the recess segment, one at the top and one at the bottom of the curved line. Each should be about ¼ inch long and split evenly between the two sheets. At this time, trace all other locator marks onto the pattern sheet as well (fig. 69). This segment also should remain secured to the stock.

The buttstock segment is the last to be

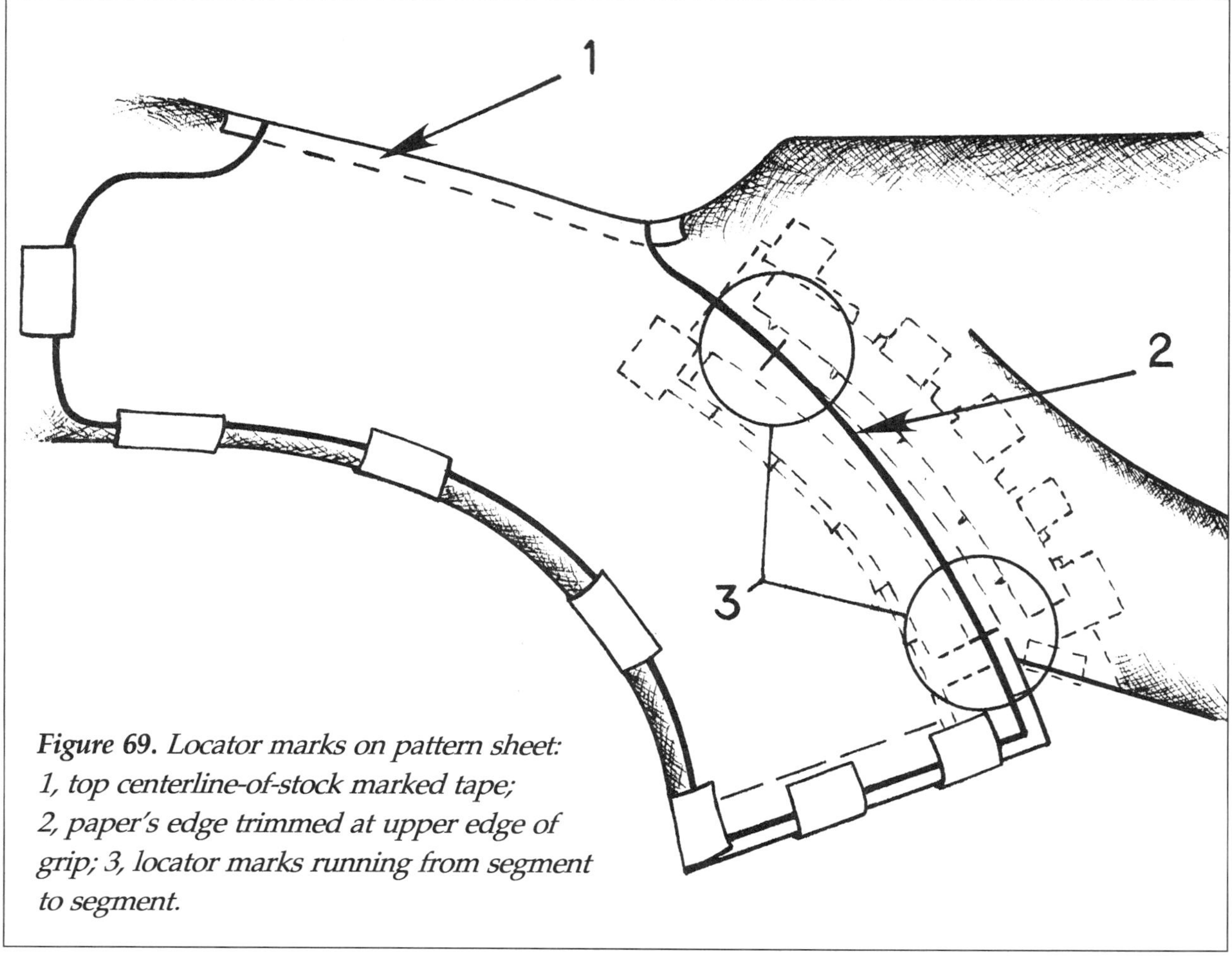

Figure 69. *Locator marks on pattern sheet: 1, top centerline-of-stock marked tape; 2, paper's edge trimmed at upper edge of grip; 3, locator marks running from segment to segment.*

made; here again follow basic layout procedures with regard to the placement of the centerline-of-stock marked tape and securing tapes for straight stocks and those with a raised cheekpiece, as outlined in figure 61. The following procedure for making the buttstock segment remains the same even if you are using an optional method for the first segment. To begin, trim the forward edge of this segment to match the lower contour of the curve of the center segment. The objective is to trim the paper to follow the contour while overlapping the rear portion of the center recess segment to ensure coverage of the scissor cuts, but without directly touching the slope of the recess. A distance of about $1/8$ inch from the slope is desirable, but it can be less if necessary to cover the gap of the

slits. The beginning carver will find that this task is not as difficult as it sounds but somewhat time-consuming.

The easiest way to proceed is to use a slightly larger pattern sheet than is needed. Place it on the buttstock with its leading edge fully covering the marked upper line of the curve on the center segment. Place a temporary holding tape on the rear edge and another about midway along the top or bottom edge to prevent shifting. You will need to trim the paper to accomplish this. Then hold the leading edge against the stock with at least two fingers spread wide. The paper should be taut and without ripples. If any are present, either you are pulling with too much pressure or the direction of pull is not in line with the rear tape. Held in this manner, the pattern sheet will not be lying flat to the wood on the buttstock side of the curved recess because the wood is higher at the upper edge of the curve. This is of no concern at this time. Trace the marked upper curve line of the center segment onto this sheet. Then make a crossmark at both the top and bottom ends of the curve; these will indicate where to trim to allow overlapping onto the center segment during the final positioning of the overall pattern. Now remove the paper from the stock, and trim along the line representing the upper portion of the curve.

This initially placed line of the curve is not the final product. Additional trimming will be necessary because the upper radius of the curve is smaller than the lower. By positioning the trimmed sheet at the lower portion of the curve, it is easy to see just how much more you need to trim so that the paper will lie flat to the wood while overlaying the scissor-cut portions of the center segment's rear edge. You may also need to make adjustments to the lines at the top and bottom of the curve that overlap other portions of the center segment.

Once you have properly fitted this edge to the curve, the next step is to determine where the remaining edges need to be trimmed. Allow enough excess to cover marked locator tapes and to accommodate pattern holding tapes. These need to be carefully placed so that they will not interfere with the area on which the design is to be traced. To accomplish this, place the pattern sheet in its correct position at the curved recess, and secure both the forward and rear edges. Some adjustment of the paper may be necessary to achieve the desired position. Then place two tapes on the forward edge, one at the top and one at the bottom of the curve, and a single holding tape on the rear edge near the center of the stock. Mark the remaining pattern lines. Portions at the top and bottom of the overall pattern that are not held by tape can

be hand-held to the wood while you do so. When this marking is completed, make a short locator mark at both top and bottom from the rear segment sheet onto the center segment, just as you did from the forward segment onto the center segment. These two marks and the centerline-of-stock mark on the underside of the buttstock will ensure correct alignment of the segments when you connect them after removal and tracing of the design (fig. 70).

It is easy to make opposite side panel segments of the forward and rear pattern shapes. The recess area segment will require a bit more work, however. There are two approaches to making the center segment for the opposite side. On rare occasions, the segment from the first side can be used on the opposite side. After use on the first side, the pattern will have holes made by the transfer tool. These holes can be closed somewhat by running the flat of a fingernail back and forth over the side opposite that from which the holes were made. Then use ink to retrace the design lines through the paper onto the opposite side. Invert the segment to conform with the recess of the second side. This procedure is not recommended for all three segments; it's only a slim possibility at best for the center segment. As a rule, you should use fresh pattern sheets that are free of transfer holes, though in this instance it may be possible to reuse the center recess segment because the area involved is so small and there are a minimal number of transfer holes. If you miss a few of these transfer holes during the transfer process, you are not likely to create a major detailing problem. The other segments, however, cover a large area and are full of holes, and it would be far too easy to miss design lines. If this procedure cannot be used for the center segment, your only alternative is to form a new pattern segment as was done for the first side.

The recess segment pattern is the first to be made and generally the first to be returned to

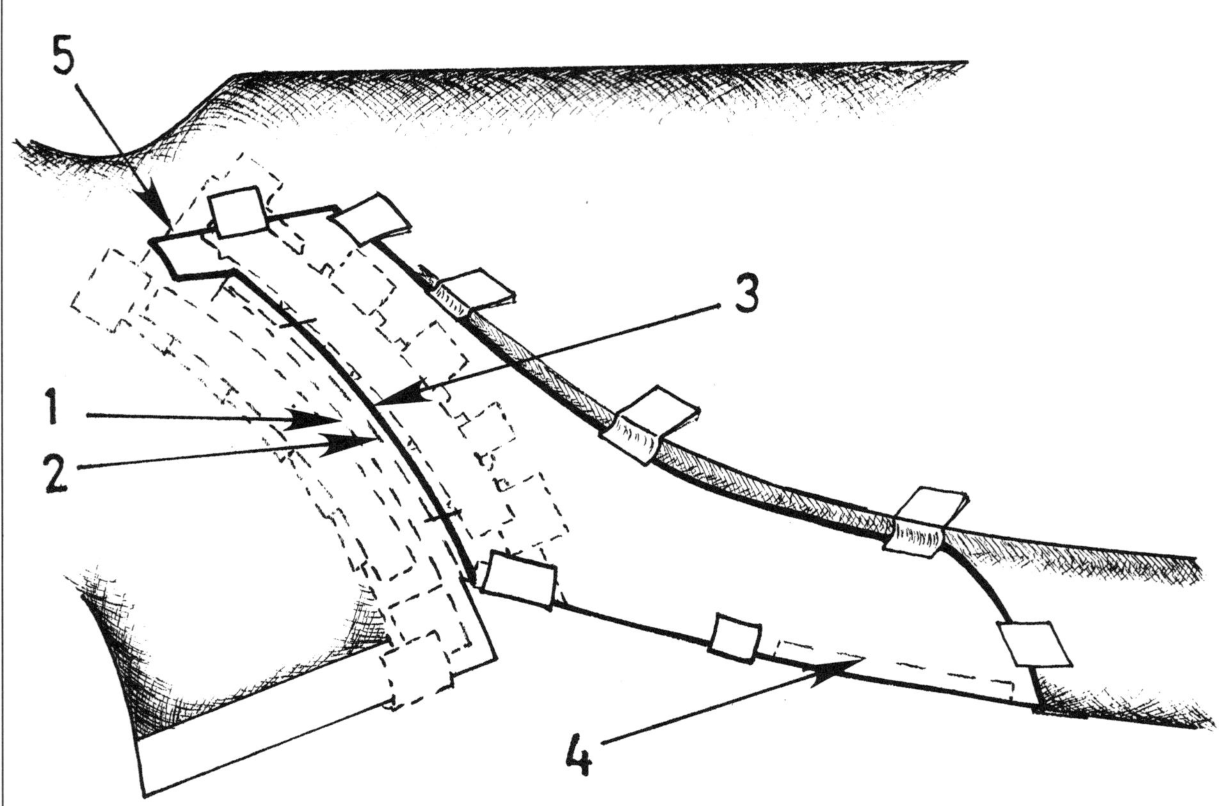

Figure 70. *Connecting the segments: 1, upper edge of grip; 2, lower groove; 3, paper trimmed to follow curve of lower groove; 4, bottom centerline-of-stock marked tape; 5, extended tab to run under forward segment.*

the stock after its portion of the design has been traced on it, although you can position the segments in any order. With experience, each carver develops his or her own preferred procedure. Aligning the locator and centerline marks on the grip and buttstock segments, including those lines that run from these segments onto the recess segment, will ensure that all segments are placed properly. Use just two holding tapes, one each at top and bottom, until you are certain that the alignment is correct. This will facilitate any necessary adjustments. Only after correct alignment has been achieved do you place permanent securing tapes around the edges of the pattern segments. If it is possible after a design has been traced onto the pattern segments, place a small holding tape at or near the center of the overlapping segments to hold them together, but without placing it on design lines. If a holding tape in the interior of the design is necessary but would obscure detail lines, use a small piece of cellophane tape or place a second interior tape over already transferred lines. When tracing design lines onto the recess segment, extend those running horizontally just a bit longer than is needed. This will serve as an aid in matching segments when they overlay each other.

Method 2. The second method used to form a curved recess pattern segment is the same in principle as the first. Instead of using a single strip that is cut and shaped while following the curve, however, this method entails a number of short, thin, overlapping strips placed lengthwise across the curve of the recess. Each is shaped and secured to the stock before the next is placed. Their exact number will vary, as stocks differ, but the procedure remains the same.

Individual tracing paper strips are precut from 1 to 1½ inches long. Depending on the characteristics of the stock, you may need longer strips to cover the wider portion of the recess at the transition area. On average, the strips should be ½ inch wide but can be more or less, depending on the ability of the paper to follow the contour of the curve without buckling and forming severe ripples. Should rippling occur, trim the strip to a lesser width. Don't worry about a very minor rise in the paper.

Place the first strip on top of the curve, with its center at the line of the recess and its upper edge about $^1/_8$ inch beyond the end of the groove at its top ending point. Affix a securing tape at the buttstock end of the strip. Then, while grasping the forward edge of the strip with the fingers of one hand, run a fingernail tip of the other hand from the tape to the recess, applying light pressure but pressing firmly enough to keep the paper taut from tape to recess line. When you reach the recess line, run the tip of the nail along the groove to create a sharp crease in the paper along that point, in the same manner as described for figure 65. Continue to hold the fingernail on the crease, and with a fingertip of the other hand, press the forward portion of the strip to the stock. Hold-

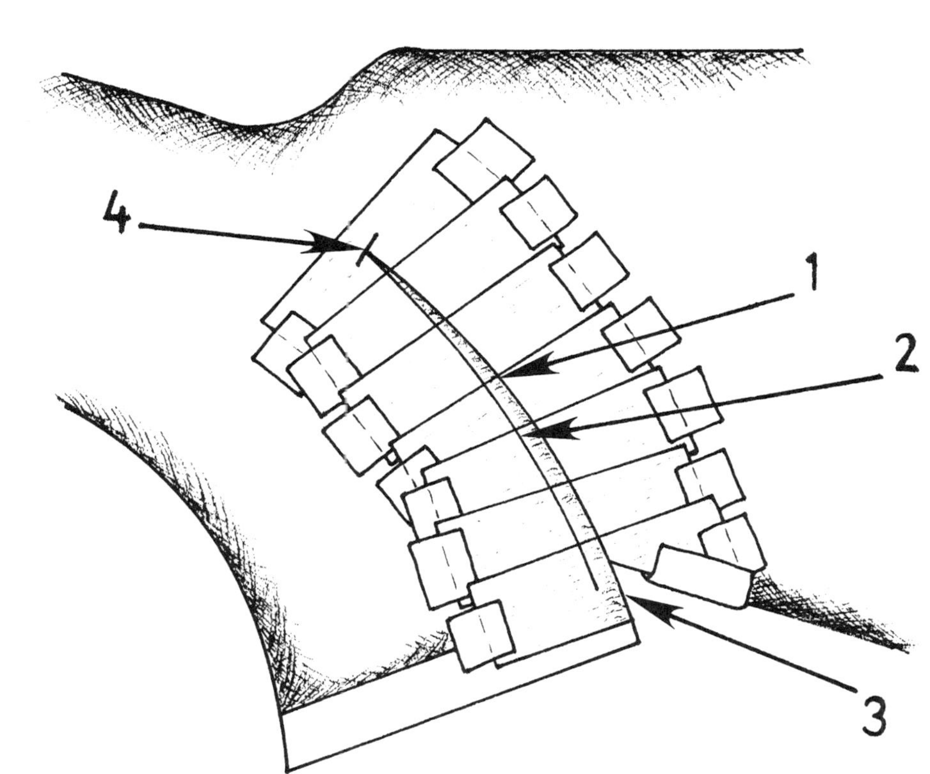

Figure 71. Applying overlapping strips: 1, lower groove; 2, upper edge of grip; 3, bottom pattern strip cut to fit configuration of the stock; 4, end of groove mark.

ing the paper thus to prevent it from moving, remove your fingernail from the groove, and use that hand to place a securing tape at the forward edge of the strip. Repeat the process with the other strips, in each case stopping just short of the end of the strip to allow an exposed amount of paper for the securing tape so that you will not have to remove the finger holding the paper. It is advantageous to cut a number of small pieces of tape before beginning to place the strips. Stick them half on and half off a table edge for easy grasping when you have only one hand to work with.

As you apply the strips, position each to overlap the one previously placed (fig. 71). Be sure to leave no gaps between strips. The drawbacks to this method are the amount of time required for placement and the bulk of tape created by the number of strips required to form the overall segment. Should one strip separate from another, realignment may not be exact. To prevent this from occurring, after the pattern has been completely formed, place a long strip of masking tape on each side of the curved recess, running its length from top to bottom as shown in figure 68. Place these about $^1/_8$ inch to each side of the crease made with your fingernail. Thus placed, all strips will be held together in position when you remove the pattern segment from the stock for design tracing. Take care during removal to prevent distortion of the segment layout. This process is a bit tedious. After this segment is removed, trim off the longer ends of the strips, thus eliminating most of the individual holding tapes.

Method 3. The third method for working a

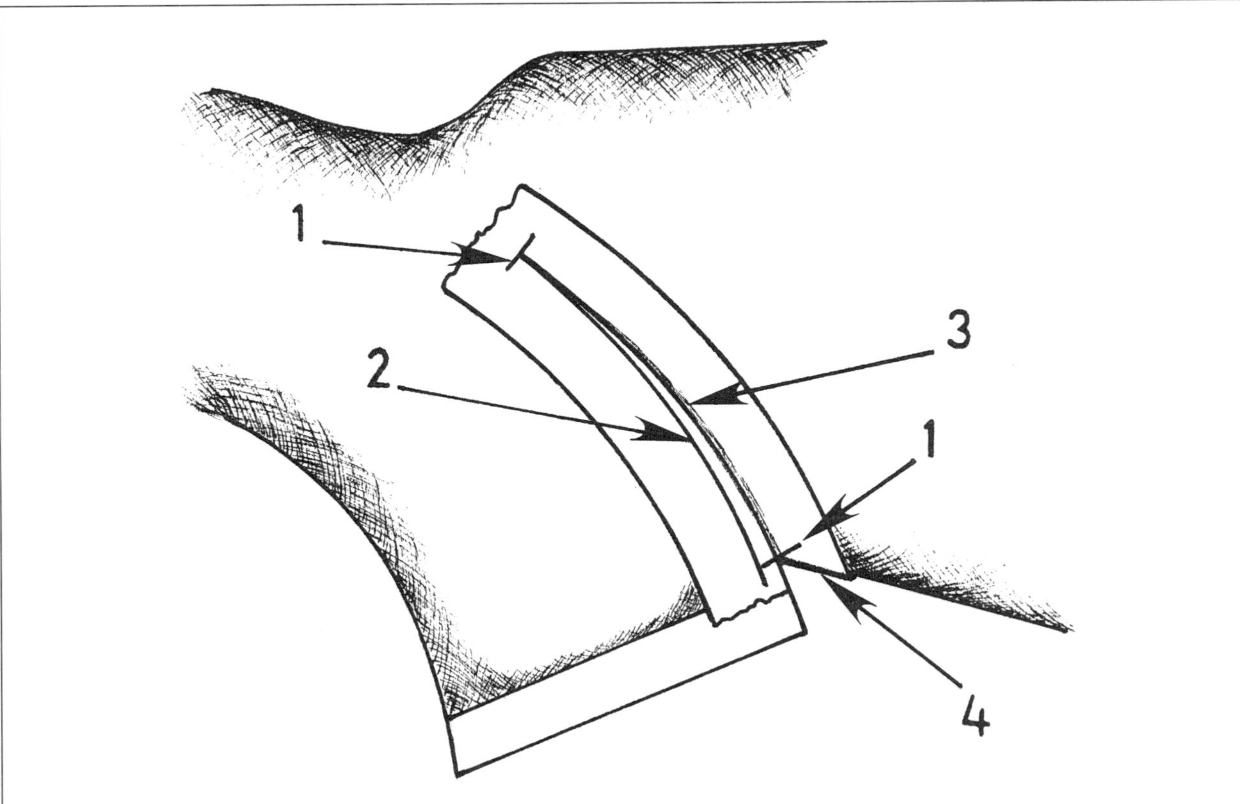

Figure 72. Applying tape directly over the curve: 1, upper and lower end of groove marks; 2, upper edge of grip; 3, lower groove; 4, tape cut to fit configuration of stock.

curved recess entails placing a strip of ¾- or 1-inch-wide masking tape directly over the line of the curve its full length, while maintaining the bottom of the recess at or near the center of the tape (fig. 72). Once applied, run the tip of a fingernail along the groove, creating an indentation on the tape that will clearly define its line. Make a crossmark on the tape at the endpoints of the groove at both top and bottom. The tape serves to provide a surface on which to trace or freehand sketch design lines. Do not alter it or remove it from the stock until the design has been completely transferred to the wood. Transfer of the design is done directly through the tape.

DESIGN PLACEMENT ON SECTIONAL PATTERNS

When planning a design layout for sectional patterns, you need to consider a number of questions regarding the configuration of the grip. You must be sure the subject matter will be compatible with any curve or recess, especially with grip types that have a longer, more sharply defined recess. The size and shape of the subject must be suitable for the space within the limits of the intended border. Pay special attention to the positioning of wildlife to achieve overall balance within the shape of the area. Determine whether the subject will overlap any part of the curved recess. In what way and to what degree will it affect the overall design? Will high detailing fall on the side area of a more sharply defined recess? Will the remainder of the design fall on a more easily observed surface? If so, how much visual distortion will occur? These questions must be asked and answered.

Sectional patterns require that you trace portions of a design onto them in such a manner that when they are assembled back onto the stock all the design lines from one section will meet with the appropriate design lines on the

adjoining section. A two- or three-piece sectional pattern will be sufficient for even the most unusual stock configurations. What follows are instructions for making a three-piece sectional pattern. Sectional pattern sections have their own locator marks, which aid in placement when returning the pattern to the stock. Designs need their own markings to determine what part of the design is to be traced onto which section. All sectional patterns use the same procedure for tracing a design and marking the original design to ensure correct positioning of the pattern section to be traced.

The first step, before removing the pattern sections from the stock, is to lightly trace the outline of the maximum area of coverage. After the line is made, remove the pattern sections from the stock. Remove each section separately in the reverse order from which they were placed. Since they are not taped together but held to the stock with their individual holding tapes, this is an easy task. After the sections are removed, match the locator marks of each section with the adjoining section and place two small pieces of tape to hold the sections together, one at the top and one at the bottom of the pattern. Try to keep these temporary tapes out of the design area. After the sections have been joined, overlay the joined pattern sections onto the design to be traced. Adjust either the design or pattern sheet so the design falls completely within the border outline. Now is the time to study the relationship of the border to the subject matter of the design and to determine if any enlargement or reduction is necessary. When you are satisfied with the placement of the design, hold the forward section of the pattern sheet to the design to prevent shifting. Remove the upper and lower tapes holding the forward and center sections together and separate the sections. Use several pieces of tape to hold temporarily the forward pattern section and the design. Trace the parts of the design underneath the pattern sheet. Draw a line the full length of the rear edge of the forward pattern sheet onto the design. This line will be the forward guide to tracing design lines that will be on the center pattern section.

Next, reverse the center section and use the side of a pencil lead to rub a light coating of lead along the crease that forms the lower edge of the curved recess of the grip. Do not rub hard, as you do not want to distort the paper. The center section has been formed with a slight rise, and you want to maintain this rise during this procedure. Flip the pattern section over and align the upper edge mark of the recess with the rear edge mark of the forward section. Do not press the center section flat to the design. After alignment, place tape at the top and bottom of the pattern section on its lower portion to hold it in place. Trace the line of the crease with a pencil. This will transfer the line of the crease onto the original design. Remove the center pattern section and trace over the transferred mark to make it more visible. Do not attempt to trace any of the design lines onto the center pattern section at this time.

The next step is to overlay the rear pattern section onto the design with its forward edge matching the lower recess mark of the center section and to trace the rear portion of the design onto it. Trace the design onto this section after applying holding tapes to prevent shifting. If the rear pattern section was not trimmed to match the exact lower recessed curve of the grip, you can ensure its correct placement by keeping the center section in place and matching the pattern locator marks of the two sections, then by placing holding tapes on the rear section. After this, remove the center section so you can apply additional holding tapes to the rear section along its forward and rear edges. Trace the portion of the design that falls in the rear section.

The next step is to place the design on the center section. This area should have a minimum number of lines. In most instances the center pattern sheet serves as a connection to ensure the proper positioning of the forward and rear sections, on which nearly all of the design is placed. A sharp curve of shallow depth will generally allow you to sketch freehand in this area to connect design lines from the forward and rear sections. This is especially true at the upper end of the curve, where the level of the stock forward of the recess line is the same level as it is to the rear. The area between the forward and rear sections gradually increases until it reaches its widest point at the transition area. How wide this area may be depends on the configuration of the stock. Even on the most unusual configuration, at some point in the upper area of the curve the level of wood will be at the same plane. If you are confronted with an area of more than $1/8$ inch, trace the lines of the original design instead of sketching them.

Do not attempt to trace design lines onto the center pattern section in the manner described for the forward and rear sections. Trace the design lines onto the center section after it has been resecured to the stock. To do this, overlay a new piece of tracing paper over the original design from which the tracings are to be taken. Trace the forward and rear pattern section marks and all design lines in between. Trim the paper to a size that will allow you to apply holding tapes without interfering with the traced lines. Reverse the paper and use a soft lead pencil to trace the design lines. It isn't necessary to trace the defining lines of the forward and rear sections. Turn the paper right side up and position it onto the intended area of the center section. Adjust the paper so the design lines join with the appropriate lines of the adjoining sections. Secure the paper and trace over the design lines. The lead tracing on the opposite side will transfer to the center pattern section. Retrace the transferred lines in ink.

If the grip is highly pronounced, a center section tracing might not be large enough to connect design lines to both the forward and rear pattern sections. If this is the case, split the difference between the forward and rear sections. Do not match the design lines of the center section to one adjoining section more so than the other. If split equally, the additional space will not be noticeable.

SINGLE SHEET EXTENDED DESIGN GRIP PATTERN

The following steps detail how to form a pattern for an extended grip area design on stocks that do not require a sectional pattern and how to easily assess design placement.

First, place a full-length sheet of tracing paper lengthwise from front to rear directly over the grip area, approximately centered over the curved recess. Secure the rear edge of the paper with two temporary holding tapes. Then, holding the paper taut, place a third tape along the forward edge. To maintain correct positioning during subsequent procedures, slip an additional 1-inch piece of tape half under the forward edge of the paper next to the holding tape, and press it firmly to the stock. This tape is to remain in position during the entire process and will serve as the forward locator tape. Make a line about ½ inch long, half on the paper and half on the tape.

Next, lightly pencil sketch lines around the perimeter and cheekpiece (fig. 73). Take off the holding tape at the forward edge, and cut along

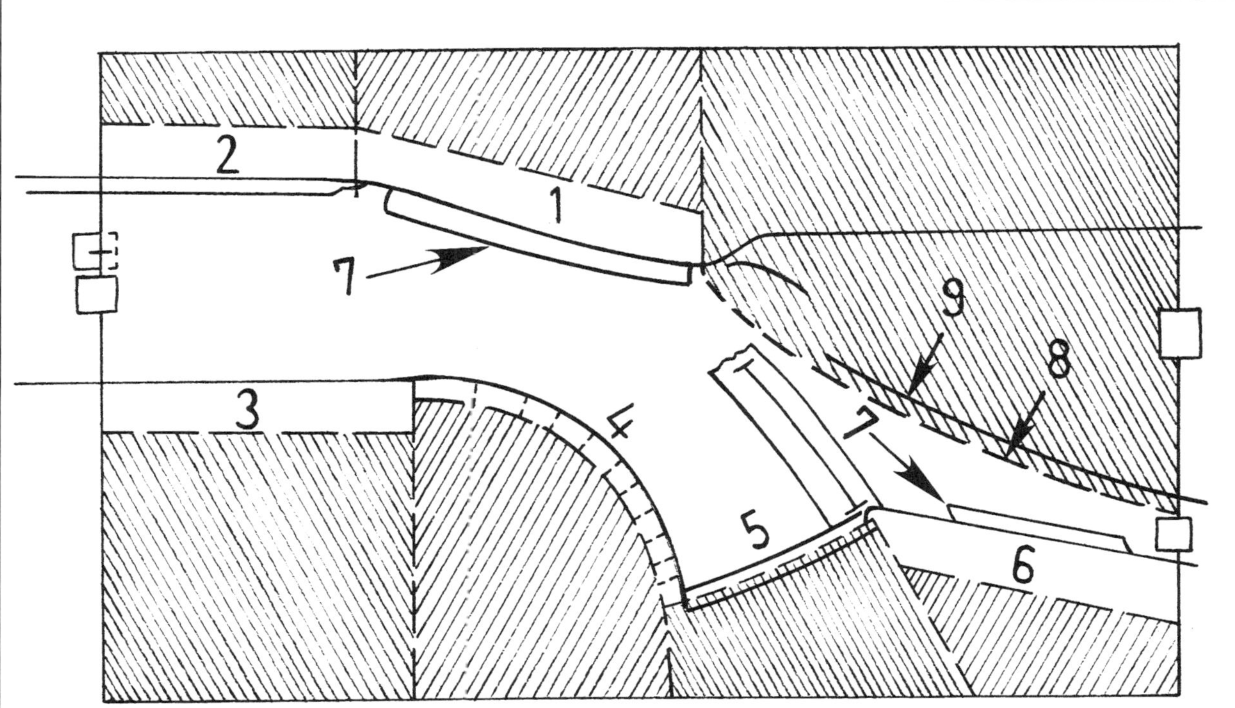

Figure 73. Trimming the pattern: 1, 2, 3, and 6, excess portions retained after shaded area is trimmed away; 4, slits cut in pattern to allow paper to conform to curve; 5, paper trimmed at center of grip cap or lower edge of grip if no cap is present; 7, upper and lower centerline-of-stock marked tape; 8, lower configuration of cheekpiece; 9, upper edge of cheekpiece.

these lines to remove excess and allow the paper to be conformed to the configuration of the stock. Be sure to lift the paper high enough to avoid accidental damage to the stock with the scissors. After cutting, secure the forward edge to the stock in its original position by matching the locator marks on the paper and the locator tape. Because this is a rounded grip, some of the paper on the buttstock side of the curve will be slightly above the level of the stock. This is of no consequence at this time and will be dealt with after you have completed the forward segment of the pattern. Be sure, however, that there is no slack in the paper from front to rear during the following procedure.

Though cuts in the paper will permit it to conform to the stock for pattern outline shaping, some areas will require additional trimming for an exact fit. Once you have done any needed trimming, align the forward locator marks, and resecure the pattern to the stock. Roll the paper at area *A* (fig. 74) over the top to the opposite side, trim it, and secure it to the wood of the stock just beyond the top of the grip locator tape. During the process, and before securing this portion of the pattern, trim away any portion of the paper at either end of the centerline-marked locator tape that prevents the pattern sheet from lying flat to the stock. After securing the grip section, fold the forward portion of the paper (*B*) over the main body of the receiver inletting. Trim the paper here so that you can secure it either to the inside of the inletting or to the opposite side of the stock.

The next area to be worked is the forward bottom portion of the pattern sheet (*C*). Trim away excess paper so that you can secure the pattern sheet to the bottom of the stock just after it makes its turn to the underside. Trim and secure the paper at this length from the forward edge to the cut made where the downward turning of the finger rest portion of the grip begins. The curved finger rest portion (*D*) is trimmed and secured in the same manner as the

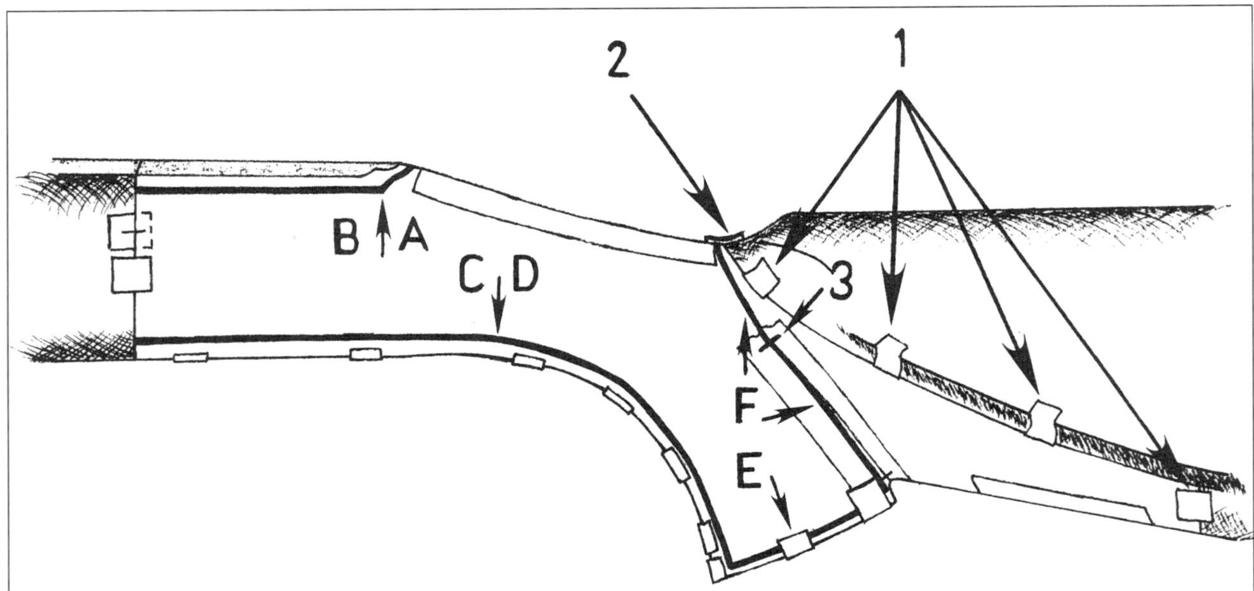

Figure 74. Line sketched along contour of receiver tang inletting: 1, securing tapes removed after lines A *through* F *are sketched; 2, securing tape removed from opposite side of stock to allow the cutting of line* F *from the top of the grip to the crossmark at the midpoint of the line (this is replaced after* F *is cut to point 3).*

forward portion, although here it is often necessary to make a series of short cuts along the sweep of the curve so that you can secure the pattern to the stock without ripples. At the bottom, trim the paper so that its edge (*E*) runs at or near the bottom edge of the grip, following its contour to the beginning of the transition area. Place the last holding tape directly at this point (*F*), attaching the paper to the bottom of the grip area.

Now that the forward portion of the pattern sheet has been shaped and secured, use a pen to trace the centerline-of-stock mark at the top of the grip onto the pattern sheet. Then lightly sketch a pencil line from the forward endpoint of the centerline mark to follow the contour of the receiver tang inletting (fig. 74 *A & B*). Begin the line $^1/_8$ inch from the inletting at the centerline, and gradually bring it to ¼ inch from the inletting at the point where you can sketch it forward to the leading edge of the pattern sheet ¼ inch below the top edge of the stock. Sketch the next line (*C*) starting at the forward edge of the paper along the lower edge of the stock at the beginning of the curve to its underside. Bring the line rearward at this position until it reaches the downward-curving portion leading to the finger rest area (*D*). From here, line *D* should follow the grip configuration at a position along its forward edge where the wood begins its sharpest curve to the extreme forward portion of the finger rest area. When reaching the bottom of the grip, run the line (*E*) rearward at a minimum of $^3/_{16}$ inch from the edge of the wood. The endpoint of the bottom grip line is determined by where it will intersect with a line traced to match the upper edge of the recess curve (*F*). On this line, draw a crossmark at the end of the curve at its top. From this crossmark, draw a line straight to the rear of the centerline mark at the top of the grip. This will complete the marking of the forward half of the pattern sheet.

To shape the buttstock portion, first remove the rear pattern holding tapes. Lift the rear half, and scissor-cut the line from the crossmark at the top of line *F* to the rear of the centerline at the top of the grip of the forward half of the sheet. To make this cut, it is sometimes necessary to loosen a holding tape that is securing the paper at the top portion of the grip on the off side. If you do so, reattach it as soon as the cut is made.

During the procedure that follows, the rear portion of the pattern sheet (fig. 74 *F*) will shift to a small degree from its original position. This will be more noticeable on stocks with a deeper curve. Because of this possibility, a portion of the pattern at the lower area of the cheekpiece (the dotted line, *8*, fig. 73) is first trimmed at a position matching the upper edge of the cheekpiece (*9*), or slightly beyond. After you fit the pattern to the grip area, you can retrim this portion of the pattern to match the lower line of the cheekpiece. You need to cut the pattern sheet above the crossmark of line *F* to ease resistance and prevent buckling of the paper along the line of the curve. After you cut the line above *F*, return the paper to a flat position against the stock, but do not attach holding tapes.

Place the tip of a fingernail in the groove of the curve at the crossmark at the top of line *F*, then run the nail along the line of the groove. You may need to hold the paper to the stock at the curve's upper edge to prevent its shifting. Your fingernail will create an indentation on the paper that will clearly define the position of the lower groove on the pattern sheet. The pressing of the paper to the bottom area of the curve will cause the rear unsecured portion of the pattern sheet to be pulled slightly forward. If this portion were secured, there would be no give, and the paper would likely tear under the pressure. Repeat the process along the entire length of the groove. Once it is complete, trace it in ink.

In some cases, it is best to draw the fingernail across the paper from the top forward portion of the sheet to run downward into the groove. This will draw up any slack in the paper. Only light pressure is needed to create an indentation; do not bear down too hard, or you risk damaging the paper. During the process, it is often necessary to hold a fingernail tip of one hand in a portion of the groove as close as possible to the next area to be indented, and make the indentation with a fingernail of the other hand. This helps keep the paper from shifting.

Before making each indentation, be certain that all previous indentations have remained in place. Upon making the last indentation, continue to hold the top of the fingernail in the groove at its bottom endpoint near the transition area, and place one or more pieces of tape across the cut line above the crossmark at the top of line *F* to maintain the position of the two sides. In all instances, there will be some degree of either overlapping or opening along this line once the formation of the recess layout is complete. After you have secured the sides of the cut above the crossmark, retrace the groove with a fingernail, this time with a single sweeping motion from one end to the other, in order to smooth out the indentation.

If the stock has a well-defined concave configuration at the transition area behind the lower rear of the grip, you need to mark the outer edge of this concave area on the pattern sheet. Hold the pattern sheet taut, with a fingernail positioned at about the center of the groove, and place a holding tape on the rear edge of the paper. Then position a small piece of tape half under the paper near the holding tape. This will serve as the rearmost locator tape. Draw a ½-inch long straight line half on the paper and half on the tape. Use ink. If your intended design will extend beyond the edge of the raised portion of the cheekpiece, trim the pattern sheet along the bottom edge of the cheekpiece where

it meets the level area of the stock, beginning at the end of the centerline at the drop of the comb. Then fold the bottom portion under the buttstock and trim approximately ½ to 1 inch beyond the centerline-of-stock mark. Secure the paper there. Trace the centerline mark and at least one crossmark onto the pattern sheet.

After you have traced all centerline and pattern locator marks, draw a full-length line 1 inch above the bottom buttstock centerline mark. Now remove the pattern from the stock. Make a scissor cut along the line of the lower groove and the line marking the upper edge of the grip curve, starting at the transition area and ending where both lines meet at the crossmark on the upper portion of line *F*. These cuts will allow you to remove the paper between the bottom of the groove and the upper edge of the curved recess.

You need now to determine what part of the design will fall in the area between the upper edge and lower groove of the recess. With the area of paper between the upper edge and lower line of the groove removed, you will be able to determine where and just what part of the design will be placed on the tape that lies underneath, covering the line of the curve. To do this, you overlay the pattern sheet onto the intended design.

Your first concern is to make certain the design fits as intended within the lines sketched on the pattern sheet. Make adjustments to the design as necessary to ensure a proper fit. Then secure the design to a white background sheet of paper or poster board, and secure the pattern sheet over the design, keeping the design with the boundary lines on the pattern. Now trace the design onto the pattern sheet. Mark off on the design sheet that area of the design that falls within the cutout portion of the groove and upper edge of the curve. Once you have completed the overall design tracing, remove the pattern sheet and resecure it to the stock, positioning it by aligning the locator marks. Now freehand sketch the lines of the design that fall within the cutout area onto the tape that runs along the line of the curve.

Remember that with the many differences among gunstocks, there is no one pattern layout that will work in all situations. With individual stocks, the area between the upper edge and lower groove of a curved recess can be relatively large or almost nonexistent. The methods presented here and through the grip pattern section are generally for the extreme cases. Extreme cases will be encountered, though only occasionally, and knowing how to deal with one is a must. When there is little distance between the upper and lower portions of the recess, it is an easy matter to draw design lines to connect with corresponding lines of adjoining sections. There are usually few detail lines in this area, with anywhere from one to four transfer holes on a single horizontal line. It is best to avoid a great amount or degree of detailing in this area.

An alternative to freehand sketching lines in that area is to trace them in soft pencil on the reverse side of the original pattern sheet or on a duplicate. Affix the pencil-marked side to the matching area of the pattern cutout, then transfer the lines to the tape by tracing somewhat firmly over the lines of the original drawn side. Draw with ink over the lines thus impressed on the tape to ensure a degree of permanence.

OVER-THE-TOP PATTERNS

An over-the-top pattern is used for a layout that connects opposing side panels with a continuous design running across the top of the grip between the action and the base of the comb (fig. 75). Layout of all other areas of each side panel is the same as described earlier for the single side panel. Place and mark a centerline-of-stock tape running along the leading edge of the finger rest area of the grip, as shown in figure 51. This tape must remain on the stock, un-

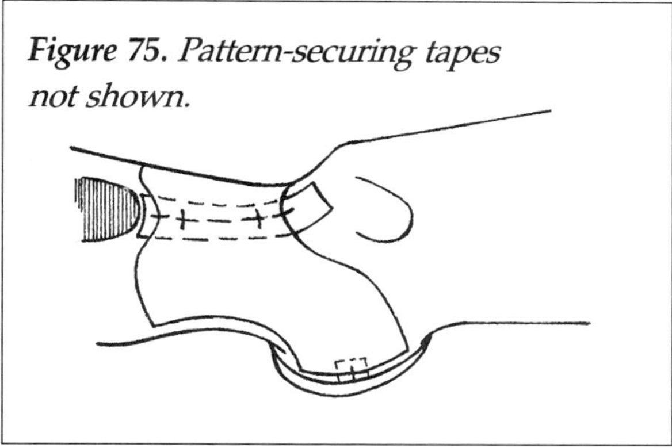

Figure 75. Pattern-securing tapes not shown.

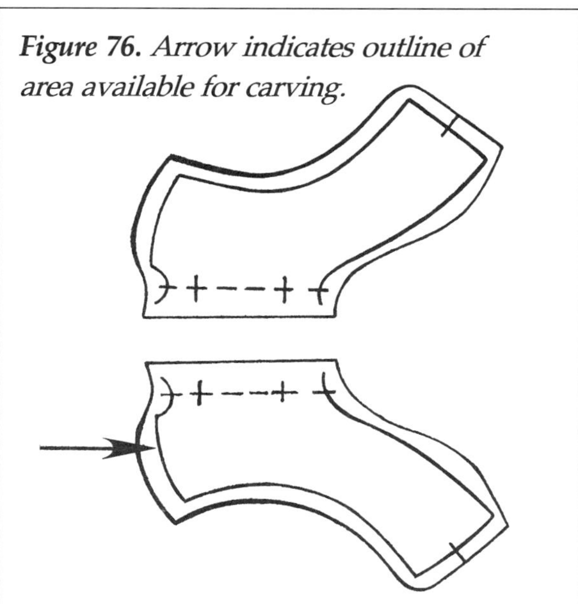

Figure 76. Arrow indicates outline of area available for carving.

changed, from the moment you draw the centerline mark on it. If the side area designs are identical, their connecting lines will easily match at the centerline-of-stock mark. The pattern for the opposite side is formed by tracing an exact copy of the first side (fig. 76). After you have matched the top centerline-of-stock mark, verify the exact placement of the lower portion of the opposite side pattern by measuring from like points on both side patterns to the leading lower edge of the design. Use centerline marks to measure also.

Shaping and design procedures are also the same as detailed for a standard single side panel layout. The extended portion that runs over the top of the grip is of a width to cover the area along the centerline mark from the base of the comb to a $^1/_8$-inch minimum from the receiver inletting.

Do not secure both side pattern sheets to the grip at the same time, as you will completely carve one side before beginning the other. If you placed the opposing pattern sheet at the same time as the first, it would be damaged during the carving of the first side. Also, do not transfer the opposite side design until you have finished carving the first. It will be necessary to grasp the side opposite that being carved throughout the carving process, and many of the transfer holes would become indistinguishable through handling. To continue the design after carving the first side, you need only to match the design lines of both sides at the centerline and measure from the forward grip centerline mark to position the lower portion of the pattern. Therefore, there is no need to transfer the design to both sides at the same time.

Transfer of the design is done through both the paper and the tape. Though the added thickness of the tape does require a bit more pressure on the transfer tool for penetration, this will present no problem whatsoever. Take care, however, not to press too hard, as is the tendency of many beginning carvers. This can result in holes deep enough to be seen at the completion of the carving or to weaken areas of wood on closely placed detail lines.

FULL WRAP-AROUND PATTERNS

Full wrap-around pattern layouts test your patience. The design not only runs over the top, but it also extends around the forward finger grip area to connect the side panels (fig. 77). The portion of the design encircling the finger rest area can be partial to full-length in height; the maximum height is from just above the grip cap to just below the trigger guard inletting, as shown by the strip area in the drawing. The total area encompassed depends on the chosen design. To place a full wrap-around design, you match corresponding design lines of both sides at the centerline mark on the top of the grip and match the centerline at the forward finger rest area.

The degree of curve leading to the forwardmost portion of the finger rest area from the leading edge of the standard placed side panel will determine the method to use in forming a pattern segment along this area. Generally, a match-line pattern is called for, for which there are two modes of application. In both instances, it is absolutely essential that you establish a centerline-of-stock mark at the top of the grip and forward portion of the finger rest area. Run a strip of tape the full length of the forward finger rest area at the center of the stock so that it follows the curve from the edge of the grip cap to the rear portion of the trigger guard inletting, as shown in figure 49. Place another strip of tape at the top of the grip, lengthwise from the drop of the comb to the edge of the forward inletting, as shown in figure 51. To create the pattern segment for the finger rest area, cut a strip of tracing paper long enough to reach from the lower edge of the grip to the trigger inletting and wide enough to span the area between the leading bend of the

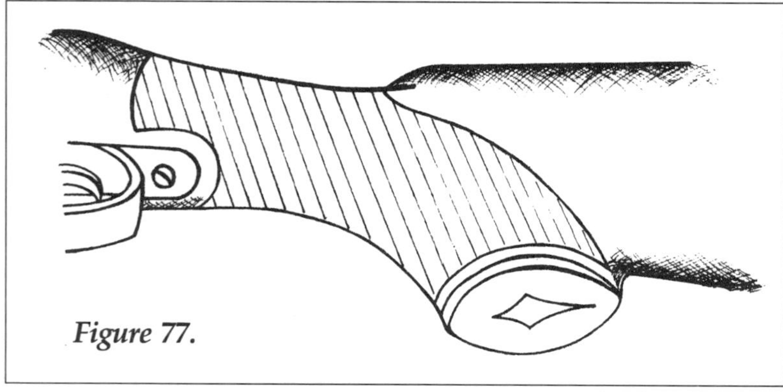

Figure 77.

grip on each side. Allow just enough excess beyond the bend so that the side pattern segments will slightly overlay this segment.

If the gunstock has an extreme curve between the finger rest centerline and side panel or between the grip's lower edge and the trigger inletting, this will create ripples on the pattern sheet. Such ripples generally will not be of too much concern, although severe ripples must not be overlooked. Deal with them as described previously for figure 67. If the design encompasses nearly the full length between the lower edge of the grip and the trigger inletting, the pattern sheet will by necessity extend beyond the design area at the top portion to run over the trigger inletting.

The top and rear portions of the side panel segments for the full wrap-around pattern are laid out in the same was as the over-the-top pattern. Extend the forward edge of the side panel segment enough to overlap the finger rest segment, and trim it at a point that will allow it to lie flat to the stock with few ripples. Place centerline-of-stock marks on the pattern segment and stock tapes as shown in figure 78. Take note that the diagram depicts a locator tape that encompasses the full circumference of the grip at its lower edge (*3*). As locator marks are to be placed at three points along the lower edge, this tape is used rather than individual tapes.

Because of the configuration of the forward portion of the grip and the number of segments

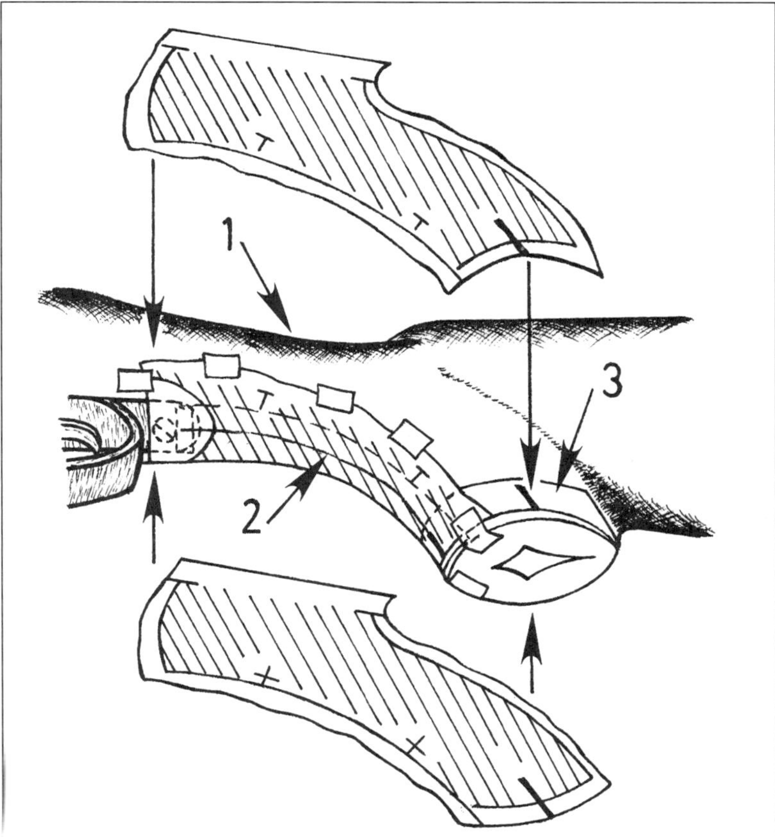

Figure 78. Marks on pattern for side panel: 1, top of grip centerline-of-stock marked tape (not shown); 2, finger rest centerline-of-stock marked tape; 3, locator tape marked at full circumference of grip.

in the overall pattern, exact alignment of locator and segment alignment marks is critical in positioning the opposing side panel segments. A T-shaped mark gives an added degree of accuracy to horizontal and vertical positioning when used in either overlaying segments (discussed in detail later) or a match-line procedure. When used in the latter, the vertical portion of the T is marked on the finger rest segment at the edge of the side segment and the top left half of the crossbar is also placed on the finger rest segment, forming an upside down L. The right half of the crossbar is placed on the side segment. When joined together in the proper position, a T will be formed. Mark the T after you have formed the segments and secured them in position on the stock. The crossmark forming the top of the T should be approximately ¼ inch in length. When positioning the segments together for the tracing of the design and their placement onto the stock afterward, all you need to do to ensure a match is to bring the edge of the panel segment to the vertical line and align the crossmark halves.

If for some reason the single strip method is impractical, there is an alternative way to form the finger rest segment. With this method, you place a series of smaller strips crosswise to the centerline mark so that each overlaps the next to avoid gaps, just as is done with the optional grip method for the curved recess. The width and number of strips you will need depends on how much of the area is to be carved and how much area can be covered with each strip before severe rippling begins. The length of the strips is determined by where the edge of the side panel will be, for when placed in its final position, the side segment must overlap the finger rest segments. If the finger rest strips turn out to be a bit longer than needed, you can trim them later, after you have removed all of the segments from the stock. If you intend to do this, first place a mark on each finger rest segment along the full edge of each side panel segment. Trimming is done beyond the mark to allow overlapping of the segments and placement of holding tapes when you return the segments to the stock. Some light rising of the paper above the stock surface in portions of the strips is inevitable, but this is not a problem as long as there is no crease or high ripple in the paper that can result in design lines being altered.

Secure the first strip at the grip cap edge, extending beyond the edge of the grip to achieve complete coverage along its full length (fig. 79). Then trim off any excess beyond the bottom edge of the grip. Place a holding tape at each end of the strip. To prevent shifting, place a smaller holding tape at the bottom edge of the stock, just off center of the centerline mark on the opposite panel side. Keep in mind that you want the side to be carved as free of tape as possible.

Though it is easier to form and position these smaller strips than the one full-length strip, and the multistrip process will more readily conform to a grip whose configuration presents sharper curves, this method has its drawbacks. Many locator marks are required to ensure the proper repositioning of each strip after removal for design tracing. And, too, the more segments, the greater the possibility for error. Though you can join all the strips into one pattern segment by taping them solidly together, tracing the design will be difficult to do

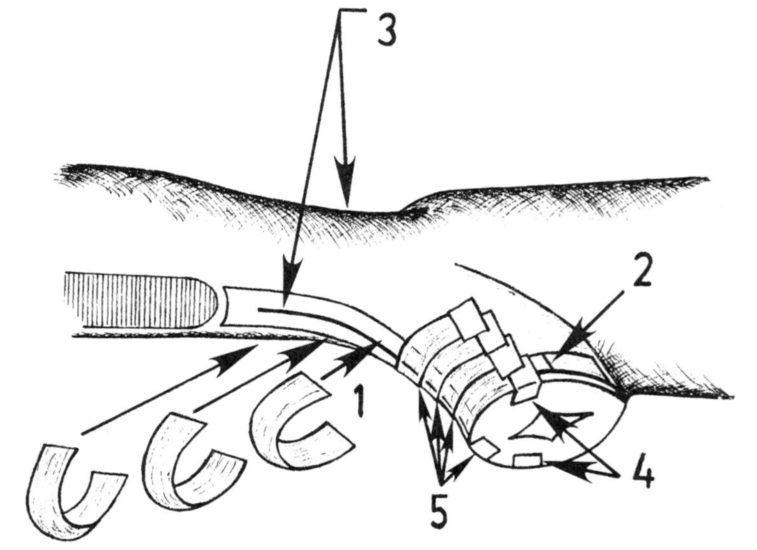

Figure 79. Applying small strips to finger rest segment: 1, strip series placement; 2, side panel locator mark; 3, centerline-of-stock mark (top not shown); 4, holding tape at ends of each strip; 5, placement of off-center holding tape to each strip.

successfully, as the joined segments cannot be made to lie flat. Used individually, each strip will require a pattern locator mark at each end to match with the side panel segment and with the strips above and below. It will also require a mark at the midpoint between the strip ends and a centerline-of-stock mark to ensure a match with the top and bottom strips. Those at the end are the T type previously mentioned, while those at midpoint are crossmarks for lateral and vertical placement. The vertical line of each crossmark runs from strip to strip, and the horizontal line runs along each strip's edge.

This method is not for the impatient nor for those lacking the determination to do a precise job. It is an optional method for use by those who possess what is needed to follow it through when other methods fail. If all else fails, you can totally cover the finger rest area with masking tape and freehand sketch continuing design lines from the panel segment, or you can have an additional design sheet from which you can cut out portions and overlay them onto the appropriate areas for either rub tracings or as is placement. Whichever method does the most precise job is the one to use.

FULL WRAP-AROUND WITH EXTENSION

The full wrap-around with extension layout consists of all of the areas covered in the previous grip sections; you will use the same methods to work those areas. It is without questions the most difficult layout to do, but it has no peer as far as function and beauty. The problems associated with this layout are the cumulative problems of all the other grip layouts presented. Nevertheless, the results are well worth the effort and your feeling of accomplishment will far outweigh that from any other type of grip design. There simply is no comparison. Note, however, that this is not a beginning carver's project; do not attempt it until you have mastered all of the methods of the previous grip layouts and successfully completed a practice piece.

Much of the following discussion applies to all areas of a gunstock and not solely to the grip. Since it is the grip area that generally presents the most bothersome situations, however, the information is included in this section.

Beginning with the wrist, or pistol, grip of a shotgun or rifle, the first step is the positioning of marked centerline-of-stock and locator tapes needed to work the specific areas as described earlier. Next, you must determine the maximum area of coverage, or the boundaries for overall design. When you freehand sketch a border, such as when a new design is to incorporate a larger area than what was removed from the stock or is to be placed where nothing existed before, you must give consideration to the overall area available for the complete design.

If you plan to use identical designs on both grip panels, the pattern is always initially formed on the cheekpiece side. If no cheekpiece is present, the line of the maximum area of coverage is determined by the position of the base of the comb and the judged approximate shape and location of a cheekpiece for the type of stock being worked. Familiarize yourself with cheekpiece shape and placement by studying firearm photographs and actual gunstocks. If a similar stock that has a cheekpiece is not available for observation, you can raise the stock to your cheek in the firing position and press pieces of masking tape onto the wood around the approximate area where your cheek meets the gunstock, then refine this outline.

Unfortunately, the size and shape of an area of any given shotgun or rifle usually will not accommodate a premade design without alterations of some sort. Those designs most likely for alteration are ones that have been created specifically for individual client viewing or display purposes at gun shows. Generally, it is the line of the border that is most affected, but at times it will be necessary to enlarge, reduce, or reposition the featured subject matter. Sketching the maximum area of coverage will enable you to correctly position any design and will clearly show points where alterations to a premade design are needed. When you are creating a new design for a specific gunstock, it will aid you in the placement of individual components that make up the complete design. Some lines of the maximum area of coverage are predetermined: the centerline of the stock at the top and the bottom of the grip, and the bottom of the buttstock. Pistol grips with a grip cap have another predetermined line, placed at about $3/32$ inch above the marked line denoting where the wood meets the top of the cap. With a full wrap-around design, the centerline-of-stock mark at the leading edge of the finger rest area is also included.

As a rule, these lines constitute the point at which the design from one side does not cross to the opposite side, if the design on both sides is identical. There are instances, however, where a portion of the design from one side overlays a portion of the design on the opposite side at the centerline area. For example, a leaf from the cheekpiece side may cross over the centerline and overlay a portion of the opposite side pattern at the top rear of the grip, while a leaf from the opposite side may cross over the centerline in the finger rest area and overlay a portion of the design on the cheekpiece side. Crossing over the centerline at front and rear from opposite sides in this way maintains balance and is very attractive. Placed properly, a single crossover can be equally appealing. Crossover carvings are best accomplished with plant subjects, but with good judgment and care, wildlife crossovers can work well too.

To best determine the area of maximum coverage, follow the steps outlined previously for the single side panel with extension. The forward and rear lengths of this design can be greater than those outlined in that section. Before you become carried away with a long forward grip extension, however, give consider-

ation to the placement of the forearm design and the effect one has on the other in relation to balance, harmony, and visual appeal. If you wish to lengthen the rear portion of the grip design, you may have a cheekpiece to contend with. In that case, the maximum area of coverage for the pattern runs from the base of the comb at the top rear of the grip, downward and rearward, to follow the configuration of the cheekpiece at its base where it meets with the flatter area of the stock. Be sure that the length of your pattern sheet is more than ample for the intended design. Its exact length depends on the design you have in mind. Here again, give consideration to balance and eye appeal. Above all else, keep it in good taste. No matter how good a carver you may be, there comes a point where too much becomes gaudy.

Sometimes portions of the line denoting the maximum area of coverage can serve as the actual line of a border; if this is the case, note the exact portion of the line as such directly on the pattern sheet. The remainder of the line continues to serve as a placement guide. In all instances, the design must absolutely remain within this area.

There are two ways to determine the placement of the design within the maximum area of coverage. One approach is to decide on the shape of a completed design, sketch its border to match the configuration of the area, and then enlarge or reduce the subject matter to fit within. The other is to determine the size of the subject matter according to the configuration of the area where it is to be placed, and then shape a border around it. Either way, remember that when sketching the line onto the pattern sheet, you must place it no less than $1/8$ inch to inletting, and the same $3/32$-inch spacing in the lower area of the grip must be placed full-length above the point where the wood of the stock meets the line of the grip cap, or above the actual edge of the wood if no cap is present. If you do not intend to have a border for your design, you should still sketch the maximum area of coverage line on the pattern sheet to aid in design placement.

There is far more leeway with floral designs than with wildlife. Individual floral components can be turned, shifted, overlaid, enlarged, or reduced to fit within the lines of a border and still look natural. Wildlife, on the other hand, must maintain a definite form and remain proportionate. By experimenting with different perspectives and poses, you can come up with a figure that will conform to a specific area. Animals can be depicted in various positions, such as a deer bounding over a fence or fallen tree or browsing, and in a head-on, three-quarter, or full side view in order to fit the size and shape of the area. With waterfowl or other birds, you can vary the position of extended wings and the angle of flight.

You can see from the above that a more concerted effort is spent on the grip area than on any other portion of a gunstock. Take heart in knowing that beginner and professional alike get out of it what they are willing to put into it. When working in this area of the stock, patience is the absolute key.

6

STOCK PREPARATION AND FINISHING

THERE IS A MULTITUDE OF INFORMATION AVAILABLE on gunstock finishing, and it's more than likely that anyone reading about gunstock carving will already have some knowledge of stock or wood finishing in general. Little will be covered here on the subject of finishes, but enough will be presented to enable the completion of a stock in addition to placing a finish on carvings. The carving procedures presented in this book require a finish on the stock beforehand. Therefore, if a stock is to be totally refinished, do so before beginning to carve. For the most part, clients who have an obviously well-used stock that is to be extensively carved will seek a total refinishing as well.

The type of finish determines the method used for its removal. If it is an original factory finish, it is likely to be either lacquer or one of the polymer-based finishes that are more predominant on higher-priced firearms. In regard to the latter, however, keep in mind that simply because a particular type of finish is on a high-priced firearm, that doesn't mean it is the best finish there is and therefore should be used on all stocks. Some finishes are far superior to others for particular purposes, and this should determine your selection. The key to correctly choosing a finish is knowing the individual characteristics of finishes and under what conditions a particular firearm will generally be used. This will be examined later in the chapter.

If total refinishing of a stock is called for, polymer or plastic type finishes are removed by sanding alone, as solvents usually have little or no effect on these types of finishes. Generally, with this type of finish, only the areas to be carved will require finish removal, and you will do so during the course of carving, not before. This will be covered later in the section on carving procedures.

Total removal of a varnish or lacquer finish can be accomplished in one of two ways. You can remove most of the finish with a quality varnish and lacquer remover and sand afterward, or you can sand alone. If you use a solvent, be certain it's the correct solvent for the job, and follow the manufacturer's directions to the letter. Beware of those that contain wax as an ingredient; many do. This type is unsuitable for stock use, as some of the wax will be absorbed into the wood and will affect the adherence of a newly applied finish.

An oil finish must be totally removed, or it will cause problems with adherence if the new finish is anything other than oil. Oil can be removed but will take considerable effort to be done properly. To remove an oil-base finish, use varnish and lacquer solvent, followed by sanding. Sanding alone will not remove oil that is just below the surface.

The most difficult situation you may encounter is a stock that has a linseed oil finish and is also deeply saturated with lubricating oil around and throughout the receiver inletting, and possibly along the barrel channel as well. A linseed oil–rubbed stock is fast becoming a rarity, because those in the gun world have become more aware of other oil finishes that offer an equally rich luster while being far superior in drying time, moisture resistance, and overall stock protection. Tung oil is highly recommended and is the only oil finish I use. I am convinced of its superiority in moisture resistance and durability. If you do run into such a situation, however, you need to first remove as much of the lubricating oil as possible, and then concentrate on removing the linseed oil, relying on the procedure for the latter to remove any remaining lubricating oil.

To remove a highly saturated area of lubricating oil, "sweat" it out of the stock by holding the saturated portion above, and facing, an open flame or burner to heat the stock considerably. Keep it far enough away to avoid scorching or burning the wood. The excessive heat will bring the lubricating oil to the surface. As soon as it rises, immediately wipe it away with a clean rag or paper towel. It is important to use a clean portion of rag with each wipe, as the object is to remove the oil, not smear it onto another area. Depending on the degree of saturation, this can be a lengthy process, as you must repeat these steps until no oil seeps to the surface. This procedure will not remove all of the oil, but it will remove enough to allow the solvent to finish the job. After using solvent, allow the wood to completely dry, then sand the stock.

Sanding requires the use of several grits in a step-down procedure to attain the desired results. Regardless of the type of finish being removed, remember that the thickness of a properly applied finish can be measured in thousandths of an inch. The starting grit of sandpaper has been debated, especially for a heavily applied finish. I do not use a grit coarser than 220. Anything coarser than this will produce deep scratches in the wood, and you will have to expend additional effort to eliminate them, removing excessive wood as well. Even when using 220-grit, take care not to overdo it.

The following are the grits best used in a step-down procedure on a gunstock, from coarsest to finest: 220 and 240 (very fine); 280 and 320 (extra fine); and 360 and 400 (super fine). I use a four-grade step-down, beginning with 220, then using 280, then 320, and finishing with 400. To simplify the step-down procedure, some prefer to use three grades only, starting with 220, then using 280, and giving a final sanding with 360. Another three-grade step-down is 240, 320, and 400. In the step-down procedure, you change to the next finer grade after the grit you are using has reached its maximum effectiveness. This point is reached when all of the scratches made by the previous grade are no longer visible.

I highly recommend the wet-dry type of sandpaper, as it offers excellent endurance, performance, and resistance to clogging, making it an ideal paper to work with. It's strong enough to withstand many brushings with a fine-bristled brass wire brush to clean it up a bit when clogging does occur. Aluminum oxide sandpaper by 3M offers these qualities and is highly recommended.

Sanding is best done using a sanding block to support the paper, although it's not often possible to use one over the entire area of a stock. Using a sanding block will increase the usefulness of the paper and produce a more uniform wood level over larger areas. Paint and hardware stores sell low-cost rubber sanding blocks. You can make your own from a wood block measuring approximately 4 by 2 by 1 inch, with a piece of felt glued to the working side. You will have to hold the paper in place by hand.

Always sand with the direction of the grain, never across it. Regardless of how fine the grade, sanding across the grain will produce scratches that, though they may not be apparent while the wood is in its raw state, will be highly visible when a finish is applied. The intent of sanding is to remove all of the old finish but as little wood as possible. Use of light pressure in the final stages is a must. Do not oversand.

Sanding alone will not produce the desired wood surface. Even after the best of sanding, small, hairlike wood fibers known as whiskers will begin to pop up when the moisture of the finish touches the surface of the wood. Before the finish completely dries, many more will rear their ugly heads. These whiskers begin to rise almost immediately when exposed to any form of moisture, even the moisture in the air while the stock is resting in a corner overnight await-ing the application of a finish. If the whiskers are not removed before a finish is applied, the finish will look as though dust settled on the surface as it was drying.

To eliminate these fibers, wet the stock with ordinary tap water to force them to rise. The best time to do this is just before applying the finish. I've witnessed several methods of apply-ing water, such as using a wet rag to rub down the stock or running water from a faucet directly onto a stock. Running water from a tap directly onto the wood should never be done. Such a practice will result in the stock's absorbing far more moisture than is desired. The best method is to spray the wood with a fine mist from a spray bottle, such as those used to mist plants. It is important to avoid saturating the wood when doing so. Mist only enough to lightly cover the surface. Some degree of moisture will be absorbed at surface level, but this will be minimal and is easily eliminated during the next step.

After you mist the stock, dry it quickly us-ing a heat lamp or hand-held hair dryer. An open flame can be used and often is, but care must be taken not to scorch the wood.

If this is all new to you, you would do well to examine the results thoroughly during and after the drying of the stock. You can determine wood grain direction by running the tip of a finger a short distance over any portion of the stock from front to rear, and then from rear to front. The direction from which the fibers have risen will feel much rougher than the other.

In order to remove these fibers, run steel wool against the bend. The steel wool will shave the whiskers off at their base. Do not apply a great deal of pressure. Use firm strokes, but let the steel wool do the work. No matter how fine a grade of steel wool you use, it is capable of removing wood, and if you exert excessive pres-sure, you may dislodge wood fibers in other areas. Grade 000 or 0000 steel wool is preferable. You can buy this at paint stores. Never use the type of steel wool pad that is intended for household use, such as those used for scouring pots and pans or those for stripping paint from doors or window frames. Using either type will quickly destroy detailing, as they are too coarse for the work intended on carvings. Rub in one direction only—against the lay of the fibers—not back and forth, as doing so will push many of the fibers down and they will not be shaved off. These fibers will then rise again when you apply the finish. Repeat the misting and the steel-wool processes until all of the fibers have been completely shaved off, determined by running your fingers over the area. Close enough is not good enough. Run your finger from the rear of the stock forward, then from the forward end of the stock to the rear. When all of the raised fibers have been shaved off, the surface of the stock will feel smooth in both di-rections. If any fibers remain, you will feel a roughness in one direction. Use the steel wool in the direction you feel the roughness. Three to four times is usually sufficient to achieve the desired results, but some areas may require more.

After sanding and removal of fibers, you need to decide whether you will use a stain. As a rule, staining is not necessary unless you want a specific color that you cannot obtain by applying the finish directly to the natural wood. In my estimation, nothing can beat the beauty of natural wood, and in most cases stock coloration should remain natural. Some wood can, however, be rather light colored and have little beauty in its grain pattern, in which case staining can give a stock some life. Should it be a client's stock that could use this attention, it is his or her choice to make.

If you decide to use a stain, I recommend the water-base type. I prefer Casey's water-base stains, which are specifically for gunstock use and found in gun stores. Water-base stains are very easy to work with and require little drying time. You can speed the drying process still further with the use of a hair dryer. After the first coat, you can easily lighten the stock by rubbing it with a damp rag, or darken it with additional stain. A water-base stain is often applied in the final stages of dewhiskering in place of plain water; in this case you can lightly rub or brush it on rather than spraying. Water-base stains maintain the same qualities with all types of finishes. Also, it is easy to achieve a specific color by blending different shades or a particular effect by placing one shade on top of another after the first shade has thoroughly dried. For example, if you apply colonial red stain to a black-walnut stock, allow it to dry, cover it with dark walnut stain, then buff with a slightly water dampened rag while the stain is still just a bit wet, you will achieve a very dark walnut color with a reddish hue that shows through more in some areas than others. The result is much like the finish found on many Colonial-era rifles.

Whether you are using one shade or more, to be sure you will achieve the desired coloring and depth, make a test run on a scrap of the same wood, and keep a record of the exact blending of stains and method of application.

Such records are invaluable in the future should you need to make a repair or wish to use the same coloring on another stock.

Removing whiskers with steel wool will not affect stain coverage when done on raw stain, but after you do so, check the stock thoroughly to ensure that all loose steel-wool fibers have been removed. Some fibers can become embedded; remove them carefully with tweezers. If not removed, a steel-wool fiber can result in a bump in the finish or, worse yet, discolor the area around it.

The choice of a finish is extremely important. You must consider the conditions to which the stock will be subjected to be certain you use the proper finish. A shotgun or rifle that is kept in a case and taken out to be used only at a range on warm, sunny, dry days will not require the attention given to an often-used hunting piece that is subjected to all that nature will put it through. For the working firearm, the necessary attributes of a finish, in the order of importance, are maximum moisture and damage resistance, easy maintenance and repair, and eye appeal. The "fair weather" firearm should have a finish that is easy to maintain and repair, but some leeway can be allowed in the degree of moisture resistance. I am, however, a bit uneasy about applying a finish that offers less than the maximum protection at all times under any circumstance. For this reason, my preferences are a quality spar varnish, followed by tung oil, then lacquer, but the latter only if applied over a good sealer.

Regardless of the type of finish you use, it must be applied to a solid base in order for the finish to adhere well and to attain the deepest penetration for maximum moisture protection. For a base, I use a thinned solution of the finish that I will use throughout the filling process and that will be the final finishing coat as well. I thin this half and half with the proper solvent for the medium being used. You will usually find the proper thinner listed on the instruction label of the product. If it is not specified, and you are in doubt, ask someone at the store where you purchased the product. Use only what is prescribed for that product. A lacquer thinner cannot be used with oil- or varnish-base finishes; they simply are not compatible. Lacquer, and lacquer thinner, if applied to an oil finish or varnish finish, will raise the finish, leaving a crinkled look. It will even do so on a seasoned finish. This generally requires that the stock be completely refinished. The thinned finish solution must be applied over the entire stock until no more can be absorbed. During the whole procedure, be sure that no area of the stock dries before you apply more finish. If an area dries before maximum penetration is reached, the rest of the solution will not be absorbed no matter how thin it may be. Should this happen, the base coat will still aid in the adherence of subsequent applications, but moisture resistance will not be as great as the finish is capable of. Many carvers do not apply a thinned base coat but instead apply the finish at full strength directly onto the stock. With such a practice, the bonding to wood and moisture protection of the finish will be inferior. Time will prove the point.

All wood has pores. Stock woods of various densities will differ in their type and number. For the finish to look good, you need to fill these pores. If you do not, the finish will appear as pitted or pock marked. With a dull finish, unfilled pores are not as obvious as with a satin or high-gloss finish, but they can be found on examination. After the thinned base coat dries, the pores will become even more evident, especially when you view the stock at an angle in a reflecting light. This is because when the base coat is applied, the medium seeps into the wood evenly, leaving a thin coating at the bottom of the pores on their side walls, and at stock surface level.

To fill the pores, you can use your finishing medium or one of the various substances that are available for this purpose. Some are clear, but most have a color or can be mixed with a stain to obtain a desired color. Always test a filler before use. Some remain gummy after hardening, and others become chalklike. Neither is acceptable. I recommend, however, that you use the finishing medium as the filler.

After your base coat dries, apply subsequent coats of either three-quarter or full consistency. Be sure to apply each coat thinly. Heavy coats will not fill the pores more quickly, but they will result in a longer drying time and take more effort to remove. Allow each coating to dry thoroughly, and lightly sand the stock between coats in order to remove the bulk of the finish at surface level. Take care not to sand all the way through to the wood, especially if the stock has been stained. If this happens, you will need to touch up the stain, and it will be nearly impossible to obtain an exact match without some degree of blemish. After each sanding, the finish will appear dull except for the recessed areas of the pores, which have not been touched by the sandpaper. Each such coat will fill a portion of the pores, until they are totally filled to the surface of the stock. At this point, lightly sand the stock with 400-grit sandpaper. Clean up all sanding residue, then apply the final finish at full consistency.

The final finish coat should be very thin. A heavily applied coat of any type of finish will not afford any higher degree of moisture resistance than a thinly applied coat. The moisture-blocking characteristics of a finish remain the same, thickly or thinly applied; it is the makeup of the finish itself that determines its moisture resistance. A thin final finish coat is far superior to one that is heavily applied, as it has a higher degree of elasticity and better resists chipping or cracking. With polymer finishes, chipping and cracking will be a result with a heavily applied coat, but these finishes generally are of a thick consistency and do not properly penetrate into the wood.

If you are completely finishing a stock, coat all areas, including the barrel channel and inletted areas, in order to provide maximum protection. This does not mean that these areas are to get the same final luster as the exposed portions of the stock, but that they are to receive an ample seal.

Most oil, varnish, shellac, and wax finishes are applied by hand, but some are applied by brush. Lacquer and polymer finishes are best applied by spraying but can be applied by brush if you do not mind the added effort of sanding and buffing necessary to achieve a smooth final finish.

Polyurethane finishes, though they do afford possibly the best protection against moisture, are prone to chipping and to developing minor cracks throughout. The latter can be attributed to the difference in expansion and contraction of the finish and the wood under various weather conditions. The better gun makers recognize that this happens over a period of time and will refinish a stock that has developed cracks in the original finish at little or no cost to the owner other than shipping fees, a fact that many gun owners are not aware of. If you apply a polyurethane finish, be certain it is on a well-prepared base to ensure good adhesion; otherwise, the finish is prone to pulling away from the wood, especially if it is heavily applied. Never use a polyurethane finish that contains a stain. It will in no way ever match the appearance of a quality finish.

7

Cutting Exercises

THE EXERCISES PRESENTED IN THIS CHAPTER WILL ACquaint the beginning carver with various procedures that will be executed during the course of carving a full design. Pay close attention to the instructions, and follow them to the letter. Should you make a mistake, repeat the exercise from the beginning unless stated otherwise, or your finished product will deviate somewhat from what is intended. These exercises will not only give hands-on experience with working tools, but also teach the beginning carver to execute exactly what is required. Many exercises will seem extremely simple in whole or in part, and indeed they are; however, do not pass them over, because each is there for a purpose that will become evident while performing the exercises in chapter 8. It is important that each exercise be completed in its entirety before moving on, as subsequent processes may refer to earlier ones.

You will need a practice stock or piece of suitable wood for the exercises that follow. Try to obtain a discarded stock from a local gun store or gunsmith who does restocking. If you cannot, a piece of black walnut from a lumberyard will have to suffice, though obviously characteristics between the two will differ. If using anything other than a gunstock, you will have to prepare it to simulate conditions as closely as possible to that of a gunstock, including sanding, staining, filling in pores, and applying a

finish, as described in the preceding chapter. You do not need to apply a thinned base coat in this instance, unless you wish to do so for practice. For the purposes of these exercises, in order to speed up both application and drying of the finish, you can use a clear automobile lacquer available in spray cans at auto parts store.

Most of these exercises are on a larger scale than will be executed during the carving of an actual gunstock, but only through practice and understanding of procedure can you gain the knowledge and ability to proceed on a smaller scale. It is expected that mistakes will be made, and they should not discourage you. Part of the learning process is discovering what does not work and why.

The initial steps for all of the exercises are the same and are not repeated after the first. Instead, it is assumed that those steps have been taken to the point of the beginning cuts. When the stock is referred to during any of the exercises, the term will pertain to scrap wood practice pieces as well.

Before beginning the exercises, you must consider how the stock will be secured during carving. Many carvers advocate the use of clamps or a cradle such as used for checkering. I prefer not to use either, as I found both to be far too restrictive. Neither can afford positioning a stock to all of the required angles. During the course of carving a full design, a stock will have to be turned many times to every conceivable position, and neither clamping to a table nor holding the stock in a cradle will provide the needed flexibility. You have to either continually walk around the stock or make cuts from awkward positions. I simply hold the stock firmly with one hand and perform the work with the other. Most carvings can be accomplished while the stock is held flat on the workbench pad. It is also beneficial to have a rolled pad upon which to rest either end of the stock to position it at an angle when needed. I use two such pads. One is an old bath towel folded to approximately 12 inches wide and held in a tight roll by heavy-duty rubber bands, one at each end and one at center. The other is scrap foam rubber rolled and held in the same manner. The towel gives a resting height of 4 to 5 inches, and the foam rubber 7 to 8 inches. They are very handy and I highly recommend them.

During carving, hold the stock with your hand as near as possible to the area being carved. This facilitates turning the stock to permit any line you are working to be easily assessable. You can rest the thumb tip of the hand holding the stock on the thumb tip of the hand holding the knife to serve as a pivot point; this gives an added measure of protection against skipping or overrunning the cut (fig. 80).

EXERCISE 1 (FIGURE 81)

An outline cut is a vertical cut that distinguishes features or an overall design from background and surrounding areas. An angled cut, called a parting-line cut, is then made to the side of the outline cut to remove a thin strip of wood. To which side this is done depends on the design. The result of these two cuts is a furrow with one straight vertical wall and the other angled away from the outlined object (fig. 82).

This first exercise is to acquaint the beginning carver with different cuts across, against, and with the grain of wood, using both the outline cut and the parting-line cut, and applying a stop cut measure with each. A stop cut is a vertical cut into the wood at the end of a detail line that is to be cut. When a stop cut is used, it is generally applied to a crossing design line at the end of the line that is to be cut next. A stop cut's purpose is to help prevent overrunning a cut beyond its intended ending. Transfer of the exercise layout will also familiarize the beginner with the design transfer tool.

First, secure tracing paper over the layout, and copy only the lines numbered 1 through 6 on figure 81. The broken line surrounding the numbered layouts is approximately where the paper will be trimmed after you trace the numbered layouts. This line, as with all of the exercises, can be either judged by eye after the paper is removed or marked as seen when secured over the layout. If done by eye, you must make certain enough paper remains around the numbered layouts so that pattern holding tapes (X) can be placed without obstructing exercise lines. When securing the pattern to the stock, position it to run lengthwise from front to rear with the grain of the wood, as depicted by the double-headed arrow in figure 81.

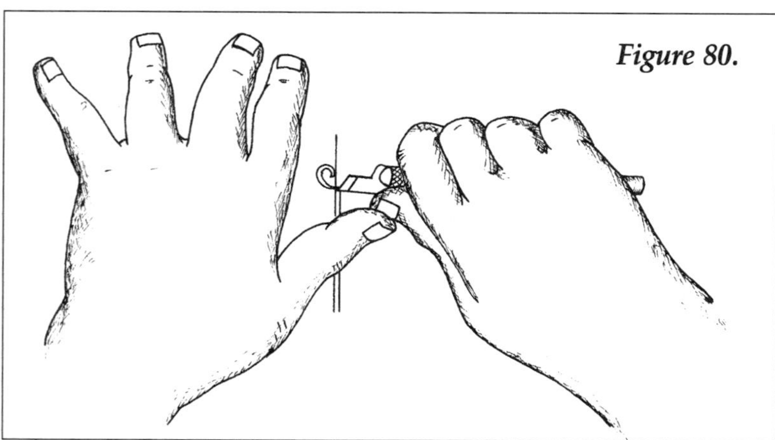

Figure 80.

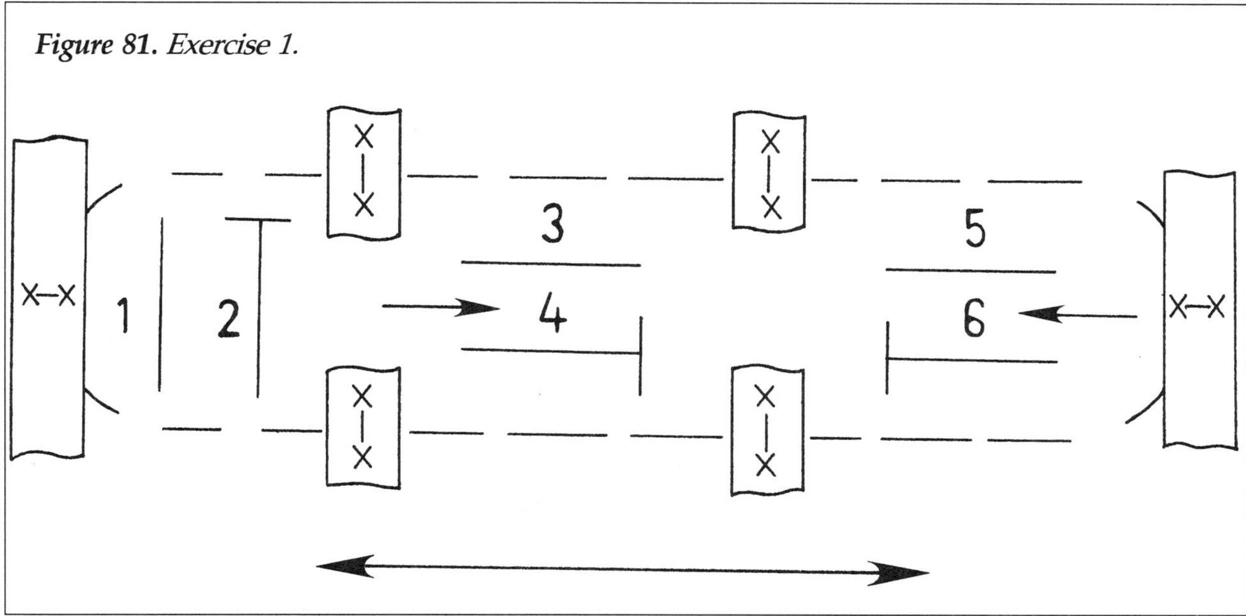

Figure 81. Exercise 1.

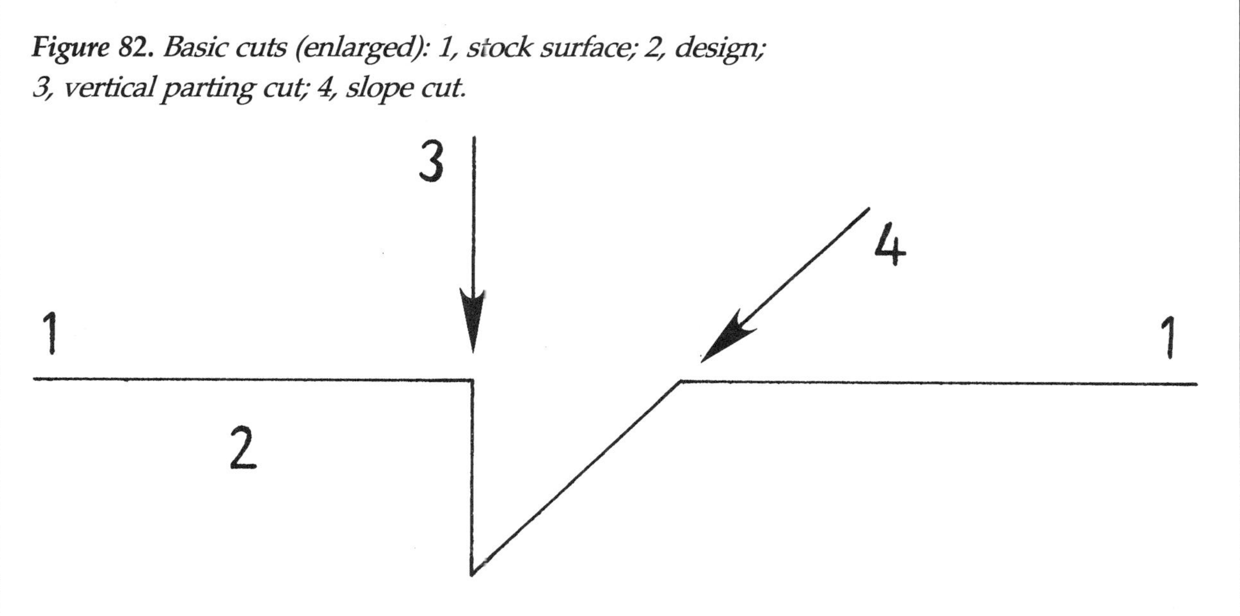

Figure 82. Basic cuts (enlarged): 1, stock surface; 2, design; 3, vertical parting cut; 4, slope cut.

After securing the pattern to the stock, check carefully that it is positioned properly and lies flat to the wood without any pulls or ripples. Also check the holding tapes to ensure that they are firmly affixed to the pattern and the wood to prevent pattern shifting during the layout transfer process.

Now begin the transferring process to layout 1, using the transfer tool to make a series of small punctures through the paper into the fin-

ish below. Maintain as straight a line as possible, and avoid staggering the punctures from one side of the line to the other. Be sure to hold the tool at a 90-degree angle to the stock at all times. Though you want to make the punctures only as deep as the finish itself, some penetration of the wood is inevitable. Keep this penetration as shallow as possible, for two reasons. You don't want to leave visible hole marks in any area that will be carved less deeply than the puncture.

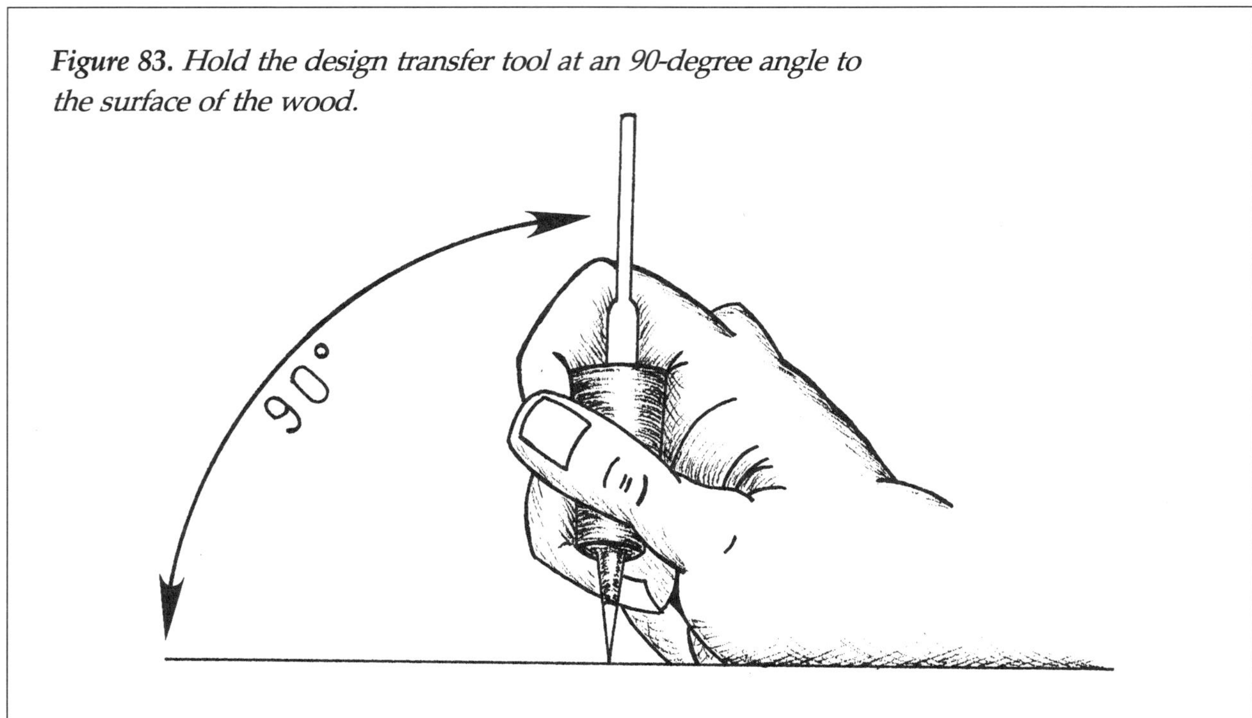

Figure 83. Hold the design transfer tool at an 90-degree angle to the surface of the wood.

Also, smaller holes create a more detailed line. The hole at surface level of the finish should be about the size of a period made with an ultra-fine-tip pen. Make the holes no more than $1/8$ inch apart, beginning and ending at the very ends of a line. For lines that curve or are part of highly detailed areas, $1/16$ inch apart or less is required.

After layout 1 has been transferred, repeat the procedure with all of the remaining numbered layouts. Be sure to transfer the short crossing lines in layouts 2, 4, and 6. After any design transfer, I highly recommend that you closely study each of the lines under magnification to ensure that all of the transfer holes are indeed present. While you do so, hold the point of the transfer tool just above the paper and retrace each line from beginning to end. Should you find that an area was missed, add the perforations at that time. The result should look like figure 84.

Remove the paper, then sprinkle a fine powder, such as baby powder, over all perforations and lightly wipe away the excess from the surrounding surface. Make certain all of the perforations have received powder. The powder will

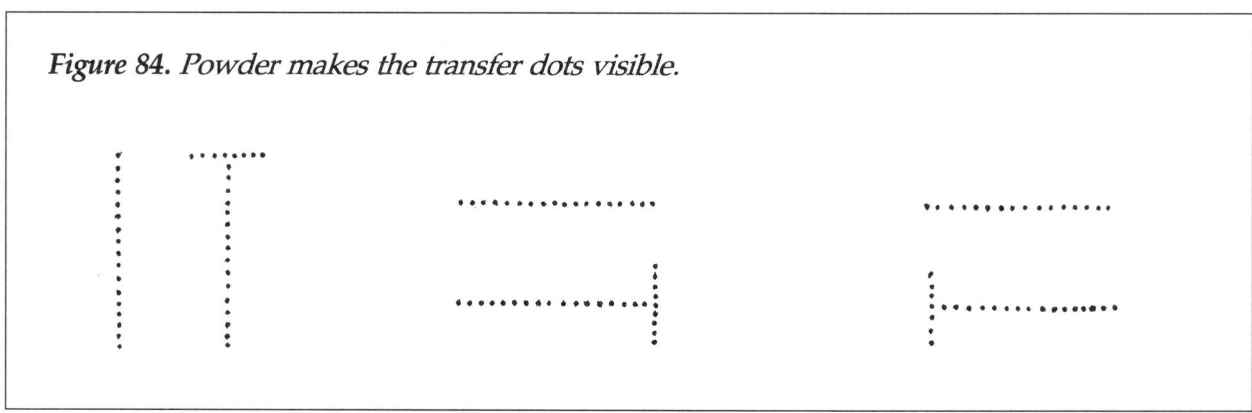

Figure 84. Powder makes the transfer dots visible.

make the transfer holes highly visible. From this point, each numbered layout will be worked separately to completion before you move to the next, beginning with layout 1 and ending with layout 6.

Line 1

Holding the slant-blade knife like a pencil when writing, use its very tip to lightly score a line connecting all of the holes of layout 1. This cut should be little more than a scratch, just enough to score a line onto the surface of wood beneath the finish, as it will serve only as a guide to prevent deflection of the blade during a second cut that will follow the same path. Keep the longer portion of the cutting edge above the perforations, serving as a visual guide to ensure that the tip remains on its intended path.

Then cut more deeply along the guide cut, using pressure enough to bite somewhat into the wood but allowing an easy flow rather than digging in. You can tell if you are digging in, because you will need to alter the force to advance the blade. When nearing the end of the line, turn the stock completely around and finish the cut from the opposite end. This will prevent an overrun and aid in maintaining a more uniform depth. Repeat this process as many times as necessary until you attain an overall uniform depth of an estimated $1/32$ inch, judged by observing the depth of the blade. Make each cut while pulling the blade in the direction of your shoulder. For easy viewing of the line from a more comfortable position when making the cut, position the stock beforehand so that the line of layout 1 is facing the appropriate direction, depending on whether you are right- or left-handed. It's important that the outline cut be straight into the stock and not angled to one side or the other. Make the sloped parting-line cut on the right side of the outline cut if you are right-handed, and on the left side if left-handed.

Since cutting is across the grain with this portion of the exercise, the parting-line cut can generally be begun from either end of the line. In this exercise, make the parting-line cut by pushing the cutting edge away from the body, doing so after you have slightly repositioned the stock so that the exercise line is running directly away from the center of your body, not your shoulder. This will give you added control of the cutting edge, as you push the blade with the thumb of the hand holding the stock while maintaining the blade's angle with the hand holding the knife.

Begin the angled cut by placing the tip of the blade on the end of the outline cut nearest you. The cutting edge should be at a 90-degree angle to the direction the cut will be made, while the knife itself is slanted at about 30 degrees. Gently push the knife forward, while angling the cutting edge downward. The tip of the blade should intersect with the bottom of the outline cut at about $1/4$ inch from the starting point. Level off the cut to maintain the $1/32$-inch depth for the remaining distance. If angled properly, the width of the trench at the surface level of the stock will be approximately $1/16$ inch. When nearing the end of the line, gradually bring the knife handle upward, while maintaining the intersection with the bottom of the outline cut. This will cause the width of the parting-line cut to decrease at the surface level of the stock, and this cut will meet with the end of the outline cut. When making the sloped cut, the tip of the blade must not go beyond the depth of the outline cut, as this will create a condition known as undercutting (fig. 85). This could be a serious problem in a highly detailed portion of a full design.

Carefully examine the completed sloped cut. If it is not at the desired depth, is not uniformly straight, or is undercut, repeat the exercise. Once you are satisfied that you have made the cut as wanted, hold the cutting edge of the

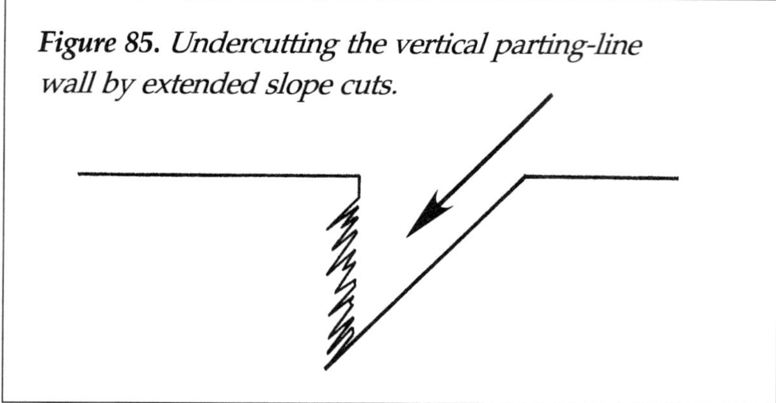

Figure 85. Undercutting the vertical parting-line wall by extended slope cuts.

slant-blade knife in a vertical position, with the tip at the bottom of the trench and the cutting edge against the vertical wall of the outline cut. While holding the knife at this position, lightly scrape the vertical wall to smooth out any rough edges. Do not cut, and do not overdo the scraping by exceeding the original width of the outline cut. The finished result should be a trench with a smooth, vertical wall $^1/_{32}$ inch deep and a sloped $^1/_{16}$-inch surface width, tapering downward to intersect with the bottom of the outline cut.

Line 2

This line is to be worked in the same manner as the first, with one exception: Here, two stop cuts will be made, each presented differently. Use an outline cut along all of the line shown, including the short crossing line at the top end as done in the working of line 1. Before starting the parting-line cut, however, make a slight vertical incision at the beginning of the line (the end without a crossing line).

Hold the knife in a vertical position, with the point directly on the end of the line, and the cutting edge at an angle to the side at which the slope of the parting line is to be made. Gently insert the tip into the stock to a depth of about $^1/_{32}$ inch. The slant of the cutting edge is just about what is desired for the angle of the parting-line cut and works to an advantage in this instance. The incision and the outline cut made to the crossing line at the top of the line will serve as stop cuts. Do not overdo this incision. Start the parting-line cut forming the trench from a distance of about ¼ inch up the line, and cut toward the small vertical incision. With the knife held firmly at an angle sloped at about $^1/_{16}$ inch from the outline cut toward the base of that cut, slowly cut into the wood to intersect with the base of the outline cut, and then bring the length of the cut to end at the small vertical incision while matching its slope. When complete, reverse the cut to run in the opposite direction toward the crossing line at the top of the line. Maintain the angle of the slope, and make every attempt to avoid undercutting the outline cut. Continue the sloped cut to the crossing cut at the end of the longer line, with no deviation such as was needed to end the cut for line 1. Check for proper depth, width, and angle of slope. Cut again if necessary. Lightly scrape the vertical wall of the outline cut and slope with the cutting edge of the knife to make everything uniform.

Before moving on to line 3, compare lines 1 and 2. Make a mental note of how you worked each one and the results when applying a stop cut and not applying one.

Lines 3–6

Execute lines 3 through 6 exactly as those you just finished, with lines 3 and 5 the same as 1, and lines 4 and 6 the same as 2. Proceed in order, and do not move on to the next line until you are completely finished with the one you are working on. Make all cuts in the direction shown by the arrow between lines 3 and 4 in one direction, and 5 and 6 in the opposite direction. The parting-line cut of line 4 will be like that of 2, but this is the only exception to the direction in which all cuts are to be made. Upon completion of each line, compare the process and results with those lines previously done.

After you have completed all of the numbered lines and noted the results, return to line 4. Score a line with the knife at the beginning of the parting line at a 90-degree angle (on the side of the parting line slope) to match the length of the crossing line at the opposite end. This length is ½ inch overall from the vertical wall of the outline cut. Now, beginning at the trench, shave thin layers of wood to enlarge the width of the slope from $^1/_{16}$ to ½ inch, terminating the slope at stock surface level between

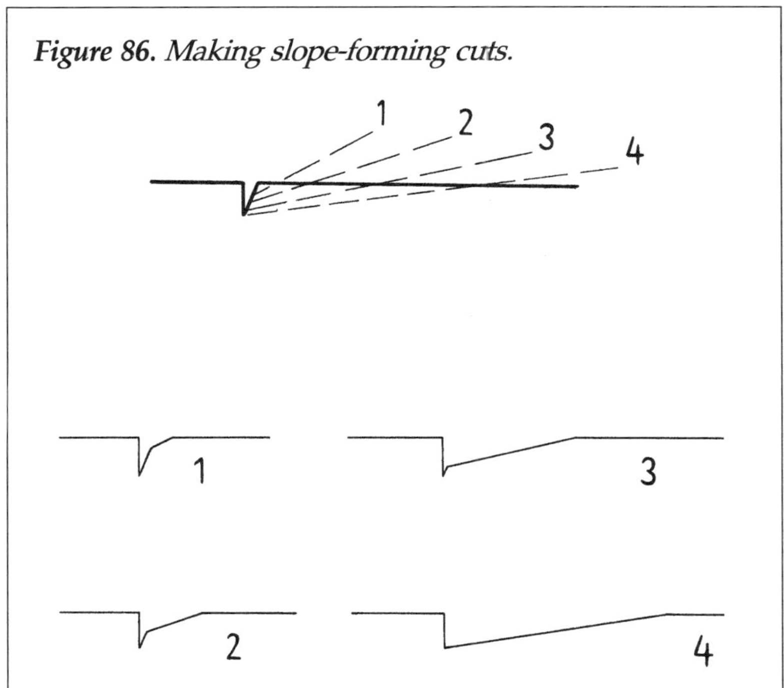

Figure 86. Making slope-forming cuts.

the ends of each crossing line (fig. 86). Make each slope-forming cut as indicated, beginning with a short reverse cut. After the slope has been achieved, lightly scrape its surface with the full length of the knife's cutting edge to make the surface smoother. Don't be overly concerned with small irregularities, but do try to make the surface as smooth as possible. When you have finished the extended sloping of line 4, repeat

the process with line 6. After you have completed both, mentally compare the different reactions of the wood when working the lines from opposite directions. You should have noticed differences in cutting across, against, and with the grain of the wood. Any carver not aware of these differences will produce sloppy work.

EXERCISE 2 (FIGURE 87)

This exercise presents the method of making crossovers, as well as procedures to follow for detail lines susceptible to chipping out. Each is a relatively simple procedure. With the exception of transferring the design, all procedures of this exercise will require continual repositioning or complete turning of the stock so that cuts can be made either across or with the grain of the wood. Work the circles in order from the largest to the smallest.

A chip-out results from side pressure exerted by the blade on wood having little or no backup support. This occurs most often with detail lines the width of that of the third-smallest circle or less. This is not to say that they do not occur otherwise, but that you need to increase your degree of caution when working on a line of this width or less. Understandably, with thinner lines, the prospect of chipping greatly increases, especially when the depth of a cut also increases. Since blade side pressure is the primary reason for chipping, to prevent the problem, you need to relieve that pressure as much as possible. To do so, avoid making initial outline cuts too deep before making a parting-line cut.

In exercise 1, there was nothing that could

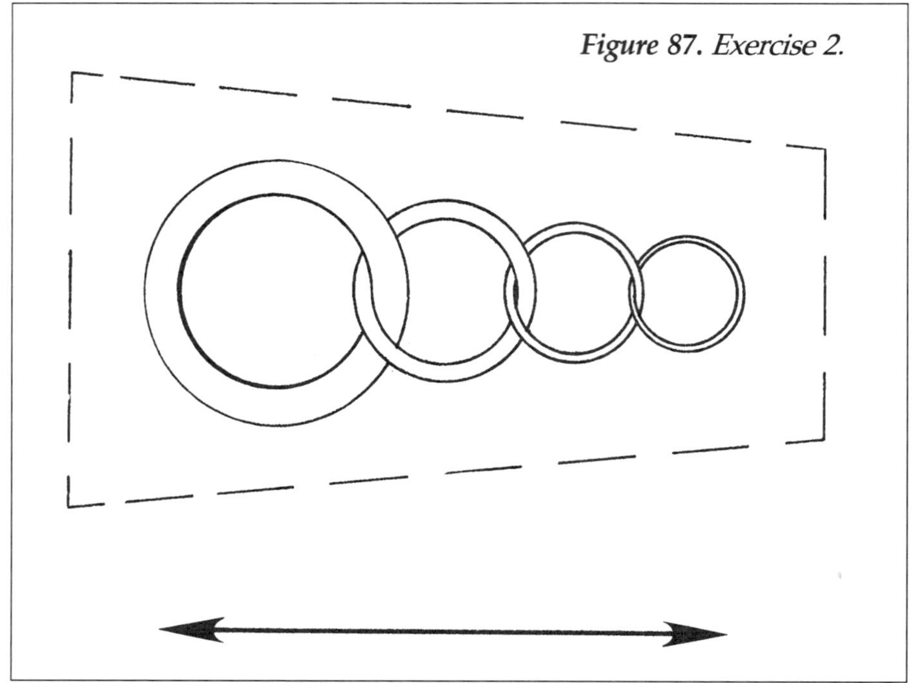

Figure 87. Exercise 2.

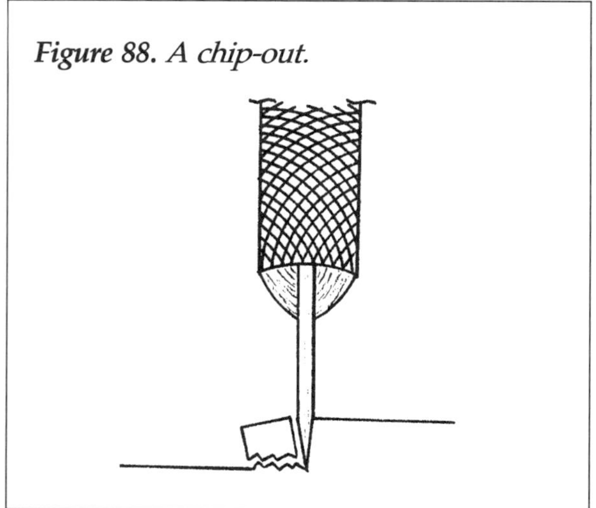

Figure 88. A chip-out.

is a high risk of chipping out portions of a design, the safe route to follow is to let the knife determine the depth of each cut. A truly sharp knife will cut even with a minimal amount of pressure. The formula to keep in mind is this: When thin detail lines require removal of wood from both sides, the stock-penetrating cut (the second cut made after the guide cut connecting the transfer holes) should be little more in depth than the guide cut and is immediately followed by a slope cut before additional vertical cuts are made to that area. Two or three light passes over a determined length of line with the very tip of the blade, making little more than a surface scratch with each pass, will achieve depth without unwanted side pressure from the blade. Next, an equally shallow parting-line cut is made using the same procedure. The process is continually repeated until the desired depth is reached. Extremely thin lines often necessitate but one very light pass with the very tip of the point. At other times, no more than a series of scrapes is needed to lower surrounding areas to the level sought. Only experience can dictate which procedure and which tool are correct at any given time.

Except when you are expanding the width of the trench after reaching a depth of $1/8$ inch, all wood removal is accomplished with the very tip and just about $1/32$ inch of the blade's cutting edge. Only an extremely small amount of wood is to be removed with each pass, and though this is not difficult to do, the process

chip away, and the outline cut was repeatedly made until achieving the desired depth. In this exercise, however, with the two smallest circles, you will use a step-down procedure to eliminate the high degree of side pressure that the next vertical cut would create. As stocks differ in grain and density, the cutting in each situation will also differ to some degree, and much will depend on whether you are working across or with the grain. When making vertical cuts around and within areas of a layout where there

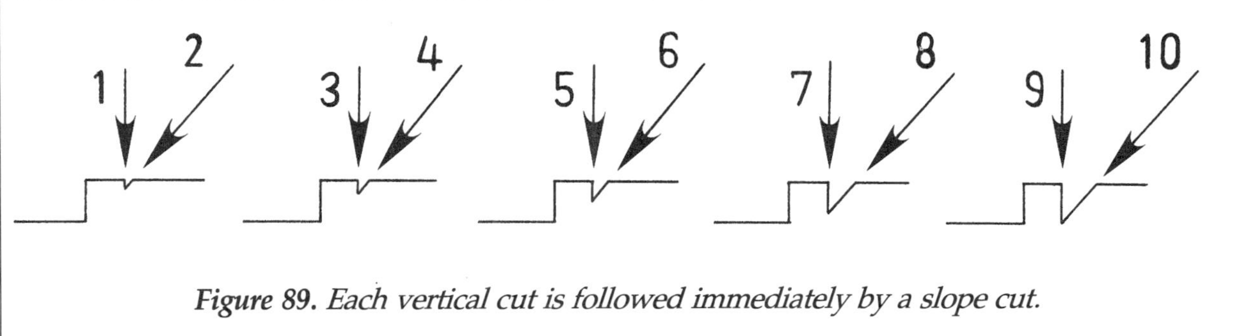

Figure 89. Each vertical cut is followed immediately by a slope cut.

requires patience and the resolve to do the job correctly. It's important to maintain the cutting edge at the peak of sharpness. If you will be doing an appreciable amount of scraping during the course of any carving, it is highly beneficial to use a second knife strictly for that purpose. With full-scale carvings, some prefer to leaving scraping until last, and others scrape as they go. I prefer the latter.

Now, place the pattern sheet from front to rear of the stock in accordance with the double-headed arrow in figure 87. The interior will be worked last, so there is no need to be concerned with chipping at this time. Begin the outside outline cut at either end, and work the entire perimeter of the layout. Then make the parting-line cut. After you have made the initial cut around the entire perimeter of the circles, expand the slope to a stock surface width of approximately ½ inch while maintaining the intersection with the base of the outline cut (¹/₈ inch). Judge the overall width of the slope from stock surface level to the parting line by eye during the course of its shaping, and

not by measuring or marking the stock in any manner.

The next step is to round off the upper edge of the circle with a softening cut (fig. 90). This will require the blade to be at its best, and touch-ups are suggested before and during the mak-

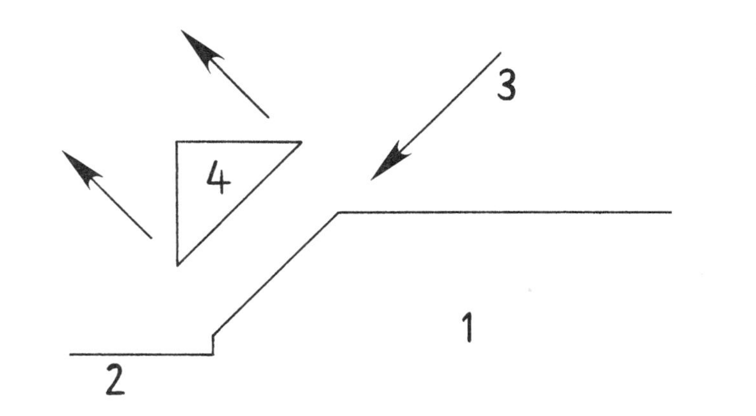

Figure 90. Softening cut: 1, raised design area; 2, lower background; 3, angle of cut; 4, removed corner.

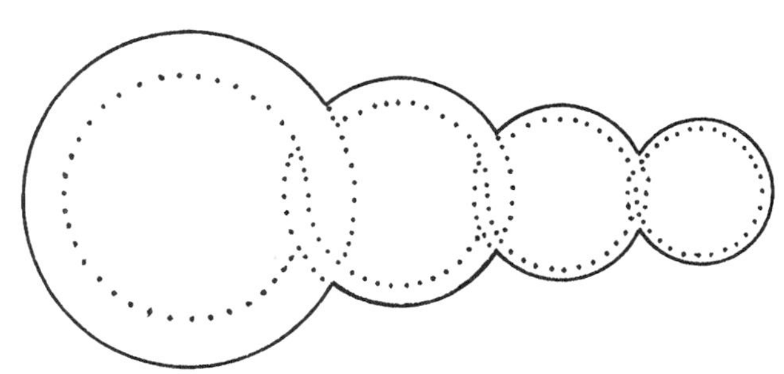

Figure 91. Only the interior transfer holes remain visible after the outside of the design is cut.

ing of this cut. Begin anywhere along the upper edge that allows you to cut with the grain. Remove the edge around the entire perimeter of the design. When reaching areas where you will begin to cut into the grain, rather than across or with it, reverse the cutting direction. After the entire edge has been angle-cut, lightly scrape the area where the wood was removed to level off any ridges caused by starting and stopping the cut. This rounding off will prevent snagging during ensuing procedures. Snags also can cause chip-outs. The interior of the layout should now be the only remaining area with transfer holes.

After you have rounded off the perimeter, turn your attention to the design's interior.

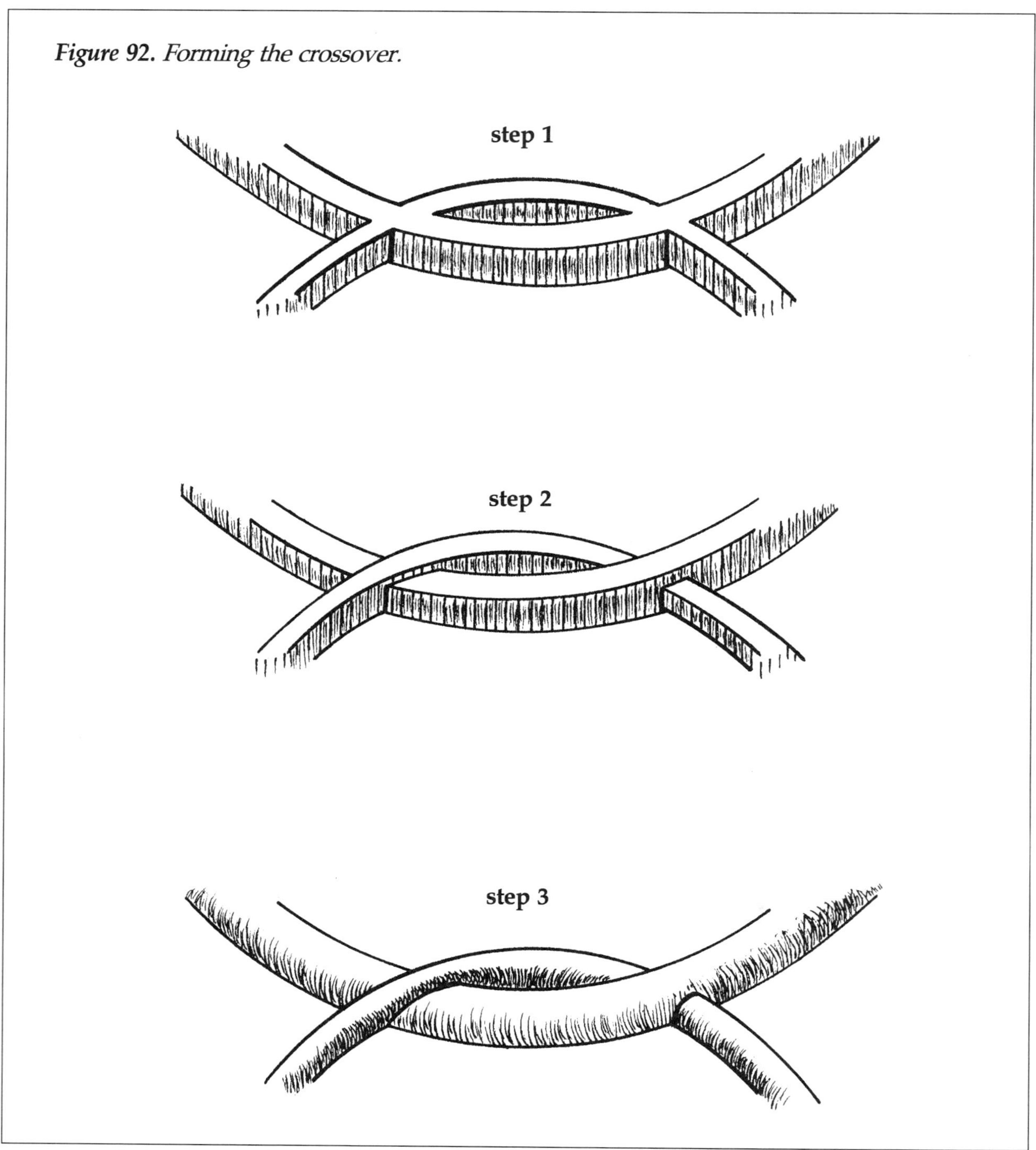

Figure 92. Forming the crossover.

Here, there is a greater likelihood of chipping out. (Should the interior have been worked first, chipping out would be more likely during the working of the perimeter.) When making the guide cut along the perforations, be sure that it does not run over onto the crossover portions of the design. Begin this and all subsequent cuts at one crossover, and when nearing another, reverse the stock and begin a connecting cut from that crossover. Work the entire circumference of the interior portion of the circle before proceeding to the next step. In other words, apply the vertical cut all the way around the interior line, and only then apply the parting-line cut. Complete each interior area of a circle to a uniform $1/8$-inch depth as shown in figure 89, then apply a softening cut to the upper edge of the circle before proceeding to the next circle.

When you work the interior of each circle, a slight peak will form at the center of the background area as you attain depth. This is because the higher surrounding wood will not allow the knife to make a flat cut. This bump must be removed and the area made flat. This can be accomplished by scraping or with a bent chisel or, my favorite for such situations, the altered dental tool described in chapter 2. This tool is excellent for leveling small areas with little risk of skipping and causing a chip-out by hitting the thin portion of a design. After I shave the area with this tool, I reverse the tool edge and use it as a scraper to remove minute ridges caused by the shaving. When you have completed this circle, repeat all of the above steps for the next one.

To create the illusion of a crossover, a portion of one circle must appear lower than the adjoining circle crossing over it

at a given point. You need to lower the profile of the line that appears to pass underneath the next circle by at least half its original height at the point being crossed, then gradually slope the line upward from that area to the point elsewhere in the design where it becomes the upper crossing line. The rise and fall of all such slopes in this exercise should be as unnoticeable as possible. After you have established the slope, round the edges by scraping to give the design its final shaping. Steps 1, 2, and 3 of figure 92 show the progression of steps necessary to form the crossover and accompanying slope.

The carving of the design is now finished. All that remains is a bit of cleaning up. First, lightly scrape any rough areas to present as smooth a surface as possible. There should be no distinct line or ridge left by the cutting process. Then use steel wool to remove any fuzz that may have resulted from scraping. Do not use excessive pressure, and move around the circles, not back and forth across them.

EXERCISE 3 (FIGURE 93)

This exercise consists of eleven interior straight lines clustered at four different spacings and

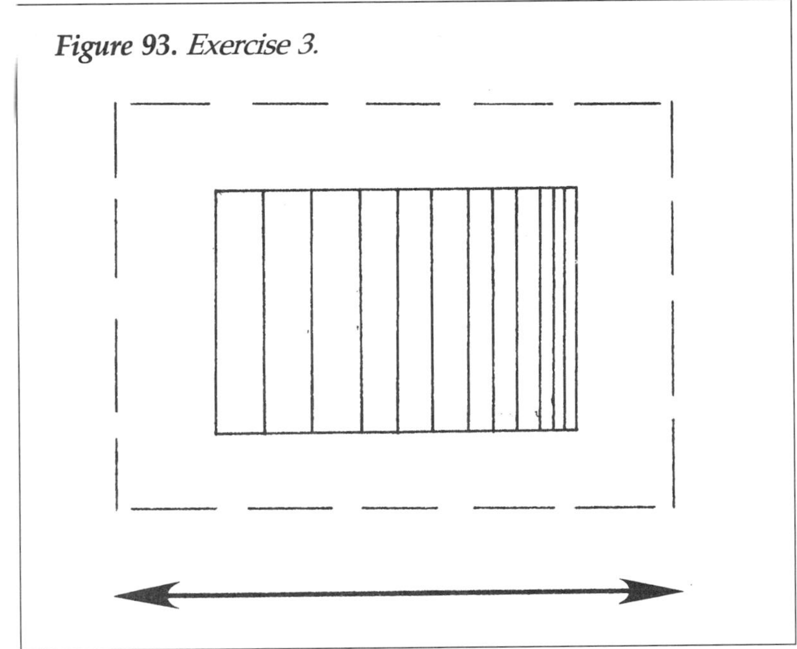

Figure 93. Exercise 3.

four side lines that form the perimeter of the layout. All lines, interior and perimeter, are to be cut at or near a depth of $1/16$ inch. The main purpose of this cutting exercise is to accomplish the carving of variously spaced lines without chipping away any wood. Should a chip-out take place during the initial setting in of the design, redo the entire layout from the beginning.

The first step (fig. 94) is to trace and transfer the design to the wood. Next, make outline and parting-line cuts around the perimeter of the design.

Then increase the angle of the parting-line cut around the entire perimeter of the design to form a slope about ½ inch wide. In this exercise, cut the interior lines after the complete perimeter slope is expanded to the approximate ½-inch width. Make a light dot-connecting cut the full length of each interior line beginning with the widest spaced and ending with the thinnest spaced. Be careful: The last three interior lines, being closely spaced, must be cut with greater care, as they will easily chip if you apply too much pressure with the blade. You can easily begin dot-connecting cuts at each end of a line to connect at some point along the line. This will lessen the chance of a breakaway or chip-out at the end of a cut at the perimeter of the design, which is more likely to happen when a single full-length cut is made from end to the other.

Step 3 shows the interior lines at their full depth, but this is not always possible, especially

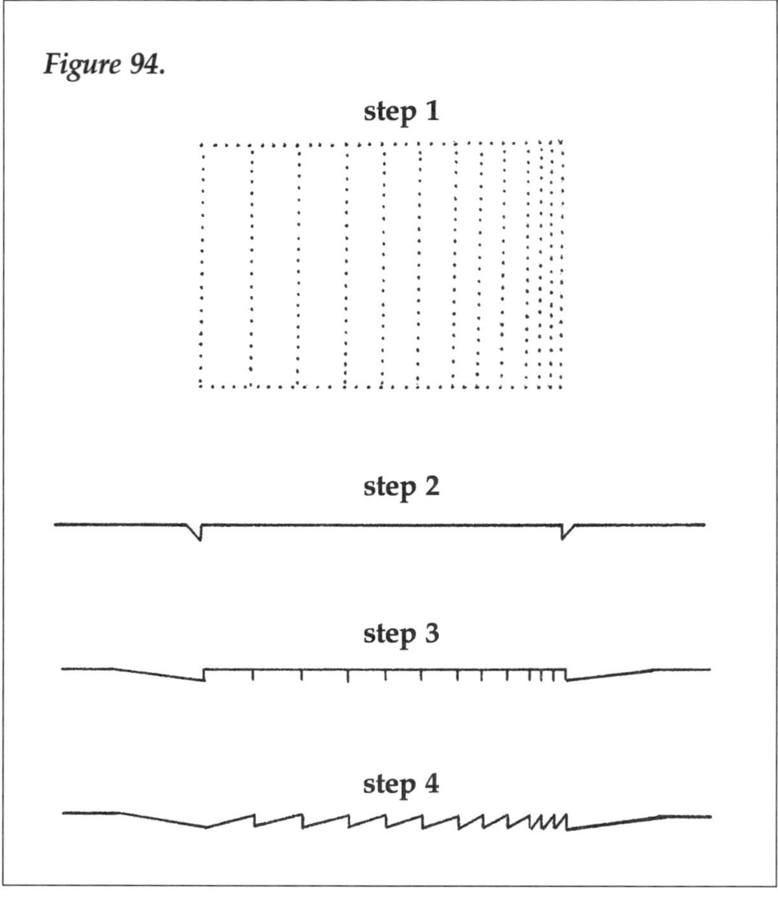

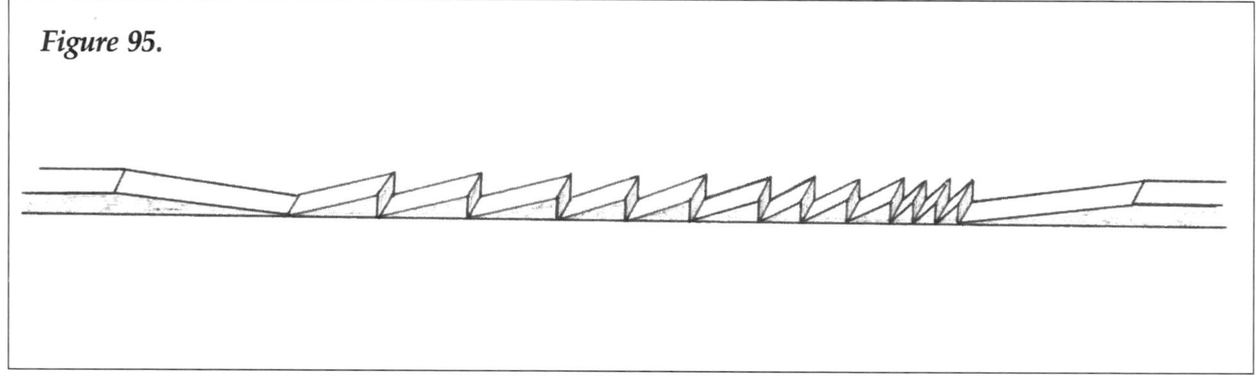

with closely spaced lines. It is shown in this manner simply to provide the beginning carver with a visual picture of the intended completed depth. This final depth is attained using the step-down procedure shown in figure 89.

Step 4 is to make a sloped cut from the top of each line to the bottom of the adjacent line. Figure 95 is an enlarged portion of the design showing the end result. Finally, make a small softening cut at the upper sharp edge of each slope. This cut is no more than would be accomplished with a single light scrape, but scraping this edge rather than cutting would more often than not cause a chip-out. This cut provides you the opportunity to straighten the line or compensate for any small irregularities along the edges. Some carvers maintain that edges of this sort should remain sharp, but such edges would be extremely fragile and would be inappropriate for a working rifle or shotgun.

After completing the softening cuts on the upper edge, gently scrape all areas with the knife blade to remove cut marks and fuzz and to square up the slope and walls of each line.

Complete the exercise by stippling the surrounding ½-inch-wide sloped area around the perimeter of the exercise. To stipple, press the scratch awl into the wood just enough to leave a very small indentation. Many carvers believe that stippling should be applied at random and widely space. I disagree, however. Close stippling provides a much better overall appearance, with an attractive, uniform look, and creates a more pronounced background against which the subject matter better stands out. Also, close stippling tends to level the background, compensating a bit for any slight roll or irregularity created while removing wood. After you

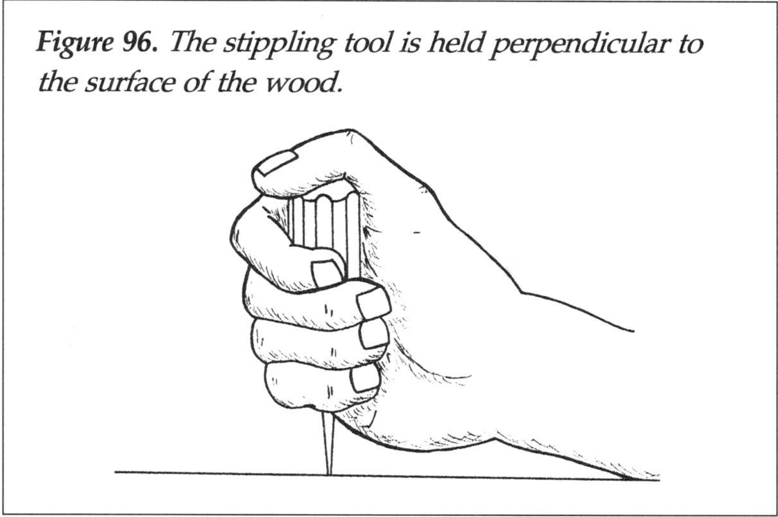

Figure 96. The stippling tool is held perpendicular to the surface of the wood.

have applied many forms of background stippling, you will decide on a favorite and use that one on most of your carvings. Keep an open mind, and do a bit of experimenting.

In this exercise, you will use both wide and close placement of stippling in order to become accustomed to the use of the stippling tool and to judge for yourself which type you prefer. Always hold the tool perpendicular to the surface of the wood rather than at 90 degrees to the stock itself. If held straight to the stock at a 90-degree angle when stippling a slope, the tool may slide into carved areas or splinter areas near previous stipple holes.

To conclude this exercise, randomly stipple two sides of the ½-inch sloped perimeter with the holes varying from close together to ¹/₁₆-inch maximum spacing in between, and stipple the remaining two sides with the holes nearly touching. Should splintering occur, it will generally be the result of the holes being place far too close or much too deep. With stippling that is slightly more than an indentation, splintering more than likely will be the result of a stipple hole's overriding onto another, especially of the tool is pressed into the wood at an angle. Make certain you hold the tool at a 90-degree angle to the area being stippled and slightly increase the distance when applying the next stipple.

Continue to increase the distance until the splintering stops. This will usually happen after one or two stipples. From this, you will learn the closest distance that successive stipples can be applied without splintering.

After stippling, place masking tape around the perimeter of the slope on the main stock surface to protect it while you dewhisker the carved and stippled areas. It's a good policy to have more protection than is actually needed to protect against a mishap that would scratch the finish. Apply a strip of tape to the finish of the stock around the entire circumference of the circled area. Be certain that all of the finish of the stock is covered to the very edge of the perimeter slopes. Expand the area of protection for the stock's finished surface by placing other strips of tape around the design. This second application of tape should expand the area of coverage outward from the design. It's best to overlap the first tape with the second tape by at least ¼ inch. Depending on the width of tape, it might be necessary to apply more tape in the same manner. Use your fingertip to press all areas of tape to the stock, especially the overlapping portions to the underlaying tape.

The same procedures outlined for dewhiskering an entire stock for total refinishing apply to dewhiskering a carved area. There is, however, a much higher risk of steel wool snags that can pull out splinters and of removing too much wood from both the design and stippled areas. To dewhisker a carved area, tear off a small piece of steel wool from the larger pad. This size will give you a better feel for detecting a possible snag and will allow you to get into tighter places. It's important to brush very lightly over both the stippling and the design, especially during the initial strokes. It is not always possible to brush in one direction on carvings during the dewhiskering procedure. Always proceed using very light pressure and caution.

After dewhiskering the carved area, use a magnet to remove steel wool particles from the carving stock and surrounding area. Follow up on the carved area with a toothbrush. Again, use light pressure. Check the carved area with a magnifying glass. If you find embedded steel wool particles, remove them with tweezers. Be careful, as it is still possible to cause a splinter.

After cleanup and removal of the tape, apply a thinned coat of lacquer to the carving and slope with a stiff-bristle artist brush. If you are using a spray finish, leave the masking tape in place, and cover all of the surrounding area of the stock with paper or plastic to protect it from the spray. Be sure there is absolutely no gap in the protective covering. Tape the covering to the masking tape at the slope's edge to form a seal in that area. Seal off any overlapping paper seams as well. Spray or brush the finish onto the design, then remove all protective covering and immediately check the stock surface for possible seeping of the newly applied finish. Should any be found, remove it quickly.

EXERCISE 4 (FIGURE 97)

This basket-weave exercise is highly repetitious. Most errors during the working of such designs, aside from incorrect layout during initial steps, stem from monotony. The exercise consists of eighteen large blocks, four squares one-third the size of the larger blocks, and seventeen vertical running segments. More basket-weave patterns appear in chapter 10, but many other such patterns are suitable for gunstock carving, and you are not limited to those presented in this book.

The first step is to trace and transfer the design to the stock. This exercise now differs from previous ones with regard to setting in the design's perimeter. In this case, make only the vertical outline cut, and no parting-line cut, around the perimeter of the design. After you have made the perimeter outline cut, the only individual transfer holes that should be visible

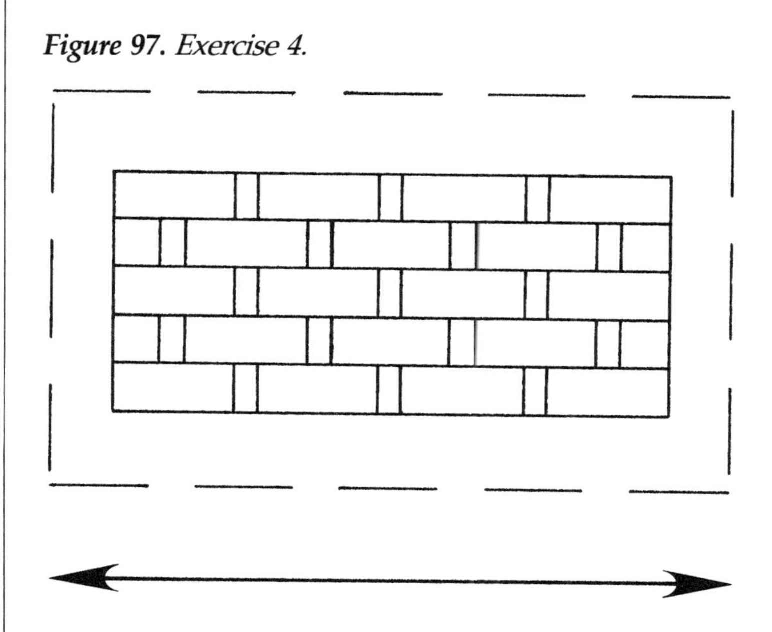

Figure 97. Exercise 4.

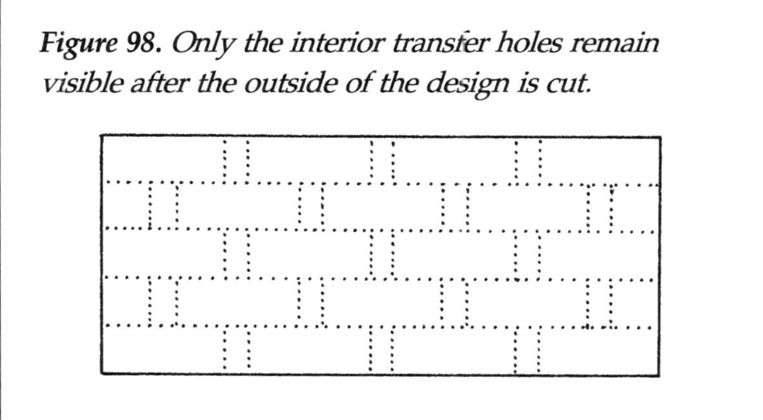

Figure 98. Only the interior transfer holes remain visible after the outside of the design is cut.

are those that define the interior lines of the design (fig. 98).

The next step is to make a transfer hole–connecting cut to all of the interior lines. Each line is to receive one additional deepening cut along its length at this time; use just a bit more pressure than you used to make the transfer hole–connecting cut. All lines beginning at the perimeter that are not continuous to the opposite side should be cut from the perimeter and stopped when they intersect another line. Interior lines should start and stop at intersecting lines. All continuous lines from perimeter to pe-

rimeter should be cut from each end and made to joint somewhere along the line's length. Cutting from the perimeter and connecting the cut along the line in the interior of the layout will prevent you from running the cut over onto the surrounding stock surface. Always take advantage of the ability to make a cut inward from the perimeter to prevent overrunning onto the stock surface. Divide into thirds each of the design's longest segments, running from left to right. This does not have to be a precise measurement. It's best to work each segment to completion before proceeding to the next segment. Start at the top left of the design and work across the top row.

Score a light reference mark from side to side of the segment or use a pencil to mark the section into thirds. The longest segments at final shaping will have their highest points at the center of their widths from side to side, with two equally formed slopes, one on each side of the center portion of the segment. Each sloping section is made downward and away from the center section (fig. 99). Treat the four smaller segments at the end of rows 2 and 4 as longer segments. They are a third of the overall length of a full-size segment, so their respective slope should be cut downward and inward from the perimeter of the design. Do not attempt to make a slope with only one cut. Use a series of cuts from side to side to deepen the slope as shown. Form all slopes to maximum depth of $^1/_{16}$ inch, and as shown in figure 86. During the sloping process,

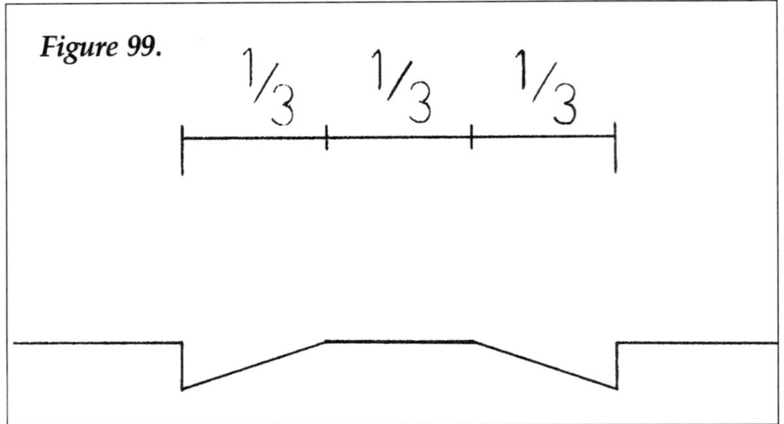

Figure 99.

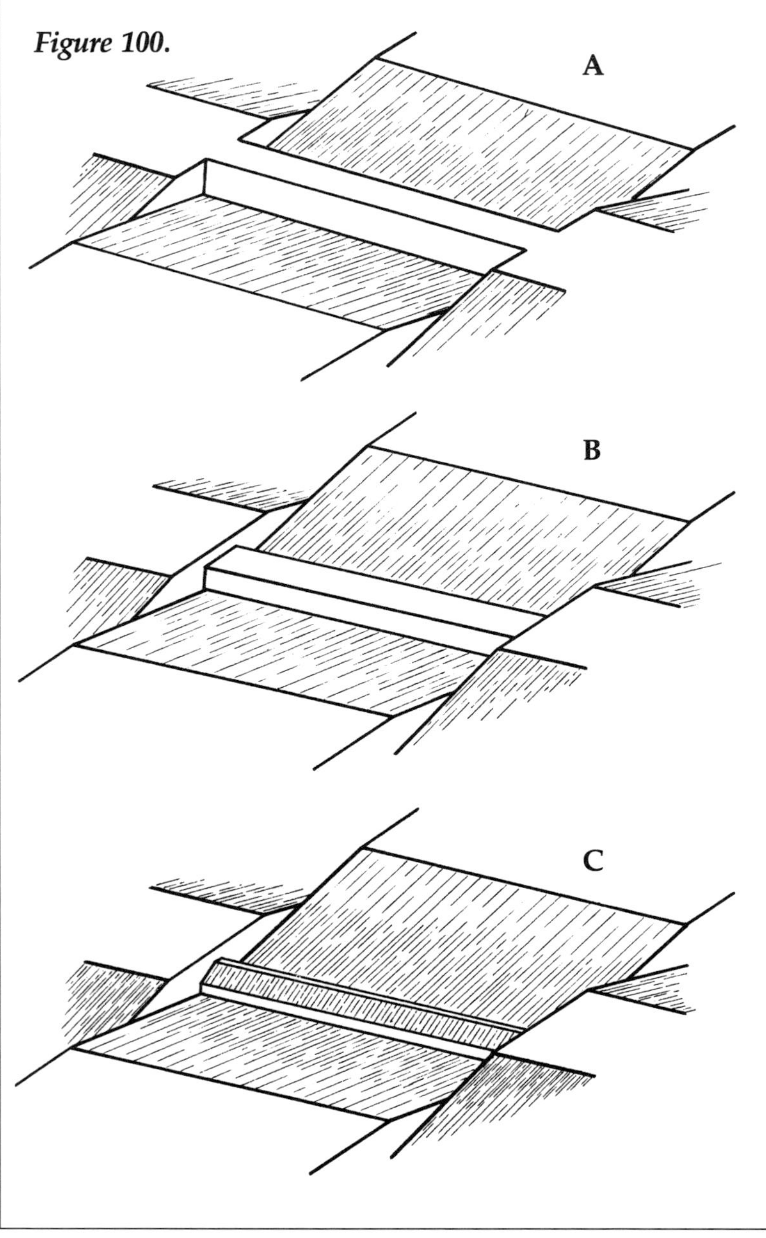

Figure 100.

you will need to make downward cuts running with the length of segment to form a sharp vertical wall on each side of the slope. Be careful not to undercut what will be the side walls of the slope when making side cuts to form the slope.

Once the center portion of the square is at stock level, perform the final shaping by lowering the height of the thin vertical segments by approximately one-third and rounding off their corners (fig. 100). Then round off the top portion of the slope to blend with the higher center portion of the square. Do this by scraping from side to side with the cutting edge of the knife blade. The width of the center portion will be reduced just a bit by the scraping, but this is intended. When finished, each square should have a uniform roll from one end of the block to the other, with the highest point at the center. The maximum depth at the lowest point of all squares should be as close as possible to $1/16$ inch.

Now, place tape along the edge of the design to mask off the surface of the stock, and dewhisker the area. Remove the tape, clean up the area, and apply the finish. Examine the right-hand portion of figure 101. Note the final shape of the lowered vertical segments and their relationship to the higher areas, which appear to run under. Above and to each side of the

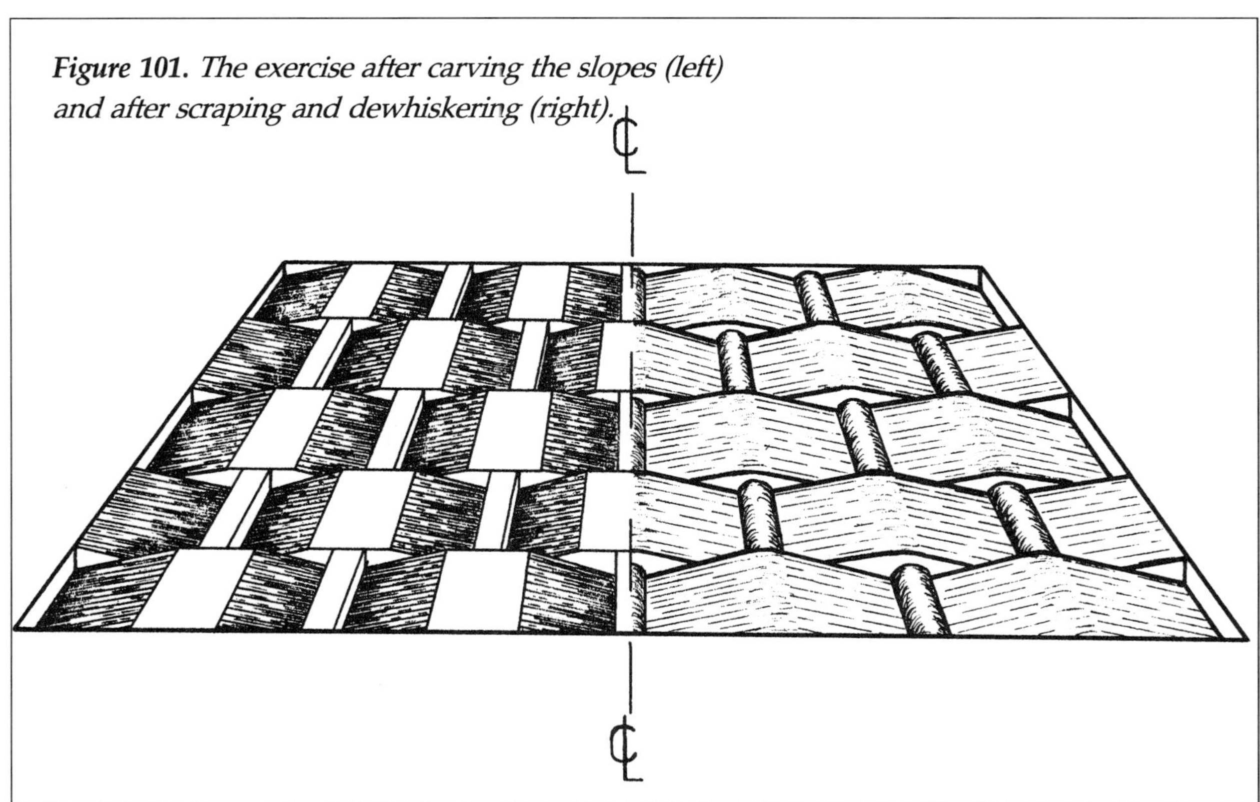

Figure 101. The exercise after carving the slopes (left) and after scraping and dewhiskering (right).

vertical segments is a small flat area; this is the wall of the adjoining block. These areas are of no consequence, as they are so minute that they will not be noticeable.

If you complete the first three rows without making a mistake, you can end the exercise at that point or continue to carve the entire design. If you make a mistake during the working of the first three rows, complete the entire exercise. If you then make mistakes in the fourth and fifth rows, redo the exercise from the beginning.

When you apply a basket-weave pattern as an actual design to a gunstock, use a pattern of alternation to avoid mistakes, especially when all segments are of equal size. This means establishing a row or column in its entirety from which to follow a pattern when you cut an adjoining row. Though the layout generally is not critical, there are times when either the high or low point of a perimeter segment would be beneficially placed at some portion of an accompanying border design. Consider such things beforehand when using a border around a basket-weave design.

EXERCISE 5 (FIGURE 102)

One of the most important lessons to learn in any form of carving is how to execute levels, because they are the means of achieving a three-dimensional appearance. Levels are of greater importance with human and wildlife forms than with floral designs to achieve realistic results.

In this exercise, a partial animal torso is carved. There are three major levels to be executed when carving the torso. They will give a three-dimensional appearance, and little contouring will be necessary. The finished maximum depth around the perimeter of the torso should be about $3/32$ inch. The initial step, however, is to create a ½-inch-wide slope around the design that will end at the base of the design at a depth of $1/16$ inch. The additional $1/32$ inch will be added later.

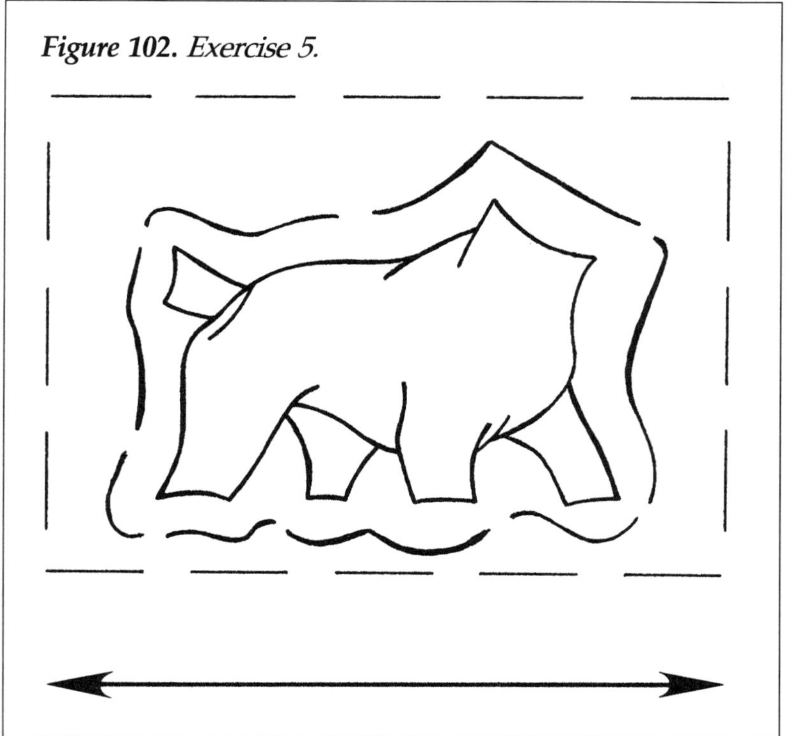

Figure 102. Exercise 5.

uniform levels may not be an easy task for a beginning carver. In most cases, however, wildlife torsos that are determined to be at three levels can generally be worked at but two levels. Portions of the torso at mid-level that are near the higher level can be carved at that level, and those that are near the deeper level can be treated as part of that level. Then both levels can be contoured to attain the appropriate effect.

The next step is to make cuts connecting the transfer holes to those lines within the interior of the torso. Then shave the tail and left legs to leave about $^1/_{32}$ inch above the background level of wood (fig. 103).

First, trace and transfer the design to the stock. Then make the vertical outline setting-in cut and parting-line cut around the perimeter of the design. Expand the parting-line cut to a ½-inch-wide sloped cut completely around the perimeter, then smooth the side walls of the design and expanded parting-line slope by either using a file or scraping with the cutting edge of a blade.

You now need to examine the torso to establish various levels. The left front and rear legs will be the most deeply carved portions, and the right legs and torso the highest. The portion of the tail shown, though at midpoint of the torso, should be considered part of the deepest level, on the same plane as the off-side legs. The wood constituting the overall depth of the design is fairly thin, and dividing that depth into three

Round off the upper sharp edges around the entire perimeter of the design, including those of the deeper levels. The blunt ends of the neck, tail, and legs need not be rounded off.

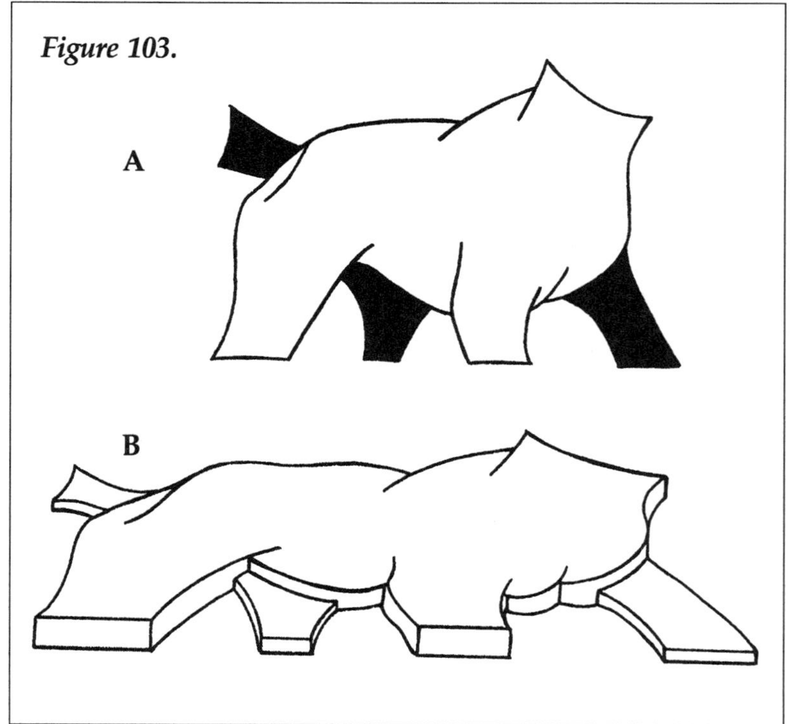

Figure 103.

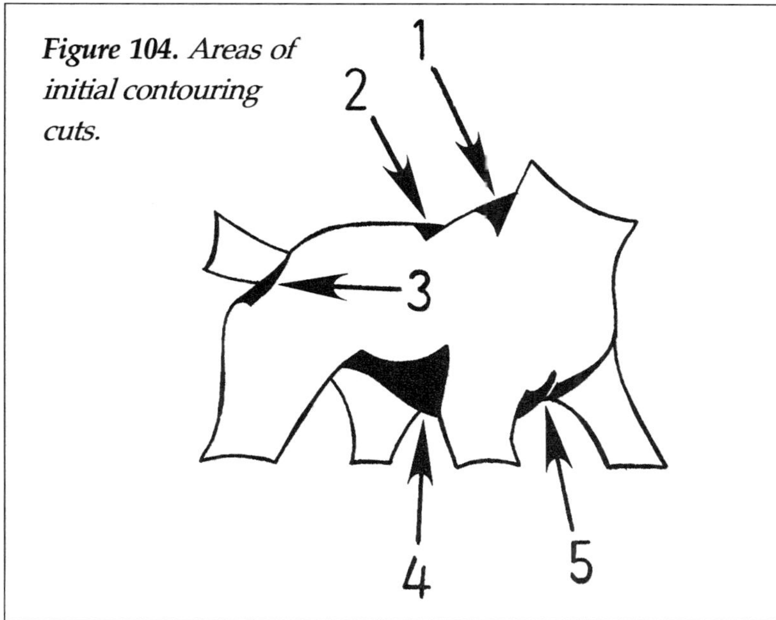

Figure 104. Areas of initial contouring cuts.

they may have to be slightly deepened during the process to achieve the angle sought. Should deepening be necessary, remain conscious of the angle and do not make the deepening cut such that it will exceed the angle to an excessive degree.

Work area 2 of figure 104 in the same manner. Upon completion, scrape both areas to remove obvious cut edges and to blend the areas with the surrounding wood. Also slightly round the higher upper edges

Portions of interior lines near the perimeter of the design may be affected by rounding off the edge, and you may have to recut them.

Now contour the darkened areas shown in figure 104. Judge these areas by eye; do not mark the stock in any way.

Begin with area 1. Turn the stock so that you can make a simple angled push cut from the perimeter of the design toward the interior of the design. Place the tip of the blade directly at the lowest point of the previously made vertical cut, which defines the neck. This is the base of the design. Maintain the position of the blade's point at the base of the design and angle the blade so that the cutting edge at the upper portion of the design will meet the end of the neck-defining cut. The lines you cut earlier will act as stop cuts during this procedure (fig. 105), but

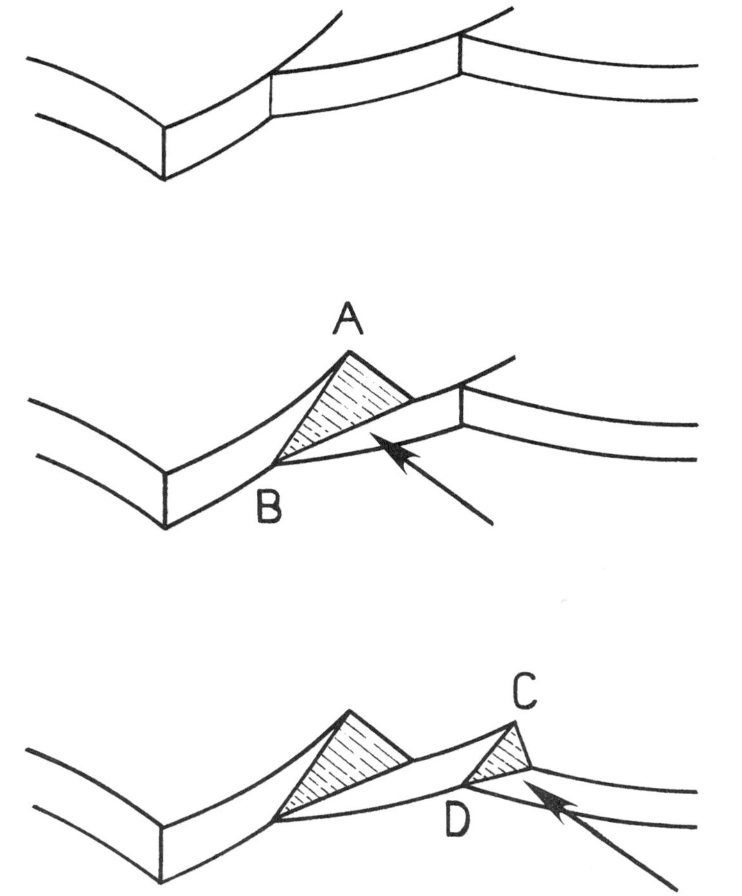

Figure 105. Enlarged neck and back view from top of design. Top diagram shows areas 1 and 2 before cuts. Middle diagram shows angle of cut from A to B in area 1. Bottom diagram shows angle of cut from C to D in area 2.

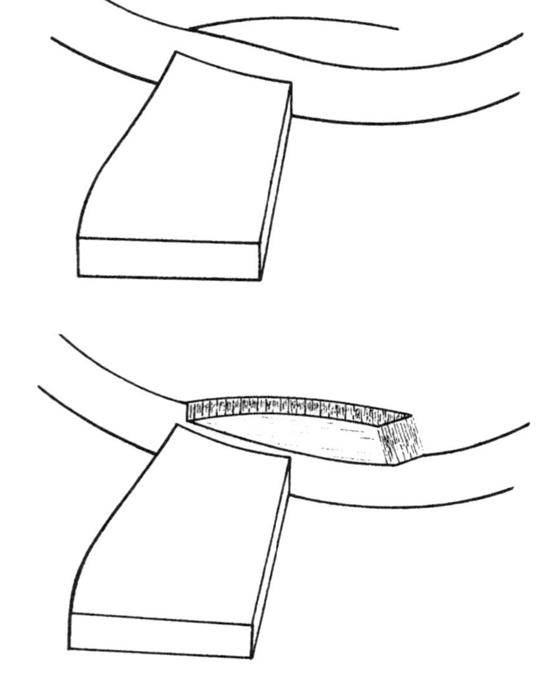

Figure 106. Enlarged view of the rump area before cutting (top) and after cutting (bottom).

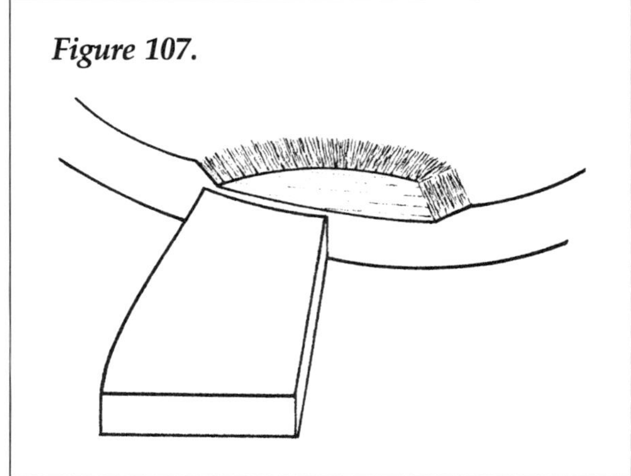

Figure 107.

and the upper edge of the interior line to blend with the surrounding area, and scrape them to eliminate cut markings. Round the upper edge along the inner line a bit more than usual to create a softer, less pronounced line than those in areas 1 and 2 (fig. 104).

Area 4, the stomach area, is the largest of the areas to be contoured and is chiefly responsible for giving the correct torso shape to the overall form. To gauge where to begin the contoured slope from the interior to the underside of the torso, draw an imaginary line between the end-

of the lines you cut earlier, but leave them high enough to be well pronounced.

In area 3 of figure 104, remove the wood from the length of the interior cut line made earlier to the perimeter of the rump. This should be a flat cut, starting at the perimeter of the design at the upper portion of the tail and running the length of the line, curving upward as it nears completion. Keep the depth uniform throughout, at a level just about a blade thickness above the height of the tail, except for the upturn at the end (fig. 106). Upon completion of the cut, round the perimeter

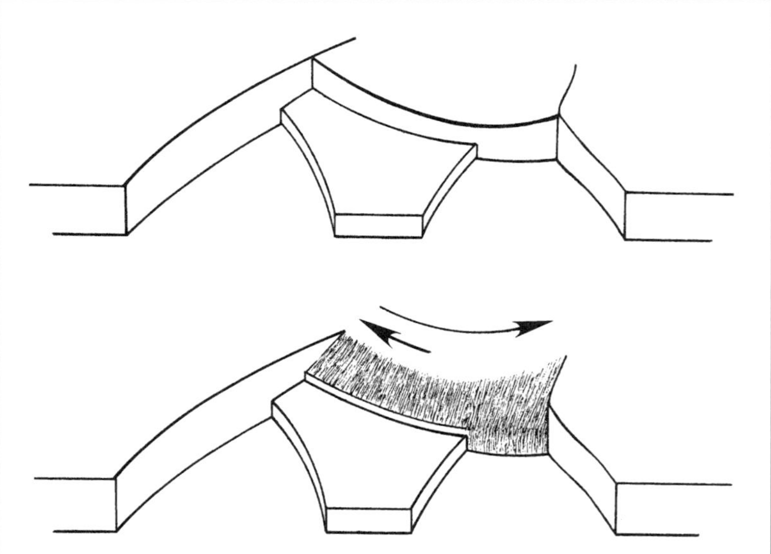

Figure 108. Enlarged view of the stomach area before cutting (top) and after cutting (bottom). Arrows indicate direction of cuts.

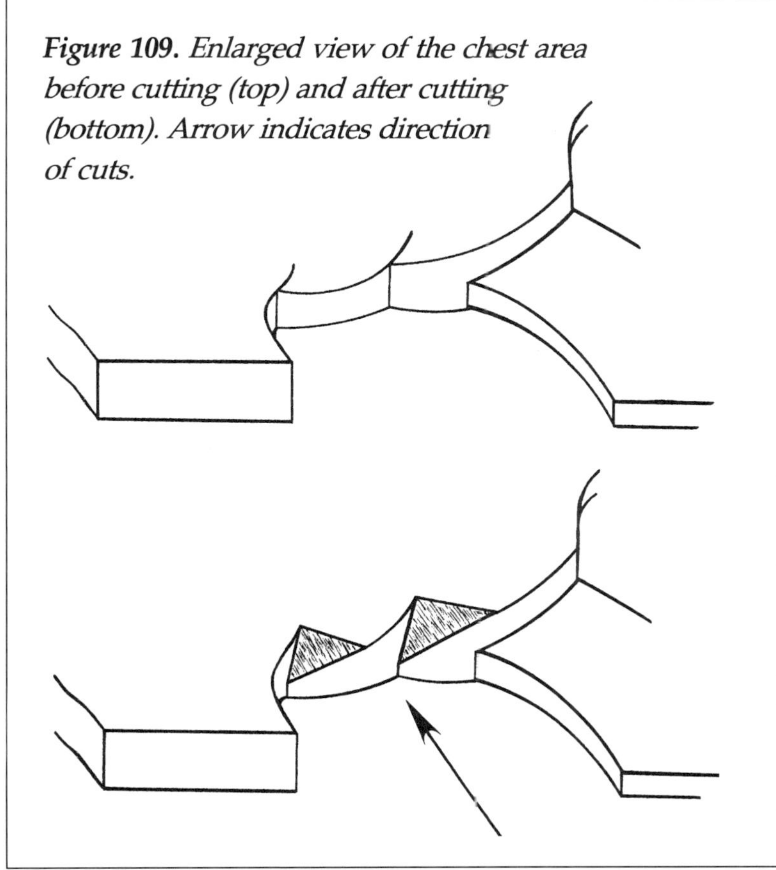

Figure 109. Enlarged view of the chest area before cutting (top) and after cutting (bottom). Arrow indicates direction of cuts.

to about a blade's thickness above the deeper-cut left leg. Keep the forward portion beyond the leg at the same slope. Slightly round off the slope along the area of the leg, then round off the area forward of the leg more severely. Scrape the entire area to blend it into surrounding areas and to remove tool marks (fig. 108).

Area 5 is cut in the same manner as areas 1 and 2. Make the first cut to the right side of the muscle dividing line, then cut from that line to the leg. Round and scrape the high sharp edges of the leg and muscle dividing line in the same manner as the other areas (fig. 109).

Now it is time to bring the overall depth of the design to

points within the interior of the upper portions of the right side legs, allowing for the roundness of the torso. Notice that the curved upper line of the shadowed area marked 4 in figure 104 is curved and has a sharper rise as it nears the front leg–defining cut. This will aid in creating the lean, muscular shape of this particular animal. The angle of the slope should run

$^3/_{32}$ inch. Use a file or knife to form a groove around the entire perimeter of the design directly at its base (fig. 110). This will give a shallow-carved design a higher-appearing image. Next, stipple the entire ½-inch-wide sloped area around the design. Then mask off and dewhisker the surrounding stock area and apply a finish.

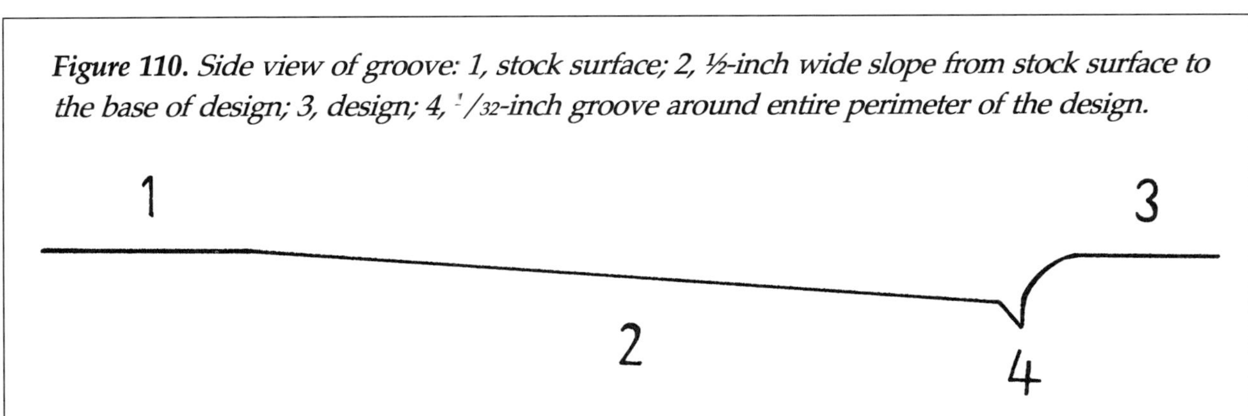

Figure 110. Side view of groove: 1, stock surface; 2, ½-inch wide slope from stock surface to the base of design; 3, design; 4, $^1/_{32}$-inch groove around entire perimeter of the design.

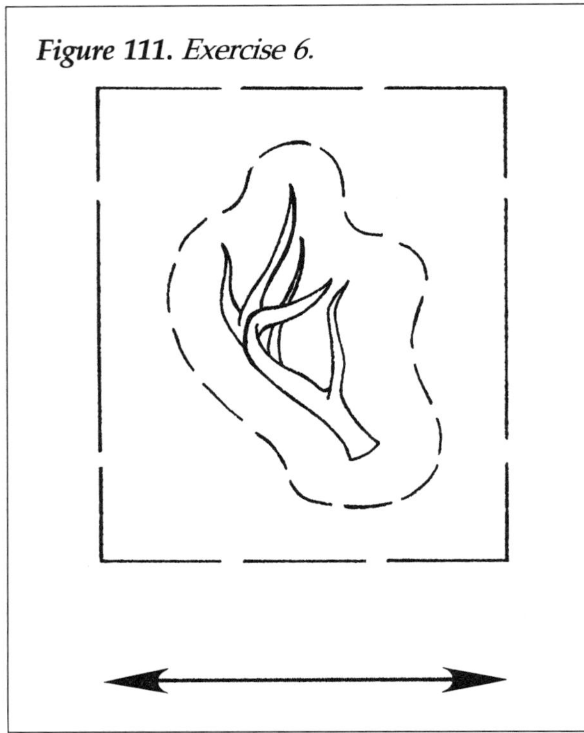

Figure 111. Exercise 6.

EXERCISE 6 (FIGURE 111)

This exercise presents curves, crossovers, a particularly small area of wood removal, and numerous opportunities for chip-outs. You also will learn how to prevent the tips of an antler from breaking away during initial setting-in procedures and the carving of the overall design. This design has an irregular full-cut border around it that is $1/32$-inch below the stock surface level and sloped from that level to the base of the design. The depth of the design from stock surface level to background level is about $3/32$ inch, sloping upward from the base of the design's perimeter to the base of the border cut. This slight depth of the border cut is enough to clearly distinguish a recessed background from the surrounding stock surface level.

Unlike previous exercises, you should transfer the line of the border to the stock at the time of design transfer. Make a vertical cut to deepen the initial hole-connecting cuts of the design and border. Next, make parting-line cuts first to the outside perimeter of the design to separate it

from its surrounding area, then to the inside line of the border. Remove background wood as with other exercises, thereby deepening and widening the slope from the design to the base of the border. The background area between all portions of the antler should be at the $3/32$-inch depth and be uniformly smooth.

When nearing the antler tips during hole-connecting and initial deepening cuts, do not bring the opposing side cuts together to form the point. This surely will cause a chip-out or breakaway of the tip. Such a chip-out can be compensated for, but not without unnecessary additional work and deviation from the original design by shortening the antler. The safe procedure is to make the transfer hole–connecting cut and initial deepening cut to one side only of each branch, with each cut extending from $1/8$ to ¼ inch beyond the tip. Then make

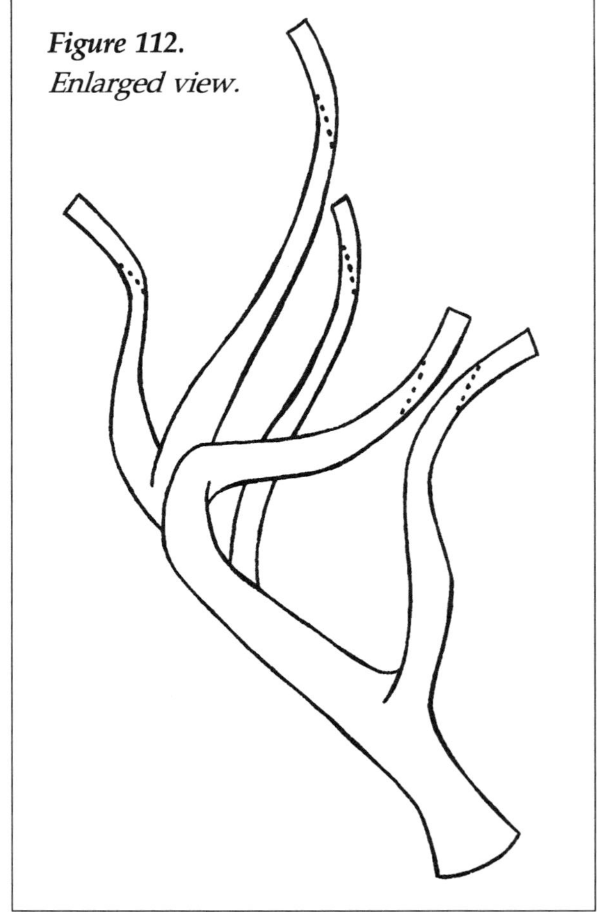

*Figure 112.
Enlarged view.*

the cut to the other side of each branch, following the transfer holes until about $^1/_8$ inch from the tip. From that point, run the cut parallel with the opposing outline cut, maintaining $^1/_{16}$ to $^1/_{32}$ inch between them, until ending at the same distance beyond the tip. Next, make a straight cut across to connect the ending points of both lines. Remove the surrounding wood to the background level. The transfer holes defining one side of the pointed tip will remain visible; ignore them at this time (fig. 112) and cut the tips of all antlers in this manner.

When you begin background wood removal, start with the small area surrounded by the second and third branches from the base of the antler at the approximate center of the design. Because no other wood has been removed, you won't have to worry about chip-outs when working this area first. On future designs, always work areas of this sort first for that reason.

Uniformly deepen the vertical cut around the perimeter of the area, and pick out the wood by inserting the blade at a slight angle. Using a modified dental tool, as described in chapter 2,

wood removal in such areas will be relatively easy. It is important to set in the outline of the antler with vertical cuts before you try to remove any wood. Attaining the full $^3/_{32}$-inch depth during initial wood removal is not always possible in small areas without damaging the walls of the antler as wood removal becomes deeper. If you reach a point where damage is likely to occur, stop. The remaining depth can be attained during subsequent procedures.

The pick-out method can be used in larger areas where two lines meet to form a sharp-pointed intersection, such as the crotch directly above the area just worked. Here, though, to bring the area coming to a point to the proper depth, along with the remainder of the area, insert the cutting tool at a near flat angle that will intersect with the bottom of the vertical cuts following the outline of the design.

Lowering the background areas between portions of the antler is best accomplished in gradual steps done equally to both sides. First, connect the transfer holes with a very light cut, and then follow the step-down procedure. This

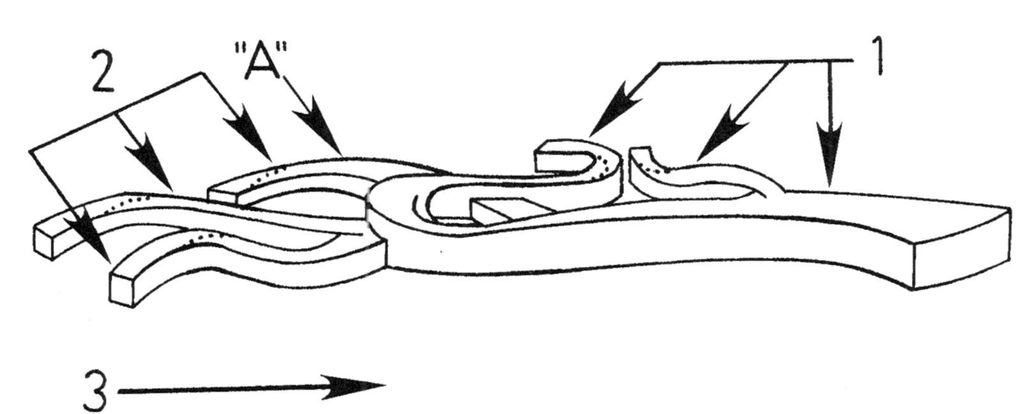

Figure 113. Side view of antler levels: 1, high portion of design; 2, low portions approximately half the height of 1 (the small area of branch A between the high portion is scraped down to the height of the low portions); 3, direction of lowering cuts made with the grain of the wood.

will ease the side pressure exerted by the blade, and the possibility of chipping away the fragile tip will be greatly lessened. After you have removed excess wood beyond the tip, the extreme tip of the antler will be somewhat above background wood level. While maintaining its shape, lightly feather the wood downward so that the tip will gradually end at background wood level. Remember, do all cutting and scraping in this area from the tip of the antler toward the body of the branch. This area is best worked with a freshly sharpened blade. Once you have removed all background wood between branches of the antler and that which forms the slope to the border, scrape the background area smooth.

The next step is to create levels. The first and third antler branches from the head are at the highest level, and the second, fourth, and fifth portions are at the deeper level. Bring these lower portions down to half the height of the higher ones. When doing so, make a flat cut fully along the length, starting at the extended end beyond the tip, and stopping at the line of the higher portion (fig. 113). After all levels have been attained, make another flat cut to form a slope from near background surface extending upward to end at least $1/8$ inch past the last visible transfer hole (fig. 114). Take great care not to cut into the grain when forming this slope, as a split or chip-out can easily occur. Make no cut from the tip end upward unless cutting with or across the grain. The ideal situation is to make the tip cuts from the higher level to the background level; however, this is not always possible when cutting with the grain. Even when cutting with or across the grain, make the slope with a series of light cuts and not with a single cut.

After making the slopped cut, you likely will have to re-mark the transfer holes defining the pointed tips, as most will be present but only lightly visible.

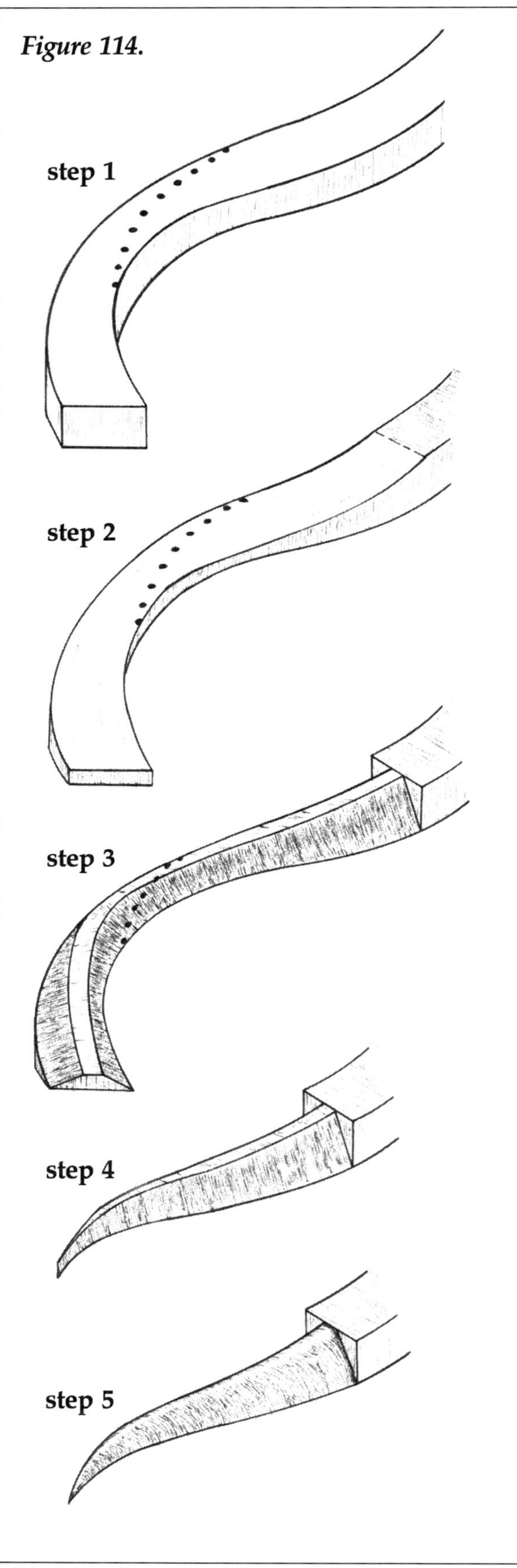

Figure 114.

Take note that the line of the cut along the upper portion is maintained slightly off center. After you make a like cut to the opposite side, there will be a long, narrow, flat strip the entire length at center of the branch. Gradually diminish the width of this flat area, and fade it out at the tip. It's best to do one branch at a time following the steps shown in figure 114.

When working antlers, perform all cutting and scraping very slowly and lightly, as all areas are very fragile until final rounding is complete. Because they are so fragile, all tips, whether they are at the higher or deeper level, must be shaped to end at background wood level. This helps to prevent them from snagging clothing during use of the firearm. When you remove surrounding wood to background level between the branches, immediately slope the tips of that branch.

Shape the longer portions of the antler branches by making a small rounding cut to opposite upper edges, then scrape to attain the final shape.

When carving a full-size animal with antlers, the animal itself is carved to completion first, the longer portions of the antlers second, and the tips of the antlers last. The downward slope along the very tip is placed during the working of the full length of the branch.

In this exercise, there are two areas where a line runs from one portion of a branch into the interior of another, and an area where one line runs within the same branch of the antler. Each is to define either a curve or an exit point of another portion of the branch. While rounding off these branches, scrape from above the line of the first antler branch from the head toward the first interior line (fig. 115). This will present a rounded perimeter between the first and third branches and a sharper, less rounded edge on the interior portion of the first branch. Work each like instance in the same manner. Steel wool used later during the dewhiskering pro-

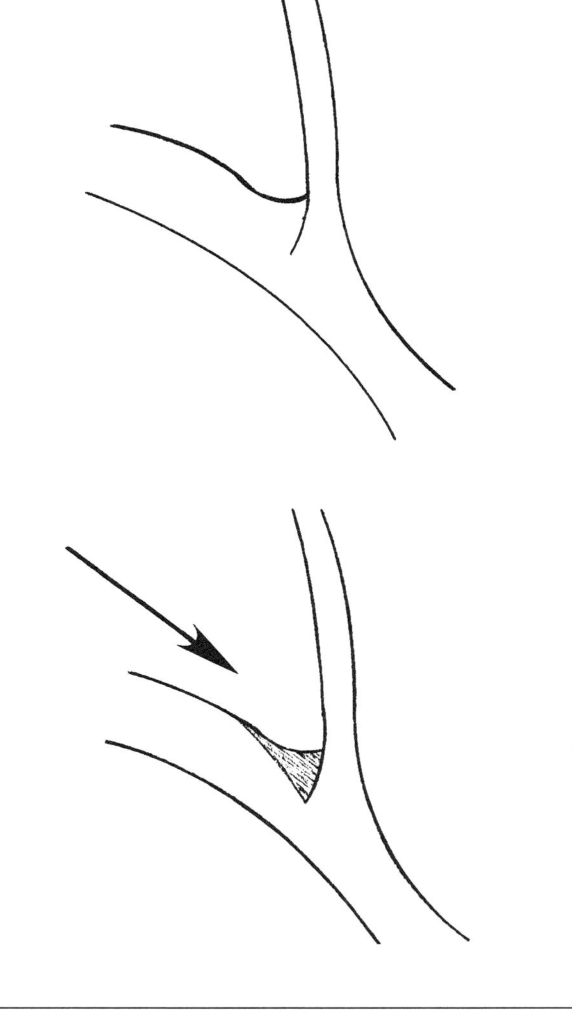

Figure 115. Before (top) and after (bottom) a light cut is made where the branches join.

cess will generally soften the interior edges to the desired shape.

After you have rounded off all portions of the antler, stipple the background. Then place masking tape around the border onto the surrounding stock surface. Dewhisker and clean up the area, then apply a finish. Repeat this exercise as many times as necessary to work it to completion without error.

8

Full-Scale Carving Exercises

THIS CHAPTER CONSISTS OF THREE FULL-SCALE CARV-
ing exercises, encompassing all of the procedures outlined in the preceding chapter. The first, an elk, is a buttstock design with border. The second, a mourning dove in flight, and the third, an oak leaf, are not presented with borders. You could add a straight cut or floral design border to the dove to create a complete design, but all three designs can be used without a border.

The oak leaf seems to be the leaf most used for carving. Perhaps this is because there is such variety in the genus both in leaves and acorns, and many make attractive accent or feature carvings. A full design for both forearm and pistol grip using the oak leaf appears in chapter 10.

These three exercises are the last to be worked. After you successfully complete these designs, all that remains to produce noteworthy gunstock carvings is continual practice, for it is only through practice that you can become proficient. Don't expect that you will complete these exercises perfectly. Look at your mistakes as part of the learning process. Some mistakes are minor; others are of a more serious nature. Regardless of any mistakes you might make, carve all exercises to completion so that you can study them afterward. Compare your completed carvings to the drawings. If you made

any mistakes, reread the instructions for that area to determine what you did wrong. Be encouraged by areas that you did well. Your completed carvings will show you in which areas you are strong or weak, and that is the purpose of these last three exercises. Only hands-on experience at carving a full design can identify these strong and weak points.

If you are a beginning carver, do not be concerned with the time it takes you to complete an exercise. What is important is that you learn the various procedures and when to apply them. Both speed and skill will increase with knowledge, patience, and practice.

The three exercises are broken down into steps as they are to be worked. The text is accompanied by diagrams, most of which are presented as viewed from stock level in order to show the width, depth, and type of cut to be made. Each carving has a maximum depth of $1/16$ inch at the base of the featured design.

Should you decide to lay out any of the exercises on a stock as you would under actual layout conditions, use the buttstock pattern layout segment described in chapter 4. If you are not concerned with placement but simply wish to work the carvings, you do not need to apply the rules of pattern layout. The elk exercise begins with instruction on layout for those following the rules of pattern and design layout.

If you are not following those rules, begin the exercise with the transfer of the full design to any location that will fit on the stock.

WILDLIFE CARVING EXERCISE: ELK

Preparing the Design for Carving
The first step in preparing the design for carving is to form a tracing pattern sheet. Secure it firmly to the stock as described for figure 33 in chapter 4. Your pattern sheet need not be as large as that shown, however, as it is not for a full buttstock carving. You can shorten the pattern to run forward from the buttplate to the approximate position of the upper and lower *B* as shown at midpoint of the pattern. At this point,

make marks like those labeled *A* to give both a horizontal and a vertical line. When using a shortened pattern sheet, position the forward locator tape to compensate for the change in size and mark it at the centerline of the stock before you place the paper. After you have secured it to the stock, place all remaining area marks *(A)*. Then remove the pattern sheet and connect the area marks with a solid drawn line. The next step is to position the design within those lines.

This particular design was created for a Monte Carlo type buttstock. It generally will need to be reduced for use on other types of stocks, in which case the pattern layout shown in figure 28 will be more appropriate. If the overall design is too large for the gunstock you

Figure 116. Wildlife carving exercise: elk.

are using for this exercise, you will need to fit it to the area available for carving. These instructions show you how to form a border around any design to meet a specific area when working with individual components. If the complete design, as presented, fits the area available for carving, use it for this exercise.

First, trace the elk and the grass onto a piece of tracing paper, and secure it to a clean sheet of white paper. Tape the white paper securely to a flat surface to ensure that it will not shift. Then place the master pattern sheet over the design, centering the elk between the upper and lower area lines and positioning it enough forward on the buttstock to allow space for the border design. Use a tracing of a segment of the border design as an overlay to gauge the proper distances from buttplate to border and border to elk. The outside edge of the border is best kept at no less than ¼ inch from the buttplate edge. When certain of the placement of the elk, tape the overlaying master pattern sheet securely in place. Then trace the elk and grass onto the master pattern sheet.

Next, freehand draw a light pencil line around the outline of the elk, running from the forward and rear portions of the grass. This line will be irregular, as it is to follow the contour of the elk. Then remove the master pattern sheet.

In this design, there are seven individual segments that make up the border. Note that all but one are placed running the same direction. The segment nearest the grass at the lower left runs in the opposite direction. This was done to create a near-equal distance from the border to front and rear legs, but this is a matter of choice and does not have to be adhered to.

Determining the placement of each of the segments is accomplished by following the freehand sketched line. Trace two segments of the border design onto individual pieces of tracing paper. Secure both segments to a sheet of white paper several inches apart, one with the traced side upward and the other facedown. For the facedown segment, retrace the design through the paper onto the upward side. Then place the master pattern over the desired segment to be traced along the freehand line. Note that in most instances, a single border segment can be used either following the same lay and direction, or flipped over in alternate segments to give an entirely different look or to allow a more balanced appearance.

Note that the freehand drawn line is a general guideline, and some deviation may be necessary during the course of the border layout, such as when an area will be too close to the design or to an area of the stock that is to be avoided. Take note of how segments on the exercise design were positioned to curve around the nose and the forward and rear portions of the antler, and also to take up space between the antler and rump; too much open area here would cause an unbalanced effect. Each border segment must be positioned to give balance to the overall design. To accomplish this, it will be necessary to play with the layout a bit until you are satisfied. In the example here, three segments at the top of the layout run from tip to tip, but the two lower segments on each side extend somewhat onto or beyond an adjoining segment. The overall layout is entirely presentable, however.

After you have traced both the feature design and the border onto the master pattern sheet, place the master sheet on a white surface to allow a higher degree of visibility. Then carefully check all areas, and perform any necessary touch-up at this time. Resecure the master sheet onto the stock, using the marked locator tapes for correct positioning. Before proceeding, thoroughly recheck the positioning several times, as the next step—the transfer of the design to the stock—is a commitment to placement from which there is no turning back.

Transfer the overall design as outlined in chapter 7 for exercise 1. Then remove the master pattern sheet from the stock and keep it at hand for quick reference during carving.

Carving the Design

There are twenty-one steps in the carving of the elk, grass, and surrounding background area, and six additional steps for each segment of the border. Each step is illustrated in an accompanying box that shows the actual width and depth of the cuts. Most of the finish in the carving area will automatically be removed during the carving process. Whatever remains is then removed when scraping to shape, smooth, or blend areas together. Finishes of the epoxy type will usually peel off without much difficulty if you insert the cutting edge of the knife blade between the finish and the surface of the stock, then gently slide it along the surface of the

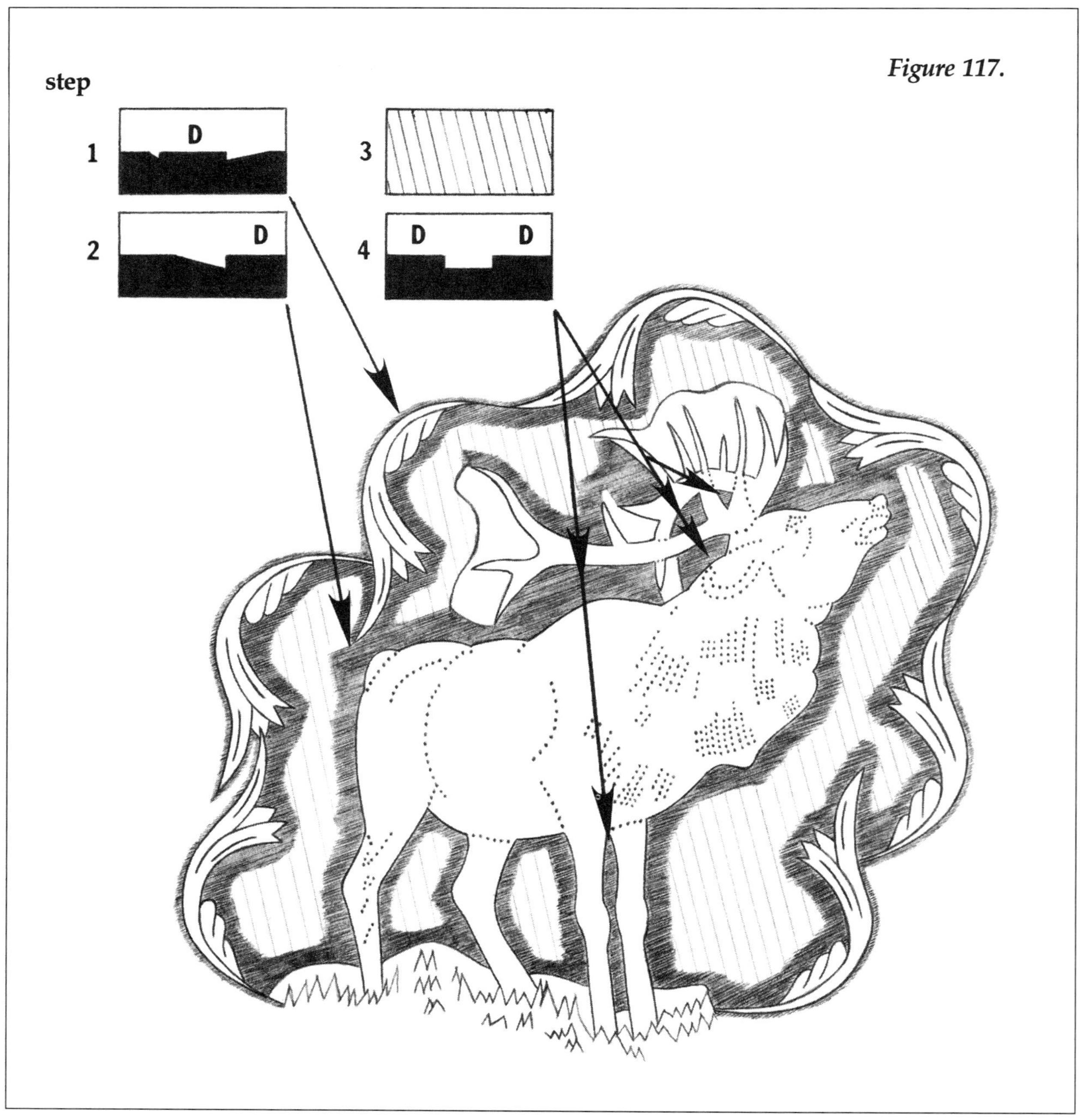

Figure 117.

wood. Only a very light scraping is necessary afterward. During the transfer procedure of closely positioned design lines, this type of finish will crack or lift, making its removal fairly easy.

Step 1. The first and second steps involve separating the feature and border designs from the surrounding stock surface and background area with cuts outlined in chapter 7 for figure 82. Step 1 is the separation of the border; *D* represents the border design. Cut away both sides of each border segment in their entirety, as shown by the shaded area in the diagram. Note that the detail on the left side of the diagram is more shallow than the right, and that the right presents a much longer sloped area. The left side represents the outside of the border, and the right represents the interior side.

Step 2. In this step, you make the parting-line cut around the perimeter of the elk, also shown by a shaded area, with *D* representing the elk design. Note the untouched areas around portions of the antler and above the grass, shown as a solid white area. As the antler is the last area to be carved, this wood is left untouched at this time to protect fragile tines. The area above the grass will be removed well before then.

After cutting, use a file to square up the vertical walls of the border and the feature design. I like to use a file riffler for this purpose. During the squaring-up process, take care not to file into any portion of the design. Smooth off the vertical perimeter wall, thereby removing all rough edges created during the cutting process, while maintaining the line of the design. Do not be concerned if a small groove develops on the background surface at the base of the design during this process, as in order to completely smooth the design's wall, the file will be certain to come into contact with the background. Such a groove will easily be removed when you level off the background surface later. Keep any

groove at a minimum, however, as the deeper it becomes, the more wood you will have to remove to eliminate it, which could mean exceeding the intended depth of the background surface.

Next, soften the upper edges of the elk and the individual segments of the border as described in chapter 7 for figure 90. The only areas to be left untouched during the softening process are the nose and the portion of the ear along the design's perimeter. In this instance, with the exception of the ear and nose, the slope of the softening cut around the entire body of the elk is made to the base of the design, where it meets with the level of the background wood. You can use the same riffler that you used for squaring up to remove the groove that might have formed. During this procedure, smooth the softening cut so it doesn't show any knife marks. When smoothing the background wood where it meets with the design, lightly use the riffler to ensure that the line to the edge of the design where it meets the background flows evenly.

Step 3. Remove the background area marked in the diagram with diagonal lines. When removing background wood, be careful not to remove too much. Try to achieve an even upward slope from the base of the elk to the base of the interior portion of the border design. You can leave this area rough cut until completion of the border and the elk, but it is good to level and smooth it before proceeding to the next step. Note that the area around the antlers remains untouched at this time.

Step 4. Remove the wood between the forelegs. (Note: If you wish, you can remove this wood during one of the earlier steps.)

Step 5. Remove the wood along the area of grass. Match the level of surrounding background area. Then cut the lines forming the grass as closely as possible to those presented, although there is a great deal of leeway in this

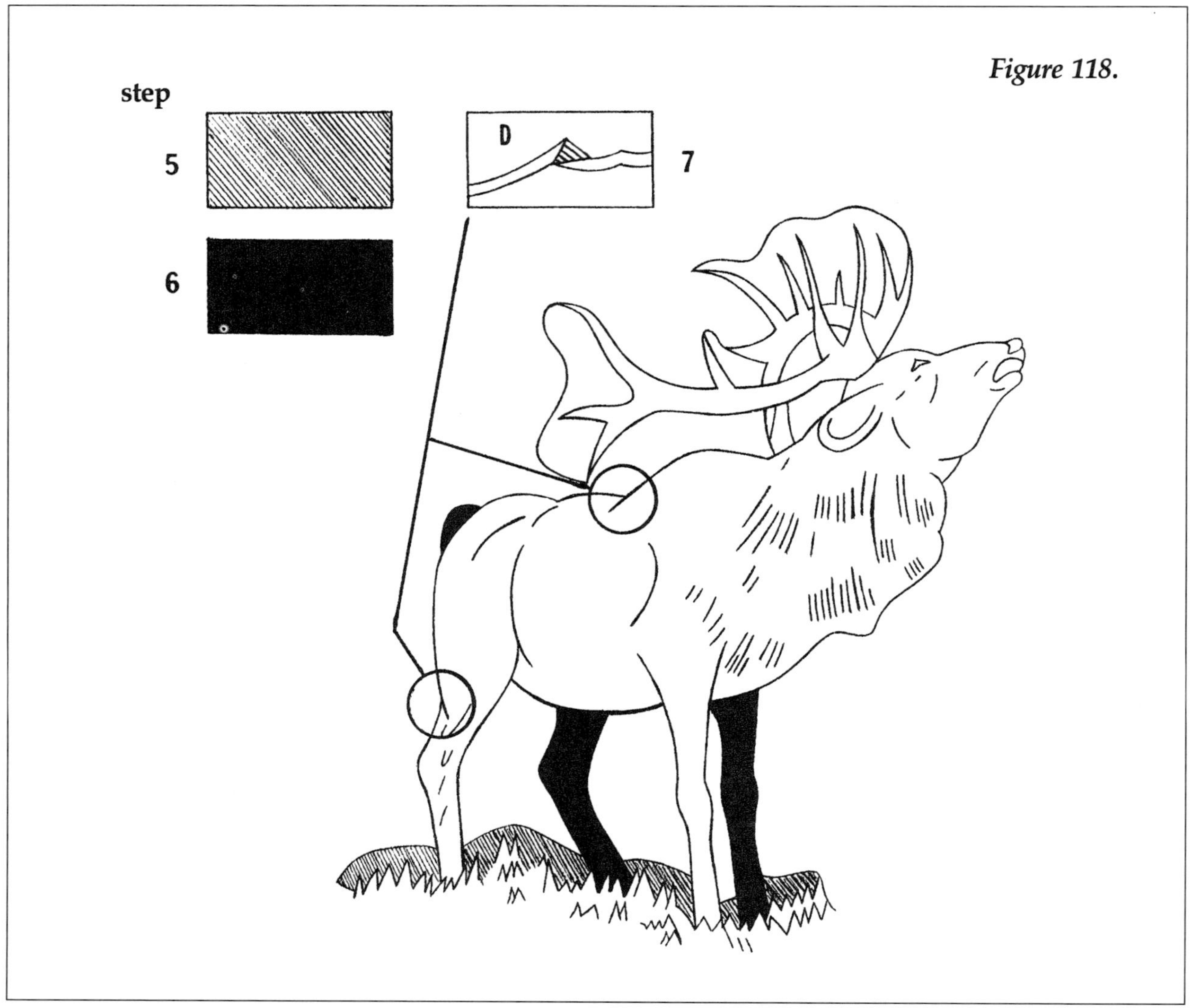

area should a minor degree of chipping out occur. Next, taper the point of each blade of grass so that it ends very near the background surface. Should it become obvious that chipping away of the extreme point will occur during this procedure, make the cut from the base of the point on an upward slope. After completing all cuts, use the edge of the blade to lightly scrape each blade of grass to a final smooth shape. This is best done from the pointed end to avoid chip-outs.

Step 6. Establish the levels within the feature design, as instructed in the exercise section in relation to figure 103.

Step 7. Cut the circled areas to give shape and perspective to the bone and muscle structure, as was done for figures 104 and 105.

Step 8. In this step, you contour the rear portion of the stomach (S) where it meets the hind leg (L). Make a very light, straight downward cut along the length of the line that in the diagram depicts this portion of the stomach. Then make a cut to each side in the manner shown. Lightly scrape the sharp edge created by the cut at the upper portion of the stomach to achieve a round, smooth finish, then scrape the edge of the longer sloped cut at stock surface level on the leg portion in the same manner.

Step 9. Contour the lower portion of the

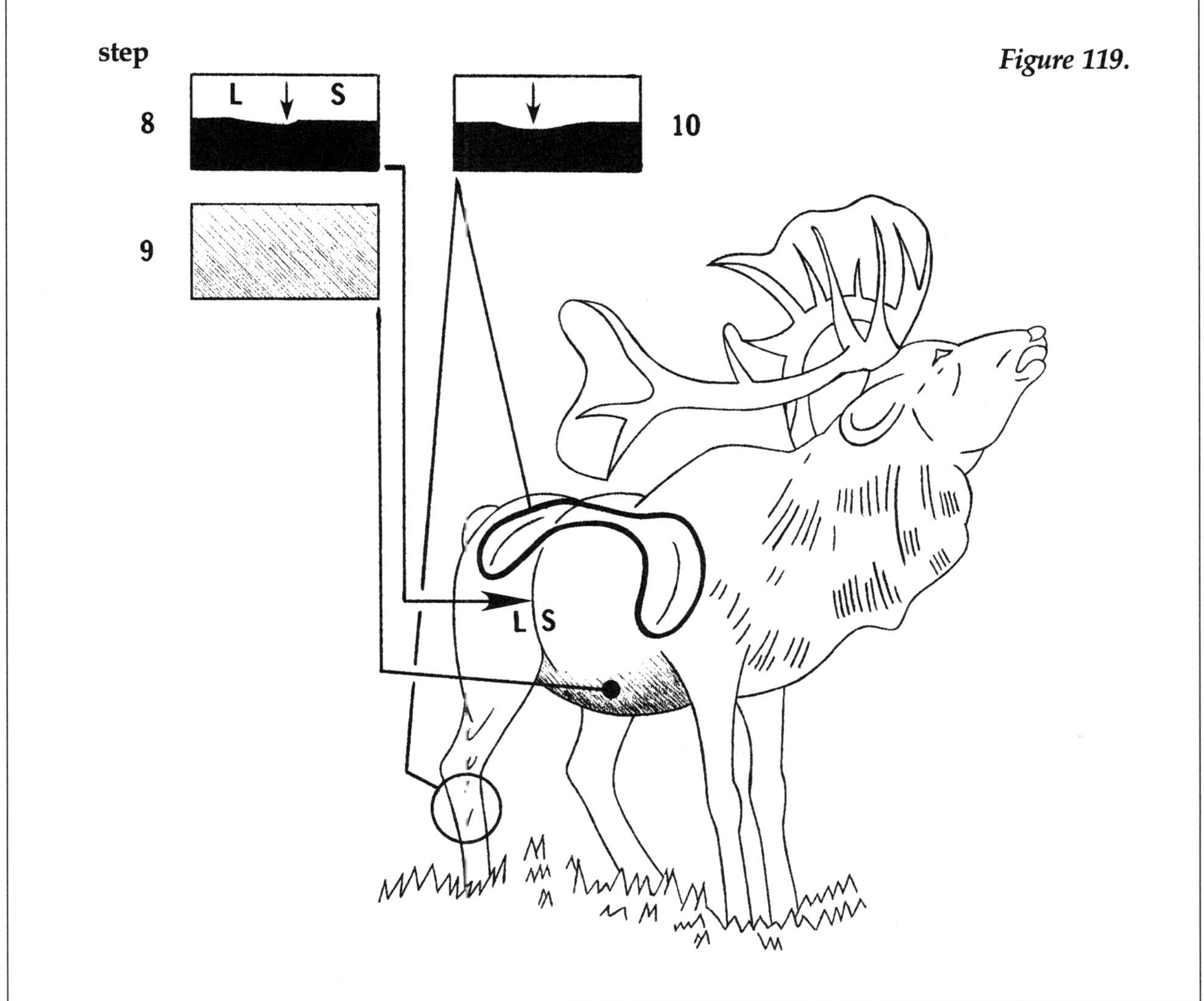

Figure 119.

stomach between the fore and hind legs. With but one exception, contouring this area of the elk is done in the same fashion as outlined in chapter 7. If you compare the lower portion of the rear stomach line of figures 108 and 118, you can see that the line of curve of the elk extends onto the lower portion of the stomach in an upside-down V. After making the necessary vertical cuts to the leg and stomach lines, run the point of the blade at a flatter angle, thus bringing the area between the two lines forming the V slightly lower than the rounded curve of the stomach and the line of the leg. The difference is in depicting the proper perspective between the torso of a lean, muscular dog and

that of a large, big-boned animal of considerable weight. These minute details have a definite impact on the overall perspective of a design. It is important that you remove only a very small portion of wood to lower this area; wood removal to just about the thickness of the blade at the point of the V is ample, and from that point graduate the slope downward to blend with the lower stomach curve. Afterward, lightly scrape with the cutting edge of the blade to smooth the area to blend with the lower portion of the stomach. Also round off the sharp upper edges of the stomach and leg at this time.

Step 10. In this step, you make lines that define the contour. They show where rolling depressions will be made rather than a sharply defined cut line, indicating areas that protrude because of underlying bone or muscle. The arrow in the diagram indicates the position of the line. Note the width and roll upward from each side of the line. You achieve this by first making an extremely light angled cut to each side along its full length. Near the end of the line, the angled cut is barely more than a scratch that is brought inward to meet the end of the original cut line. Using these lightly made cuts as a guide, create a depression with a half-round file. Only two or three light brushes of the file are necessary. Depth is of prime importance in both the cutting of the guide and the use of the file. Beginning carvers often exceed the desired overall depth. It is better to cut too shallow than too deep, as the area can later be deepened if needed, but wood filings cannot be replaced.

The width and depth of contour-defining lines differ from one subject to another, as well as from one area to another within the same design. These are left to your discretion, and it is recommended that you do some homework on animal anatomy. Most times depth and contour can be judged by carefully observing shaded areas of drawings or photographs on which the design is being based. In this instance, the forward stomach contour line above the foreleg is to be only half the depth of that of the rump area.

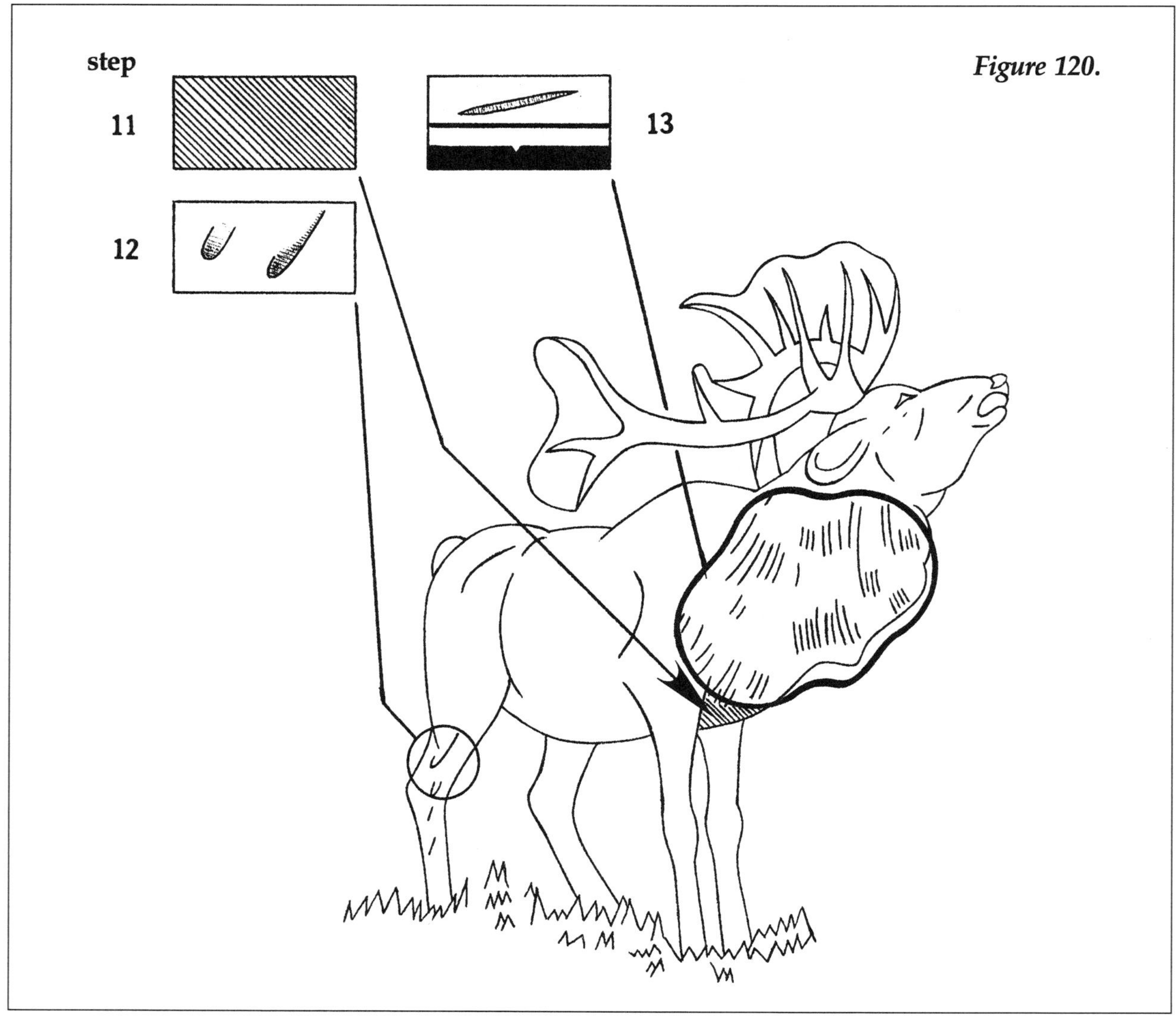

Figure 120.

Step 11. You now work the slope from the upper portion of the leg line to the perimeter line of the chest and from the leg line to the dark heavy line defining step 13. This area is a continuation of the type of slope executed on the lower portion of the stomach. Figure 89 in chapter 7 shows how the slope continues from the upper portion of the off-side leg to the area of background wood.

Step 12. Next, you create two areas of depressions that will add an appearance of underlying bone structure. Each is formed as a shallow depression beginning with a cut along the lines shown in the diagram. Feather out the depression of each area using a modified dental tool or the tip of a kinfe. Slightly round the upper edge along the line of the cut by scraping, and blend it with the depression. The depths of these depressions are no more than the thickness of the knife blade.

Step 13. In this step, you make extremely shallow V-cut lines as done for the guide cuts

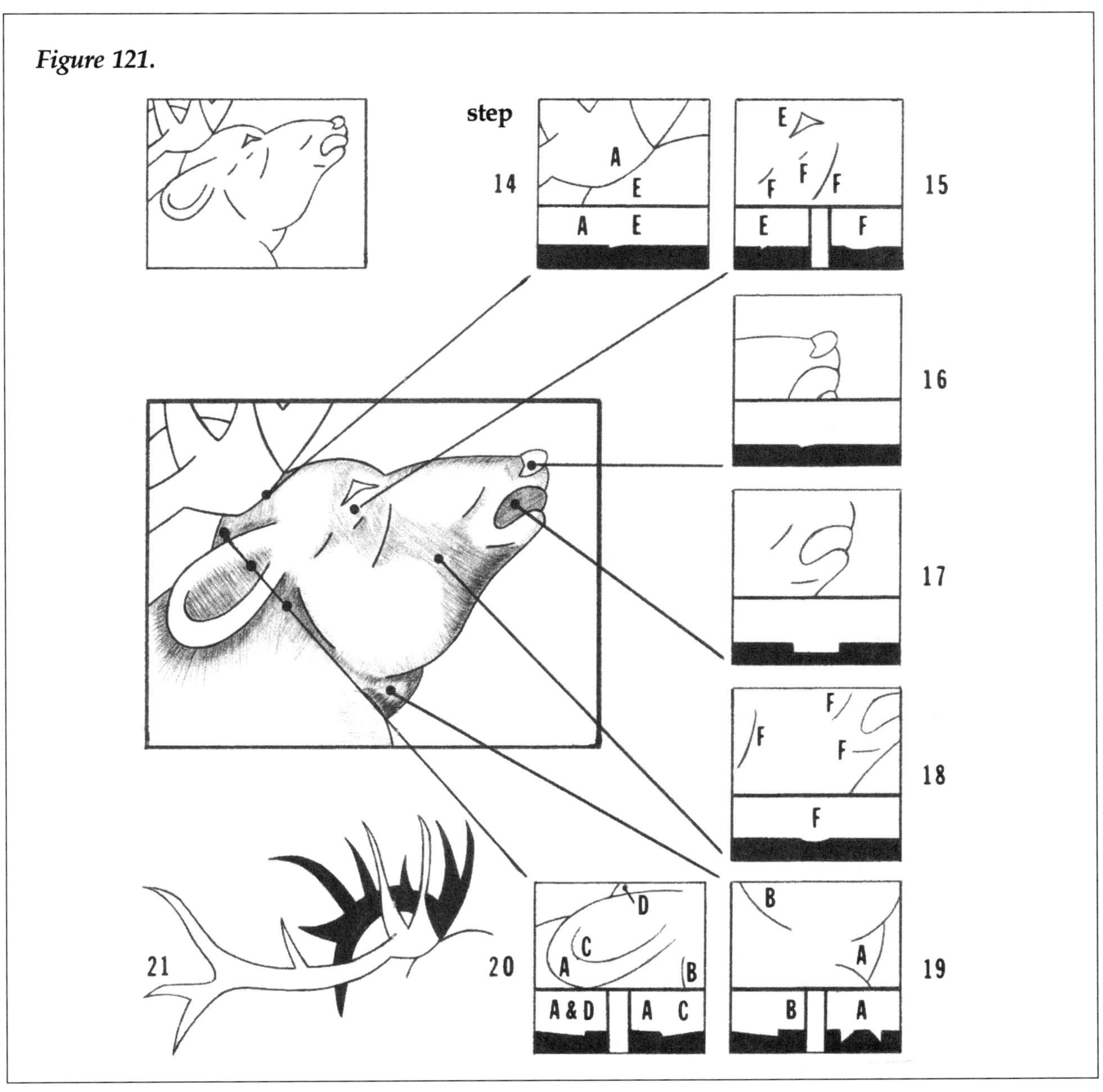

in step 10. Here, though, no file is used afterward. Beginning carvers often have some degree of difficulty with this area. Most have a tendency to go far too deep and end their cut lines much too abruptly. Where lines are close, the top portion of the angled cut should be made to intersect with the top portion of the angled cut of the line next to it. The angled cuts from each side of a line are brought together at the end of the line as shown in the diagram. Some carvers like to give a wave effect to the wood's surface within this area before cutting the lines, in order to make the elk hair more distinct. You can experiment with this on a practice piece to see whether it is to your liking.

Step 14. Now you make a shallow parting-line cut to define the antler (*A*) from the head area (*E*). The slight slope is made on the head side as shown, then rounded off by scraping. Though shallow, this separating line will be clearly visible after a finish is applied.

Step 15. This step involves the eye (*E*) and three contour-defining lines below the eye, marked *F* in the diagram. The lower portion of the diagram depicts the types of cuts required. Cut *E* is a vertical cut defining the outline of the eye. In this case, this is all that is required other than a light scrape around its perimeter to create a small, almost indistinguishable slope outward. *F* shows the same type of depression as in step 10, but on a smaller scale. These depressions, in combination with later steps, will give shape to the head. Once again, these depressed areas should be very shallow.

Step 16. Now, the remaining line toward the interior of the head is completed in the same manner as around the eye. The perimeter softening cut will have already removed some wood on each side of a portion of the nose, defining its outer perimeter. Take care when making this cut, as the small area of the nose at the perimeter can easily chip out during this process. Carefully soften the portion of the nose

along the perimeter of the design by scraping either along its outside line or inward. Chipping may occur if you scrape outward.

Step 17. Remove the wood within the mouth at a level plane to half the thickness of the overall height of the design, leaving the sides vertical. Only lightly soften the upper edge around the perimeter of the mouth, as a sharper look is sought here.

Step 18. In this step, you make three more contour-defining lines. The line at the extreme left is the same line shown at the extreme right in step 15. Here, you are contouring the area between it and the lines near the mouth. The lines nearest the mouth are formed like those of step 15. Give special attention to the area between them and the upper edge of the mouth. After forming the two recesses as shown in the diagram, round off the upper edge of each recess nearest the mouth to blend with the softened upper edge of the mouth cut. This will create a slight rise around the entire perimeter of the mouth. Extend the center of the upper line somewhat during the scraping process to run between the edge of the mouth and the nose. This means the width will be reduced to do so, which in turn means the depth is to decrease also. Lightly scrape the area to the rear of the mouth behind and between the initially placed lines (*F*) to make it just a bit flatter than the upper and lower part of the raised portions, leaving the rear area visible but less pronounced. Note the shaded area between the mouth contour-defining lines and the line shaped during step 15. Scrape this entire area as shown to form the protrusion of the rear jaw area, with a gradual concave rounding to the perimeter of the design that extends from the line at the extreme left. During this process, the concave area is shaped to blend with the mouth contour lines. Scrape all contoured areas to effect soft, gradual blending. Leave no harsh lines.

Step 19. This step focuses on the lines defining the upper rear of the jaw running from the ear (marked *B*) and the lower jaw area at the perimeter of the design that is the beginning of the neck (marked *A*). The lower portion of the diagram shows the type of cuts for each area. The letter *B* in the left diagram appears above the raised forward jaw area, with the lower line of the cut sloping upward and away toward the larger area of the neck. The deepest part of the vertical cut along this line, shown in the diagram, is at the area of the ear, from which point it becomes more shallow as it nears the end of the line at the midpoint of the jaw. The degree of slope from this line coincides with the gradual rise of the vertical cut, until it forms but a very light line. Where it connects with the lower jaw line in area *A*, it once again is gradually cut deeper, until ending at the perimeter of the design.

The slope from the line of this cut is also widened to coincide with the depth. Make this gradual slope to the perimeter with two light cuts rather than trying to achieve it all with one cut, as you will have better control of the blade, allowing more precise detailing. Area *A* shows the deepest part of the sloped cut at the perimeter of the design. Create the same type of slope with the shorter line toward the rear, from its end within the interior. Once you have cut the area to shape, soften the line of the upper edge of the jaw with a light cut, then scrape it smooth and round it. Soften the upper edge of the shorter rear line with a slight more angled cut to the rear, then smooth it by scraping. Scrape the raised area between the lines to a more rounded shape, leaving but a slight hump while sloping it downward from the interior to the perimeter of the design.

Step 20. The last step in the shaping of the head is in and around the ear. For the area between the antler and the ear, apply a standard parting-line cut along the line of the ear (*D*),

with a slight upward slope toward the antler. Scrape the base of the antler to conform to the same slope and to the slope of the perimeter softening cut, in which case you may have to reestablish a portion of the line separating the antler from the head. Some of this area will have already been brought to shape while squaring up and softening the perimeter edge. Cut the remainder of the line more toward the rear curve and lower interior portion, as shown in the darkened lower left diagram. Scrape the slope of the perimeter softening cut to blend with the cut placed along the balance of the ear line. The ear line ending within the interior of the design near line *B* should be a gradual rising cut from about midpoint of the lower portion, fading out at its end.

The sloped cut following the line of the lower portion of the ear within the interior of the design begins where it meets with the perimeter softening cut. Scrape the intersecting slopes of the ear and line *B* toward the rear to blend the two together. The shaded area in the picture part of the diagram indicates the overall area needing scraping. Eliminate any bump that may have developed where the two slopes intersect in order to present a smooth transition. Soften the upper edge of the ear by scraping.

Form the inner area of the ear by making a longer sloped cut from near the top of the ear's perimeter to intersect with the base of the initially made vertical cut that defines the inner edge of the ear. The area of the sloped cut is shown by the shading in the design drawing, and the degree of the slope in the right side lower box of the diagram. Scrape the upper edge of this inner part of the ear and the recessed portion to soften and round them smooth.

Step 21. Carve the antlers as outlined in text and drawings in chapter 7. These are the standard procedures for the carving of all antlers.

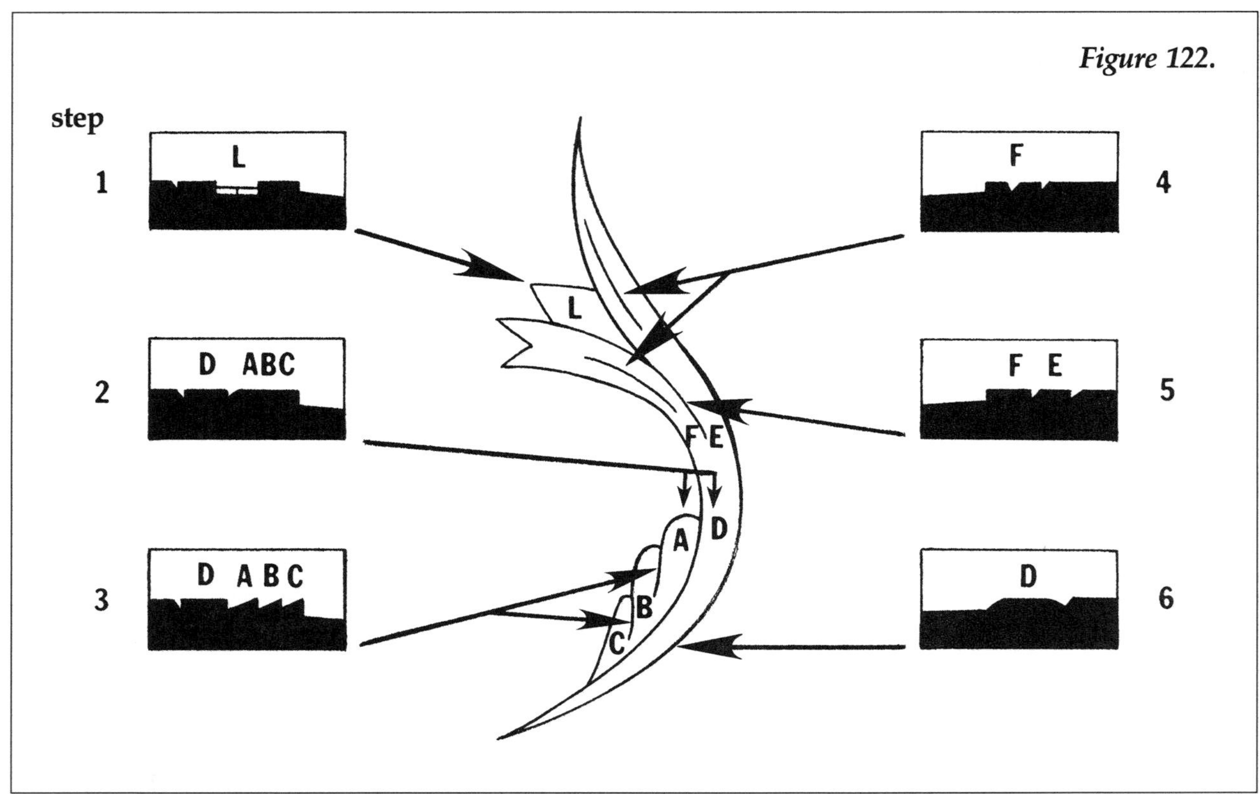

Carving the Border

After completing the feature design, finish carving the border segments as follows.

Step 1. Cut the area marked *L* in figure 122 to a level plane at half the height of the overall segment, or cut it exactly as shown in *A* of the right lower diagram of step 19 above. If following step 19, the base of the vertical cut should be at half the height of the overall elevation of the design. Both methods will achieve nearly the same results.

Step 2. In this step, the main body of the segment (*D*) is separated from the three protrusions along the inner portion. Make a separating cut straight down on the main segment side, with a slight sloping cut on the protrusion area.

Step 3. Make a sloped cut from the outside line of area *A* where it meets with line *B*. Cut another slope from the *A–B* line to intersect with the base of the cut of the main portion of segment *D*, then another from the *B–C* line to the base of the outside *A* line. Make the same type of cut from the outside upper edge of line *C* to the base of line *B*. (Note: This is the type of cut used in exercise 3 in chapter 7.) The sloped cut within the *B* area is to blend with the ending of line *A* and that within the *C* area with the ending of line *B*.

Step 4. In this step, you make a parting-line cut to the outside of the segment (shown on the right of the diagram) and a V-cut at the center of the two longest split segments of the design, marked *E* and *F*. The cuts shown below the letter *F* are lines on the divided main portions of the design, designated by arrows. Slope these cuts and fade them out at each end. This can easily be accomplished by lightly running a V-file along the groove after you have made the initial cut to serve as a guide. By beginning and ending lightly at each end of the line, you can easily form the proper type of groove. Two passes with the file are all that are required.

Step 5. E and *F* in the diagram represent the two outward-branching portions of the main body of the segment. Cut the line between, which is a continuation of the *F* side branch, by making a vertical cut with a small sloped cut afterward to the *E* side.

Step 6. Now round off the entire perimeter of the segment in the manner shown, and lightly soften all interior cuts by scraping to remove obvious or sharp cut edges. This includes the inner edges of *E* and *F* (step 5), as those lines cross over the area marked *L* to join with the perimeter slope, and the line between *A* and *D*, between the main portion of the segment and three protrusions marked *A*, *B*, and *C.* Lightly scrape the sharp upper edges of *A*, *B*, and *C* to remove extreme sharpness. When scraping to achieve a smooth, blended surface, be careful not to eliminate detailing. When nearing ends, scrape in a direction along a line or toward the main body to avoid chip-outs. You should wind up with all perimeter edges near background level, with virtually no side wall at all.

When you have completed all of the segments, study the entire design with a very critical eye. Point up any areas that may need it. Check the background between the border and the elk to ensure that it is uniformly level and reasonably smooth, especially in the little niches and corners throughout the design. You should have no problems with access to these areas, as the rounding-off procedure will have allowed ample room. The altered dental tool is ideal for smoothing in more raised or difficult areas.

Once you are satisfied, it remains to stipple the background. This is accomplished as outlined in figure 96 in chapter 7. In the instructions on stippling there, it was stated that the tool must be held at a 90-degree angle to the stock at all times. Here, though, there is one exception: Should there be any danger of leaving a tool imprint on any part of the design, you may need to angle the tool slightly away from the

design. Do this with care, however, to avoid the possibility of the tool skipping or sliding onto the design or causing a chip-out.

After stippling is completed, mask off the stock surface around the perimeter of the design with tape, following the contour of the outside parting-line cut immediately at its edge where it meets stock surface level. You will have to place many short lengths and even very small pieces to accomplish this. After the tape is in place and you are certain the stock surface is protected, brush the design area with steel wool as detailed in chapter 6. After dewhiskering the design, clean away loose particles of steel wool and check over the entire design once again. Areas that need additional scraping or pointing up will be very obvious at this time. Do so if necessary, then brush the area with steel wool again. Remember, do not use steel wool with too much pressure or for too long a period of time, as it will remove wood and affect detailing. After dewhiskering, close your eyes and lightly run the palm of your hand across the design in all directions to discern any sharp or grabbing areas. Soften any such noticeable areas. This will prevent clothing snags that could tear out portions of the design when the firearm is in use. When you are totally satisfied, the design is ready for a finish.

WILDLIFE CARVING EXERCISE: DOVE
Some of the most beautiful carvings feature birds. With their wing feathers and flowing lines in flight, their beauty is unsurpassed by any other wildlife subject. This particular dove was chosen for the exercise because the feathers of its extended wings combined with the flair of the tail feathers are a delight both to behold and to carve. The sense of accomplishment at a job well done in the execution of bird feathers is just as strong for me today as it was over twenty years ago.

Just seven steps are necessary to complete

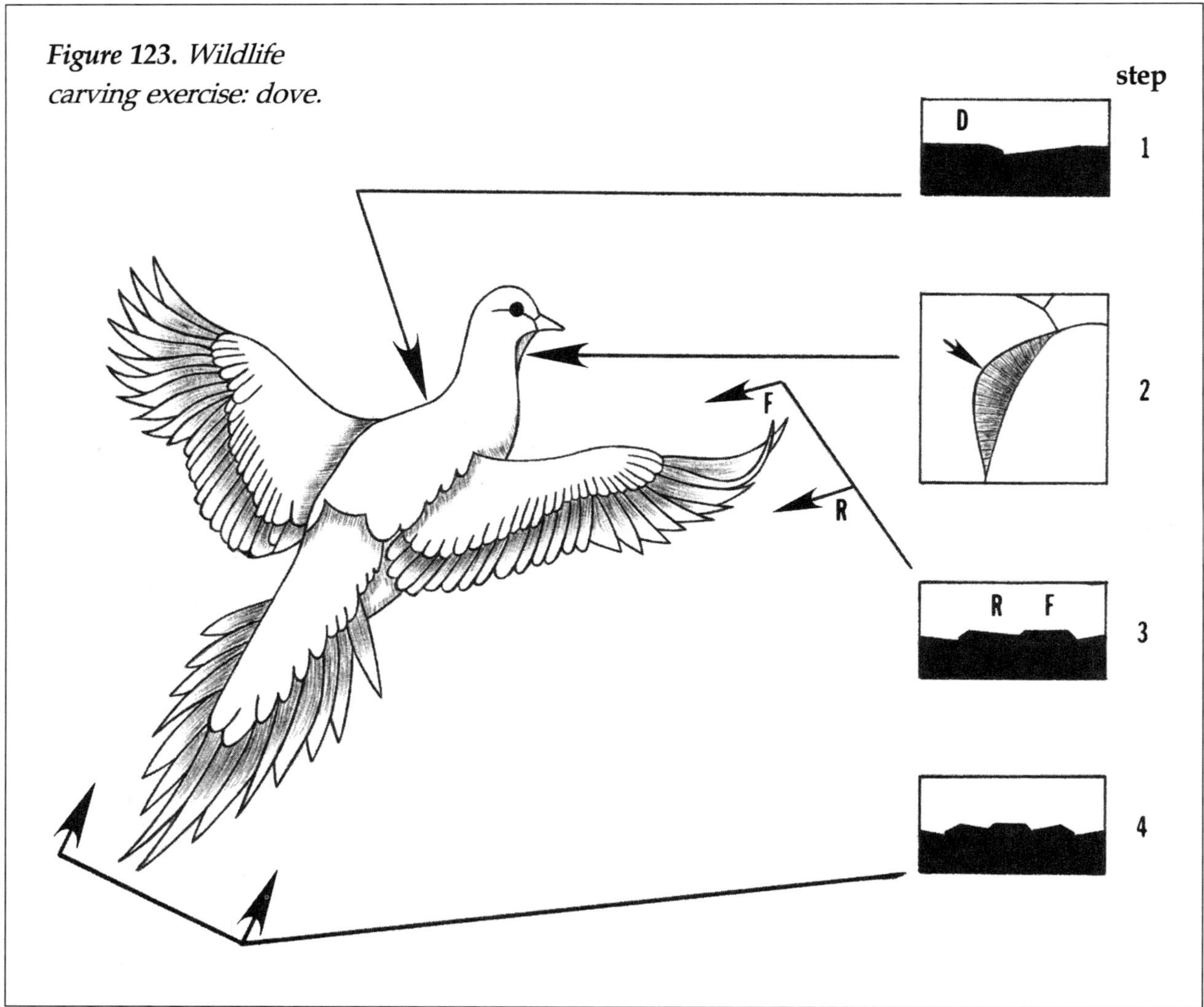

Figure 123. Wildlife carving exercise: dove.

this exercise, which features no border. You will find, however, that completion time will be near that of the entire carving of the elk exercise. The degree of difficulty in this exercise draws on your patience and ability to deal with monotony, and you will learn a lot about carving—and yourself—during its working. Not only will it show how much attention you paid to previous instructions and exercises, it is a true test of a beginner's desire to be a gunstock carver.

This exercise is also a buttstock design. Place and transfer the design as instructed for the elk in the preceding exercise, lightly dust with powder, and you are ready to begin the carving.

Carving the Design

Step 1. In this step, you will make parting-line cuts and sloped background cuts around the design. The portion below the *D* in the diagram represents the main body of the dove (with upper edge softening cut), and the lower portion indicates the depth of the parting-line cut and sloped background cut angled from the base of the design upward to stock surface level. The overall depth of the parting-line cut around the perimeter of the design is held uniformly throughout from a minimum of $^1/_{16}$ inch to a maximum of $^3/_{32}$ inch. In the future, which depth you use will be your choice. For this exercise, maintain the depth at $^1/_{16}$ inch.

The initial vertical cut along the edge of the feathers must be done slowly and with a high degree of caution. Cut only the perimeter portions (the tips) of the feathers at this time. While making the cuts to these areas, you may find that detail lines become difficult to distinguish because of cracking or lifting of the finish. The solution is to scrape away the finish.

After scraping or shaving the finish from the surface of the wood, examine the area to ensure that the transfer holes are intact. Some may be barely visible and need a slight retouching before you proceed. Because of the number of areas that can easily chip away during the initial parting-line procedure, first make this cut at a depth that is just enough to outline the curve and tip of each feather while barely breaking the surface of the wood. This cut and subsequent ones are made as detailed in chapter 7 for figure 86.

Remove the recessed areas between feathers by first making a vertical cut, then inserting the tip of the blade at an angle to intersect with the base of these cuts. This will allow you to pluck out the wood. Continue this procedure until you reach the desired depth. When making the sloped cut of the background area that brings it to its final depth and width, be sure that the upper edge of the slope at stock surface level presents a smooth, continuous line around the design while keeping it at ½ to ¾ inch from the perimeter of the design around its entire circumference. You can easily do this by using a flat mill file to lightly file from stock surface level toward the base of the design. When doing so, be concerned with the edge at stock surface level more so than the surface of the slope itself. Do not risk the possibility of damaging the detailing of the feather tips by trying to file the entire surface of the slope up to the design. You may file a large portion of the slope when establishing the upper outer edge, but stay a safe distance away from the design itself.

Making the parting-line cuts along the tips of the feathers is tedious work and requires a great deal of care and patience. The longer lines near the tip of each wing and those of the tail would appear to be much easier than the more rounded ones from midpoint of the wing to the body, but each has the same degree of difficulty. The pointed tips of the feathers are subject to breaking away if you do not exercise care during their carving. The rounded tips, though less likely to so, can suffer the same fate and are a bit more time-consuming and monotonous. The initial vertical cut at the rounded portions does not have to follow the curve of the tips, but instead can be made as a V-cut with the point of the V at the deepest recess of the curve where each feather meets with the adjoining feather. After you have reached the desired overall depth, you can easily round the tips with a downward shaving cut. During this process, scrape each vertical wall as you go to smooth them up.

Step 2. Slope the neck area below the beak as shown in the diagram, then scrape the upper and lower ends to blend with the softening edge cut of the beak and neck. Scrape the inside edge (arrow) to present a smooth transition onto the neck area, as well as decreasing the sharpness of the recessed area.

Step 3. Make an angled cut from the extreme rear perimeter of the wing to the line of the rear portion of the forward feathers. This will define the separation between the rear and forward portions of the wing feathers. Then make a shallow vertical cut to the rear portion of the forward feathers. To form the separation, follow the same procedure as when making parting-line cuts around the perimeter of the design. Cut both wings in the same manner. Since a three-quarter view is being presented, there is no need to carve the off-side wing to a deeper level as was done with the off-side legs of the elk in the preceding exercise. All that is

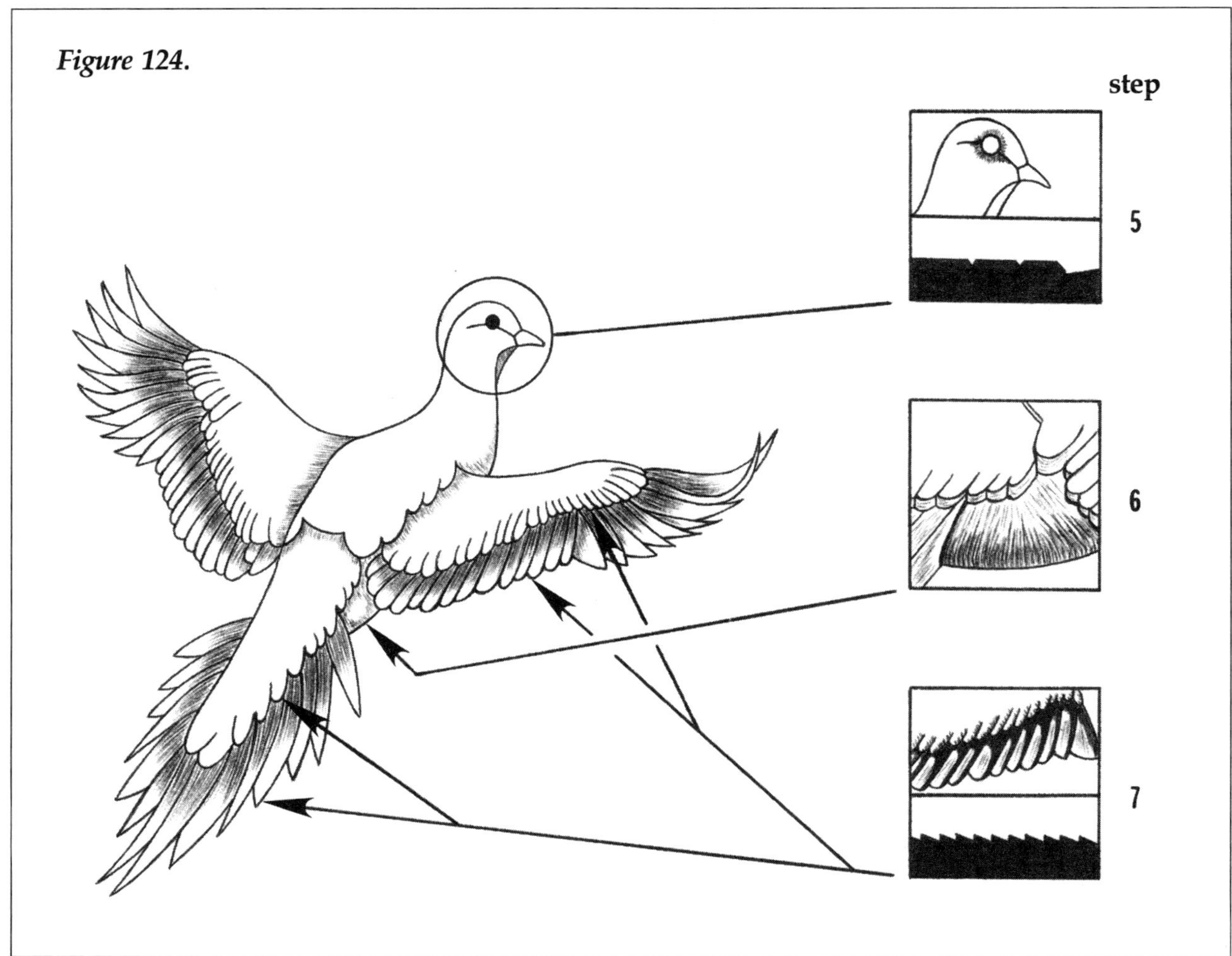

necessary is a light reduction in depth of the wing along the line of the upper portion of the back (as indicated in the design by the shaded area).

When you have completed the background slope and perimeter of the rear feathers of each wing, shape the rounded tips of the interior feathers. This is accomplished in the same fashion as the rear feathers. Here, though, remember that the area of wood at the base of the forward feathers is the interior portion of the rear feathers; *do not* cut into this area. All of the feathers of the forward row are much smaller in width than those at the rear portion of the wing, so you have to form each feather with even more caution than when you formed the rear row. Use only the very tip of the blade.

Step 4. This step entails sloping of the longer tail feathers, forming a portion of the design's perimeter, and those within the interior of the tail that connect with the line of back feathers where the wing joins the body. Slope the tips of the long tail feathers downward to end at about two knife-blade thicknesses from the base of the interior feathers. Then, cut and shape as done with the wing feathers. The diagram for step 7 shows the background slope and the slope from the initial upper edge portion at the perimeter of the design to the base of the interior feathers. Cut and slope the interior feathers of the tail in the same manner as those along the wing area. Lightly scrape the straight side edge of the interior line of the feathers to soften its appearance. To do this, slant the blade by turning the long cutting edge vertical with the point in the deepest part of the groove.

Step 5. This step concentrates on the eye, which in this design consists of a circle with a slightly downward curved line forward and rear of the circle itself. The forward line connects with the line of the beak. First, make a very shallow cut around the circumference of the eye. Using the very tip of the blade, angled from slightly outward, make a second sloped cut around the eye to cover a slightly wider area than with the initial cut. The depth of the combined cuts should be no more than what is shown in the lower portion of the diagram. Then make a cut of the same depth to the forward and rear lines, beak line included. Using the tip of the blade once again, make a small angled cut the full length of the lower side of the rear and forward eye lines and to the beak line from the direction of the tip of the beak (shown by the shadow in the diagram). Next, return to the circle of the eye and enlarge the angled cut around it. Before cutting, compare the size of the diagram with the size of the design and apply the proper reduction. Note that in the diagram, the enlarged angle cut is greater on the underside of the eye than above it. Note also that the larger angle cut of the lower portion of the eye extends only partially along the forward line. After the eye is completely formed, lightly scrape all sloped areas to smooth them off and feather them into the surrounding area. Leave the upper side of the forward and rear midpoint lines sharp. Scrape the edge of the circle of the eye to give it a rounded appearance.

Step 6. In this step, you shape the stomach area. Only a small area of the stomach is seen, yet its shaping is highly important in achieving the correct overall appearance of the design. To shape this area, make a vertical cut following the detailing of the wing, back, and tail feathers. This initial cut, like that of the initial feather parting-line cut, is best made at just enough

depth to break the surface of the wood. Then make a slightly angled cut from the outside direction of the design at a shallow depth to remove a thin line of wood from the stomach area along the line of the initial vertical cut to the wing, back, and tail feather. This is to clearly define the detail lines of these three areas and reduce the possibility of these tips chipping out. This also will present the stomach at a depth slightly lower than the line of back feathers at that area, with a slight downward curve ending at a depth that is just below the elevation of the wing and tail feathers; these feathers themselves are just a blade thickness below the line of back feathers. This means that the elevation of the wing and tail feathers is a blade thickness below the line of back feathers and the stomach is at a two-blade thickness below the line of the same back feathers. Now increase the angle of the softening cut along the outer perimeter, and scrape the stomach area to give a rolling curve to the underbelly.

Step 7. This step involves interior feather detailing, beginning with the forward row of the right side wing. The method is identical to those in chapter 7 for figures 94 and 95. The raised portion of each sloped cut of each wing feather, with the exception of the first two feathers at the tip end of the right wing (discussed later), should be toward the body of the dove. After making all sloped cuts, lightly scrape each feather along the upper sharp edge and the slope in order to smooth off rough portions and further shape the feathers to their correct proportions. Give a downward-angled light brushing with a pointed triangle file at each line ending toward the forward portion of the wing to create a smooth transition into the solid area of the wing. Finish all feather lines throughout the carving that end in the more solid areas in this manner. When shaping the last feather at the upper perimeter of the design, be sure that the slope coincides with the overall shape of the perimeter curve of the wing. Complete the forward row, then work the rear.

Now turn your attention to the two feathers noted as the exceptions earlier. The second feather crosses over the first near the very tip. To achieve the correct effect, do not make the sloped cut of the third feather to the base of the second as pronounced as those within other portions of the wing; instead, make it at only about half that depth. The high area of the second feather is to be the forward edge. This means that the slope is made downward toward the body. The base of the sloped cut of the second feather should meet the line of the bottom of the shallow slope of the third feather. The slope of the first feather is also made downward toward the body of the dove, while following the line of the forward edge of the second feather. The softening edge cut along the perimeter of the first feather will have to be reestablished afterward. Doing so will make the tip of the second feather become even more pronounced, which is what is sought. Lower the very tip of the first feather to be near the background surface during the process. After shaping the first feather, return to the second to apply the finishing touches, first angling the tip toward the background surface, then making a narrow softening cut along the forward edge from the rear line of the first row of feathers to the tip. Make this cut at a sharper angle downward than usual, and do not scrape it. This cut actually is not made to soften the edge, but to present a thin opposing slanted surface, giving an exceptionally pleasing appearance to the completed carving.

Shape and cut the back feathers along the line where the wing joins the body at a very slight, barely noticeable slope, with the high edge at the forward portion. Do not apply a slope cut to the last back feather that is in line with the rear row of the wing. Give this feather just a slight rounding at its entire edge, carrying it over to the line across the back. To better

be able to accomplish this, you will first need to remove a small amount of wood across the rearward side of the back line. The amount of wood removed along this line should be no more than you can remove with two light scrapings. Blend the rounding of the feather at each end of the line across the back with the line forming the back feathers where the wing joins the body. Complete the offside wing the same way; here, though, there are no exceptions to consider.

Once you have completed the tail, stipple the background area. After stippling, check the entire design to ensure that no area has been missed. Also check for areas that might need touching up. Then, following the procedure outlined at the end of the elk exercise, mask off the stock area around the design, dewhisker, and apply a finish.

FLORA CARVING EXERCISE: OAK LEAF
There are five steps to the carving of this oak leaf design. In most instances, veins in a leaf carving are gouged rather than raised. Though I'm not opposed to gouging veins, I do have a particular fondness for leaves that show that the carver has gone the "extra mile" in creating raised veins. The added effort is far outweighed by the result—a result, I might add, that is immediately recognized and appreciated by a client. The pointed tips at the lobes give this oak leaf its striking appearance. Though care is necessary in their shaping, you need not be as painstaking as when shaping antlers. This is not to say that leaf tips can be rushed through or executed haphazardly, but during later steps, minor errors that may have occurred can be rectified more easily than with antlers. Keep in mind, however, that if any corrections are made in the tip area, this will usually result in the shortening of the tip. Though this is not critical, your design will not be what you had originally laid out.

Two very different buttstock designs.

The design on the left incorporates two animals in proper perspective; the design on the right features a unique floral pattern.

Grip designs should complement the design on the buttstock.

Two more complicated carvings use stippling (top) and a basket weave (bottom).

Three different ways of using a game bird in a buttstock design.

Notice how both of these designs make full use of the area available for carving.

The carved area nicely complements fine hand-checkering (top) and a raised cheekpiece (bottom).

Two complete guns show how the carved areas all fit together.

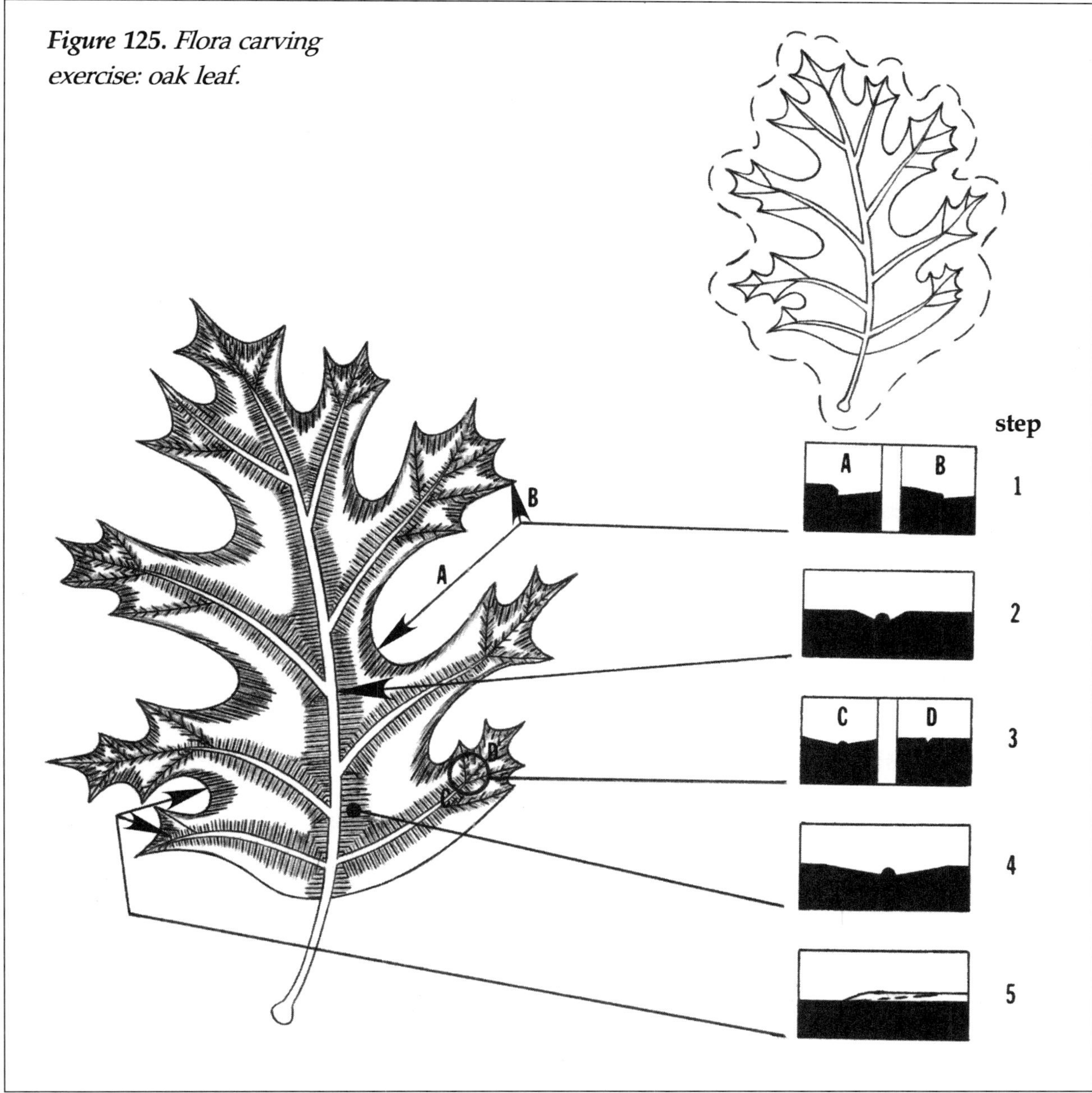

Figure 125. Flora carving exercise: oak leaf.

The oak genus includes fifty-eight trees and ten shrubs. Understandably, there are a vast number of differences in sizes and shapes of the leaves and acorns. In your carving, be certain to present the correct acorn with the leaf. The leaf in this exercise is the California black oak, which has from seven to nine bristle-tipped lobes. The appropriate acorn, shown in chapter 10, is deep cupped and elongated.

The smaller leaf depicted above the carving step diagrams is the leaf to be carved in this exercise. Generally, this will be the maximum size used in gunstock carving, and I highly recommend that you do not exceed it. The larger leaf to the left of the diagrams serves to illustrate the relationship between relieved areas of the central vein and its branches.

Place and transfer the design as instructed for the elk earlier in this chapter.

Carving the Design

Step 1. Begin by making the appropriate

parting-line cuts. Use graduated knife cuts to remove wood to form the slope of the background from the base of the design to stock surface level; the broken line around the leaf in the diagram suggests how this should run.

Next, make a softening cut around the entire upper edge of the design, after pointing up the vertical wall with a file or riffler. Shape the area between the lobes (*A*) and the lobes themselves, as depicted, then angle the pointed tips slightly downward so that they are near background level (*B*) at their ends. When shaping the lobes, make the cuts from the very tip inward. Use lightly made step cuts from this direction to prevent the points from breaking away. Once the tips have been angled, you can more safely point up with the riffler and make edge-softening cuts. When removing wood from the sides of the extended stem, take it off equally from each side in lightly made vertical cuts and outward sloped cuts afterward in the manner depicted for figure 89.

Step 2. This step involves removing wood from each side of the primary veins, which are to be presented as raised. As this exercise includes both raised and gouged portions, now is the time to establish which is which to avoid mistakes. The raised portions consist of the main central vein, which is a continuation of the extended stem, and those veins that branch out from the main central vein, running toward the tip of each lobe. At this time, you are concerned only with these raised veins. The gouged areas will be worked in step 3.

While carving the leaf, regardless of how it is positioned on the stock, be sure to always cut either across or with the grain, and never into the grain. This means that you will have to be conscious of grain direction at all times and will have to turn the stock as necessary to allow cutting across or with the grain. The initial vertical cut on one side of a vein will present no problem; however, the possibility of chipping

out a section will present itself when you remove wood from its opposite side.

The diagram for this step shows the end result that is sought for all of the raised portions. To carve the raised portions, begin with the main central vein at the area where stem and leaf meet. It makes no difference which side of the main central vein you start first, but as a matter of establishing a good working habit, complete whichever side you start the cut on from the stem to the top of the leaf before you begin the other side. Make a light vertical cut from the edge of the leaf along one side of the vein only, and stop where it meets with a branch leading to the tip of a lobe. Then cut along the branch toward the far tip at the center of the lobe. Along this path, near the lobe, smaller veins branch out to other portions of the lobe. These are the vein portions that will be gouged later. The branches from the main vein are not raised all the way to the lobe tips but instead come to a point before reaching the tip. From this point, they continue as slight V-cuts, which also will be carved after all raised portions are completed.

When the initial cut reaches the endpoint of the intended raised portion, stop there and return to the main central vein. Do not cut the upper line of the branch at this time. Instead, renew the vertical cut along the line of the main central vein, beginning at the upper line of the side branch you just completed. Continue the cut until you encounter the next side branch. Again, follow the bottom line of the side branch, and then afterward return to the central vein. Repeat this process until you reach the endpoint of the central vein at the top of the leaf. Then give each of the cut lines a sloped cut to clearly separate that portion of the vein from the surrounding wood. The depth of the sloped cut along the central vein should be no more than $1/32$ inch, which is half of the depth of the design. The slope of each branch vein should be the same depth at the area of the central vein but gradually decrease in depth and width until reaching its endpoint near the tip of the lobe, where a heavy scrape is enough to remove the necessary wood.

Now turn your attention to the opposite side of each branch. Because there will be no backup wood to support the thin line of the branch, perform the sloping procedure as outlined in relation to figure 89. Immediately after you cut the opposite slope of a branch, round the vein by scraping. This will prevent accidental chip-outs during ensuing procedures. After completing the first half of the leaf, use the same procedures on the other half. With the second half, do the initial cutting to the lower portion of the branches, followed by the central vein and upper portion of each branch. The main central vein on this side is also cut as in relation to figure 89 because of the lack of backup wood.

Step 3. In this step, you cut the grooved portions of the raised veins. The groove from the end of each vein and each of those offshooting from it should be little more than a heavy scratch made with the tip of a knife. Part *C* of the diagram depicts the general shape of the main portion of the branch as it nears its end. Part *D* depicts the shape and depth of all groove cuts. Note that on the large leaf, a series of sloped V lines has been placed along the lines that are to be V-cut to clearly define them.

Step 4. Now widen the slope at both sides of the center and branch veins by making shaving-type cuts to the larger areas and by scraping areas where widening runs over into other sloped areas. On the large leaf, the shading at each side of the veins indicates the general width sought. After you complete all the sloped cuts, scrape the sloped areas smooth to blend with the surrounding higher level of wood within the design.

Step 5. Give a final shaping with the tip of

a half-round file to each perimeter area between lobes and points of the lobes. Shape these areas so that each has an elongated slope at its center that gradually decreases when nearing the points of the lobe. The dotted line in the diagram for this step shows the degree of slope at center. When filing, maintain the direction of the stroke at 90 degrees to the perimeter line, raising or lowering your hand to achieve the proper slope for the area you are working. Next, scrape the upper edges smooth to blend with the higher surrounding areas. Unlike a natural leaf, there should be no distinct flat areas, but instead each sloped area should appear to gently roll over to blend with other sloped areas.

Once you have completed all of the carving procedures, stipple the background area. Then mask off the upper stock surface and dewhisker the carving. Check for snags, following the procedure outlined at the end of the elk exercise, then apply a finish.

Completion of these three full-size exercises will clearly show areas where you need additional study and practice. The keys to becoming successful are patience, resolve, and practice, practice, practice.

9

TECHNIQUES FOR LOW-RELIEF CARVING

THIS CHAPTER ADDRESSES THE QUESTION OF DETERmining the appropriate scale for low-relief carving (see "relief carving" in the Glossary). A false assumption is that because one-half of an animal is seen, this automatically means that one-half of the animal's scale width is to be carved. This may be sound logic under other circumstances, but not with low-relief carving. Though all other aspects of an animal's body should be to scale, an exception is made for the animal's width because of the limited depth of the carving.

For example, for an elephant whose total height within the design is 2½ to 3 inches, one-half the scale width would be $5/8$ to $11/15$ inch. Given that the average rifle stock at the widest part of the buttstock is about 1½ inches, the most eye-catching aspect of the finished carving would be the cavernous area from background surface to stock surface level that would be necessary to present half the elephant's width at scale. So much wood would be removed around the elephant's circumference that the depth of the background area would be nearly one-half the width of the buttstock itself at its thickest point. Should this same carving be done in high relief, where excess wood was allowed for such a carving during the forming of the stock, this elephant would appear as an abnormal growth, as it would protrude far too much above the surface plane of the stock. One thing

for certain—the application of either would be the topic of discussion at the shooting range for a long, long time.

Two exercises in chapter 7 demonstrated how applying levels would begin to give form to the larger, wider portions of an animal's torso. To briefly review what has been established in regard to design depth, the overall depth of the background area for all designs should range from $1/16$ inch to an absolute maximum of $3/32$ inch. Only on very rare occasions do I find it necessary to carve to a depth of $3/32$ inch, and when I do so, this is only at spots within a design and not an overall depth. There are also a few cases in which specific designs are carved at less than $1/16$ inch, such as those applied around inlays or onto the raised edge of a cheekpiece. The surrounding background wood is to rise from the base of the design at a gentle slope to the stock's surface level, and the slope at the upper portion is to blend with the surface level of the stock while as little wood is removed as possible.

The easiest way for a student to grasp the fundamentals involved in creating realistic-looking depth in a low-relief carved animal is to compare the carving process to the procedure performed by an artist creating an in-depth pencil drawing. In drawings, depth is achieved with varying degrees of shading; in low-relief carving, with varying degrees of slopes.

When tracing a design from a drawing or photograph, take note of the size, shape, location, and varying tones of each shaded area. Careful observation of shading will go a long way in enabling a student carver to apply slopes that form correctly placed and shaped structural configurations, even if he or she has little knowledge of basic animal structure. Light shading denotes slopes or depressions at or near the surface, and dark shading more depth or a recess. A sharp contrast between adjacent tones indicates a pronounced angle around the line of change, usually associated with a depression or sharply rounded area. Generally, there will always be a thin area of shading between levels that will indicate the width of a slope or rounded edge. This simply means that a slight rounding or slope equal to the width of the contrasting area takes place before the sharper decline. Gradual differences in tone with no pronounced line imply a more gentle slope, or rounding.

The most difficult area for a novice in terms of structural configurations is the head. There are, however, some basic guidelines that make rendering this area less perplexing. The first thing to learn is that every minute detail of a drawing need not be applied to a carving, only those features that are most pronounced. As you become more proficient, you can include higher detailing, but even then it's not absolutely necessary. Extremely fine detailing will be very difficult to accomplish for all but the very proficient, more because of wood quality than size. And, too, there is a point at which fine detailing is wasted effort, because if too fine, it generally is lost or appears as no more than a scratch when a finish is applied.

As the white-tailed deer is one of the most-carved animals, it will be used as an example in the following explanation of interior detail-

ing. Any member of the deer family, such as blacktail, elk, or moose, can be handled similarly. Different views are treated somewhat differently, but you can successfully work any view to completion if you pay close attention to shading. Trace the master lines of the design presented in figure 128 and follow these instructions to complete the carving. Do not make transfer holes to the areas that are darkened in the drawing.

Make the parting-line cut to all of the design and form a 1-inch slope around the entire design so that the head and antlers project approximately $^3/_{32}$ inch above the level of the background. Remove the wood in the three areas between the antlers to the same $^3/_{32}$ inch depth. Next, use the very tip of the knife to make a light vertical cut along the interior line of the nose from the perimeter of the design to the line of the mouth, the interior line of the lower jaw below the mouth, along the entire line of the jaw pouch, along the line of the head at the antler, and to the outer lines of the ear near the eye area. Do not do the eyes or inner lines of the ear at this time. Be very careful when

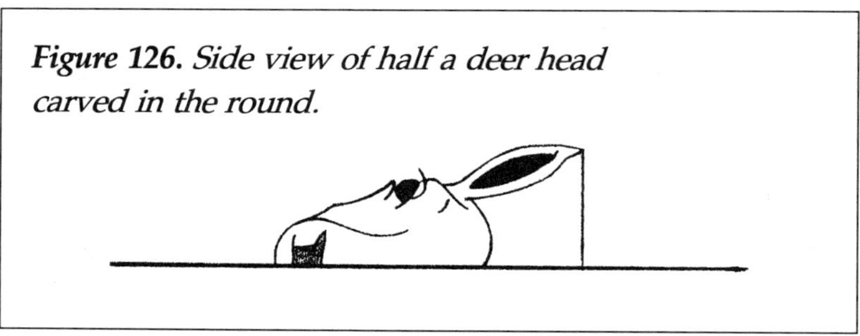

Figure 126. *Side view of half a deer head carved in the round.*

carving the area where the lines of the pouch, neck, and snout come together; a chip-out can easily occur if too heavy a cut is applied.

If you examine the drawing of the side of the head, you will note two outstanding configurations aside from the antlers. One is the large, rounded area that encompasses the ear, eye, brow, and jaw pouch; the other is the elon-

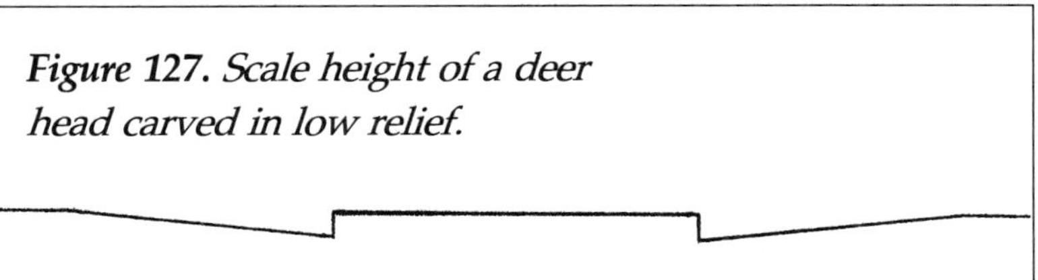

Figure 127. Scale height of a deer head carved in low relief.

gated snout, with the nose and mouth. First establish the high portions of the design: the ear, brow, eye, nose, pouch, and forward portion of the mouth below the nose. By removing surrounding wood from any of these features, that feature becomes more pronounced. You can remove as much wood as necessary to achieve the desired effect, but be careful not to overdo it or you will cause a serious distortion.

There are three major slopes that will form the proper configuration of the head. These are slopes made the length of the snout at its upper portion from the nose to the brow, along the lower portion from the mouth to the jaw pouch, and from the forward portion of the neck to the ending point of the pouch below the ear. The first major slope to be formed is along the upper portion of the snout. The darkened area in figure 128 shows the line between the nose and brow from which the slope is to made to the perimeter of the snout. The angle of the slope is shown in figure 129. The lowest portion of the slope at the perimeter of the design is to be approximately one-third the height of the design. This slope is cut in gradual steps, not with one cut. Note that each end of the slope does not run straight to the perimeter of the design. The upper portion has a slight downward curve, and the lower portion follows the detail line of the nose. Begin the cuts from a point near the center of the length and cut toward each end. Given the angle of the snout, this should

be a cross-grain cut. Make the slope as described for figure 104. The cut made to the line of the nose will serve as a stop cut during the sloping process. Graduate the cut along the line of the nose to match the slope of the next cut. The ending point of the slope at the brow has no stop cut, and you do not want to use one in this area because it

Figure 128.

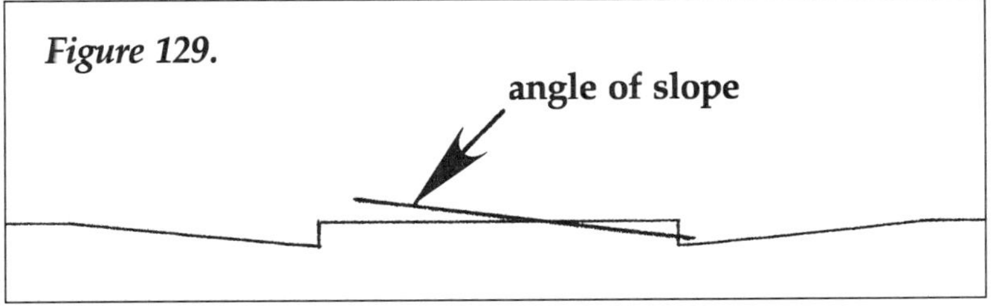

Figure 129.

might be visible after the slope and brow are formed. Using shaving cuts to form the slope, run the cut nearly to the intended line of the brow, then scrape the wood to its proper depth from the intended line of the brow toward the center length of the slope.

The second slope, made toward the perimeter of the lower portion of the snout, is made

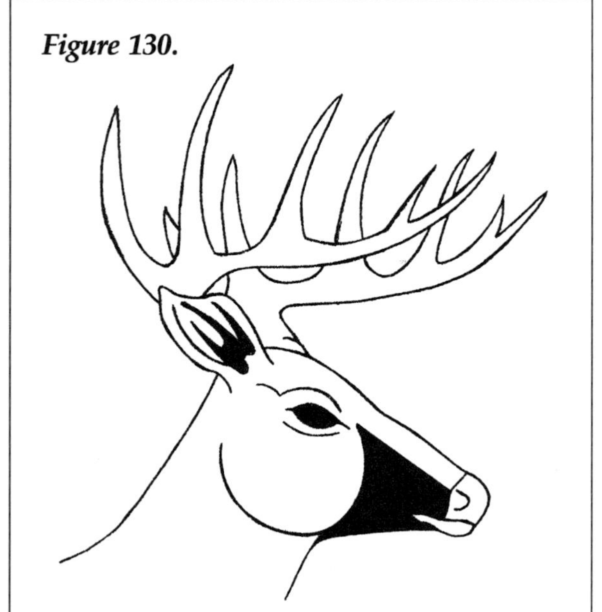

Figure 130.

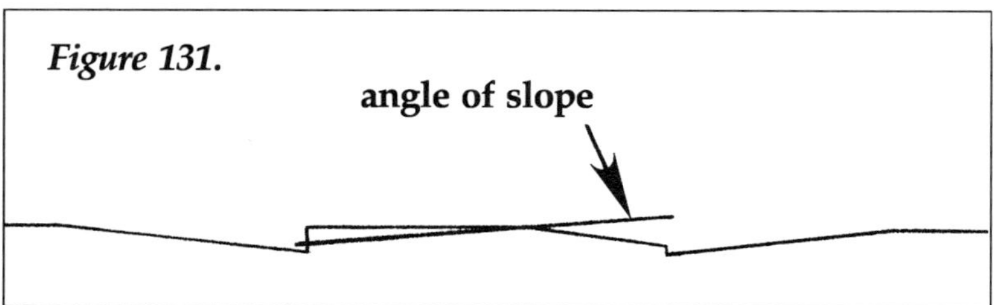

Figure 131.

tinuous slope. This will leave a protrusion of the jaw at the same level as the nose. At this point the jaw will look a bit strange, but it will be blended into its surroundings later.

The next step is to form the contour of the forward portion of the neck and the line of the pouch in the neck area. Make this slope in the same manner as the lower snout area. In this instance, however, the lowest part of the slope along the forward line of the neck is not sloped to the same level as was the lower portion of the snout. The lowest portion of the neck slope is to be about two-thirds the height of the over-all design, which will place it higher than the lowest point of the snout slope. This will put the overall design in the proper perspective.

The next step is to create the levels of the antlers, but only along the area where they meet the ear and head. These levels need only be far enough away from the head to allow softening cuts to be made to the head. The level of the far antler is one-third the height of the design above the background surface. The level of the near antler is two-thirds the height of the design above the background surface. After establishing the levels to a portion of each antler, make a softening cut around the entire perimeter of the head, with each side of the ear done last. When making the softening cut to the nose where it meets the point adjacent to the slope of the upper portion of the snout, do not blend the softening cut to the nose with the slope of the snout. The intent here is to leave the nose slightly higher than the slope. Figure 132 depicts the level of both the brow and the nose before softening and scraping. After making the softening cut to the perimeter of the head, do the same to the entire line of the jaw pouch from the eye to just below the ear. Do the same to the interior line of the nose as well. Then, use a file, riffler, or knife as a scraper

in the same manner as the upper portion of the snout. This slope, however, is longer and has a much more pronounced curve at its end in the pouch area. The cuts along the line of the pouch are done in the same manner as those done along the upper slope along the line of the nose. The high point of the lower snout slope intersects with the high point of the upper snout slope (fig. 131). As was done with the upper snout slope, the lowest point of the slope should be maintained at about one-third the height of the design. Pay special attention to the mouth area. The shaded area in figure 130 shows that the slope stops when it reaches the line of the mouth, then picks up again from the interior jaw line to the perimeter of the design; the area between the line of the mouth and the pouch is continuous. A slight scraping will match the area below the mouth with the level of the con-

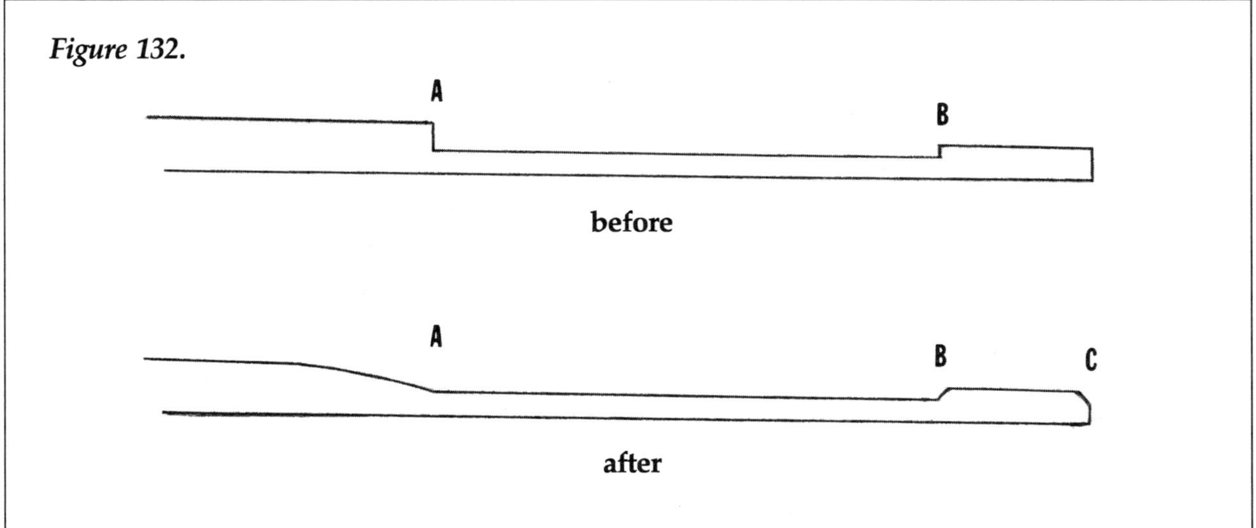

and round over the edges of the softening cuts. This will remove sharp lines so the slope created by the softening cut blends softly with the adjacent area. During this process, lightly scrape along the line where the slopes of the upper and lower snout slopes intersect.

Turn the stock at an angle so you can place the tip of the knife on the deepest part of the curved detail line within the nose area, with the direction of the blade half the distance of each end of the line. Scrape a very shallow depression at the deepest part of the curve that angles upward to stock level ending between the ends of the line. This depression is to be minute, but when a finish is applied it will be very notice-

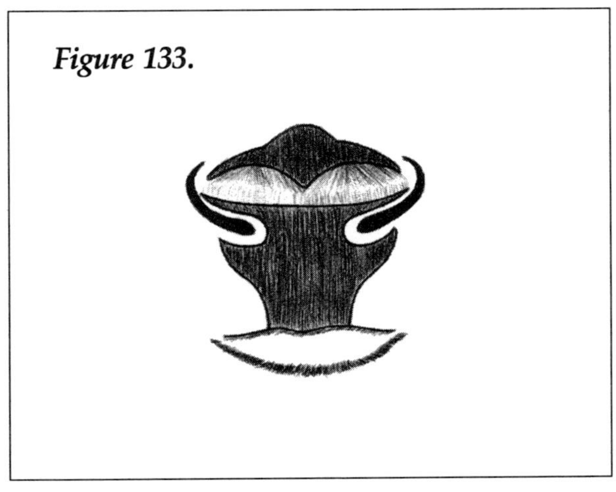

Figure 133.

able. An actual deer has a nose pad that has a curve at its top that bends and runs to the line of the upper lip. The pad is wide at the top and tapers inward until it meets with the lip (fig. 133). The tiny carved depression will accurately represent the real thing.

For the next step, use the very tip of the knife blade to make an angled cut from the lower portion of the mouth along the full length of the line of the mouth. It is important that the width of the cut be just enough to enhance the line. To make this cut, place the tip of the knife on the line of the mouth at the perimeter of the design and make a single light scrape the full length of the line. Do not apply a softening cut to the nose portion along the line of the mouth. Subsequent dewhiskering of the design will soften this edge to the desired shape. Next, angle the stock so the design is upside down. Make a light softening cut from the perimeter of the design along the short interior line of the lower jaw. Turn the stock so the design is right side up. Make several very light angled scrapes along the edge of protruding wood at the line of the mouth from the nose to the end of the snout. This will complete the nose area.

Next is the interior of the ear. Two lines define the rim of the ear: the line directly in from

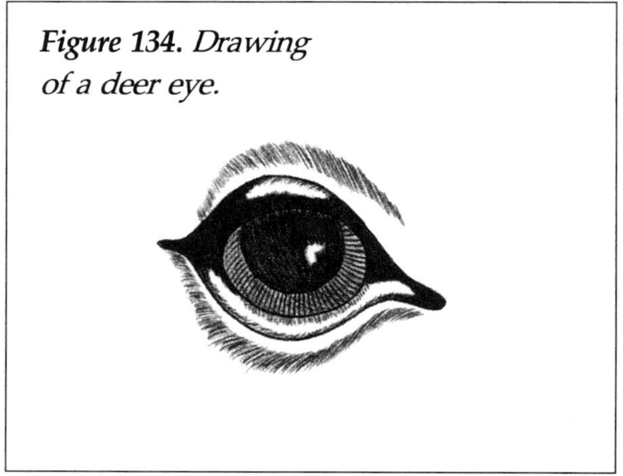

Figure 134. Drawing of a deer eye.

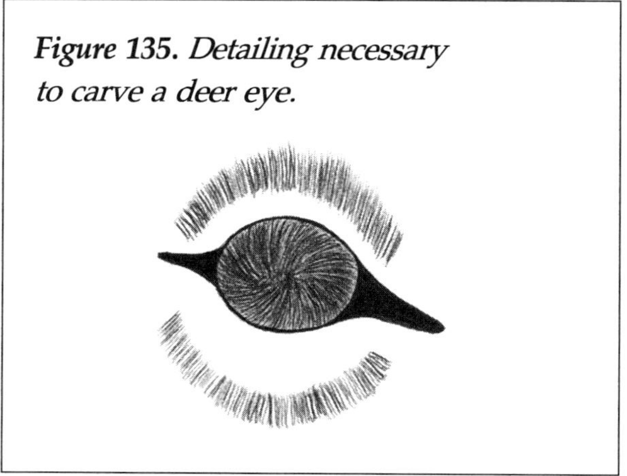

Figure 135. Detailing necessary to carve a deer eye.

the rear portion of the ear and the edge of the shaded portion directly in from the forward portion of the ear's perimeter (fig. 130). All other portions of the shaded area can be cut in freehand. First form a depression approximately equal in depth to the thickness of the knife blade between the defining rim lines of the forward and rear portions of the ear. Make a vertical cut, little more than a heavy scratch, along the length of the ear's forward and rear lines. Remove the wood between by cutting, scraping, or filing. Next, cut a very shallow depression (as depicted by the shaded area in the figure), but try to maintain the line of the depression closely to that depicted in the lower portion of the ear. Increase slightly the depression along the line at the lower portion of the ear. Make this depression as you did for the nose interior. Round over

any sharp edges of the interior rim areas and the depression.

The last feature to be detailed is the eye. You do not need to detail the lids or any other points of fine detailing associated with the eye as when it is carved on a larger scale. At this scale it is necessary to outline only the major configuration of the eye. Figure 135 shows all the detailing necessary. The first step is to use the tip of the knife to make connecting shallow, vertical insertions along the complete perimeter of the shaded area. Next, make two curved connecting cuts opposite each other at the beginning of the elongated side areas to form the complete circle of the eyeball. Make a thin, shallow, sloped cut outward and upward around the outlined eye cut. Do this only to the perimeter outline cut, not to the interior curved cuts that complete the circle of the eyeball. The depth of the cut should be no more than a heavy scratch; this will be enough to clearly separate the line of the eye from the surrounding wood. Use a knife or skew chisel to scrape the edge of the cut at the areas both below and above the line of the eyeball at the perimeter of the outline cut to elongate the trench to about $^{1}/_{16}$ inch in both of these areas only, not all of the way around the total eye layout.

Starting at the extreme outer point of either elongated portion of the layout, scrape or cut a shallow slope to the curved line of the eyeball. Do the opposite elongated area the same. Use the tip of the knife to point up the circumference of the eyeball if necessary, and to soften its outer edge. The softening cut in this instance is to be more from the interior of the eye than is done to other areas, so that afterward the entire area of the eyeball can be scraped round. The bone and muscle structure above the eye of a deer present a distinct hump, very similar to the hump of the human eyebrow. To present this hump you do not need to remove a large amount of wood. Lightly scrape the area directly above the eye shown as *A* in figure 136. Perform additional scraping to the area marked *C.* Allow a slight distance between *A* and *C* that is not scraped. As the wood is scraped from either side, this area between will become more pronounced. The offside hump (*C*) has been greatly exaggerated in the figure to show the line of the hump. Never apply a distinct line outlining the hump as depicted. During the formation of this hump, gently scrape the surrounding wood to form the rise. The same type of hump is present below the eye, but this hump is much smaller. Check the areas where you scraped to make sure there is no visible concave impression or distinct line at the edge of the scraped areas and surrounding areas of higher levels of wood. If there is, extend the scraped area to feather out any visible line.

Finally, carve the antlers in the manner described in chapter 7. As you dewhisker the

design you will see how many areas are rounded off to give the intended final result. During the dewhiskering process, study the design. Some areas might need a bit more shaping before the finish is applied.

A major difficulty for beginners is handling depth properly, both the overall depth of the design and that of detailed areas within the design as well. The tendency is to overdo, which will create a situation very difficult or impossible to correct. Until you become proficient, take each step slowly. The finished product is your chief concern, not the time of completion.

Until you become more skilled, avoid straight-on views and confine yourself to broadside and three-quarter views unless working on a practice piece.

Blending of adjoining surface areas is a major key to creating realistic-looking carvings. It may be helpful for the beginning carver, rather than blending areas immediately, to wait until a few steps later, when adjoining areas have been worked, to gain a better perspective of the overall area. When blending, unless you are knowledgeable about structure, pay strict attention to shading and to tones within shading.

When you feel that a design is complete, study it well after dewhiskering, and make any corrections before applying a finish.

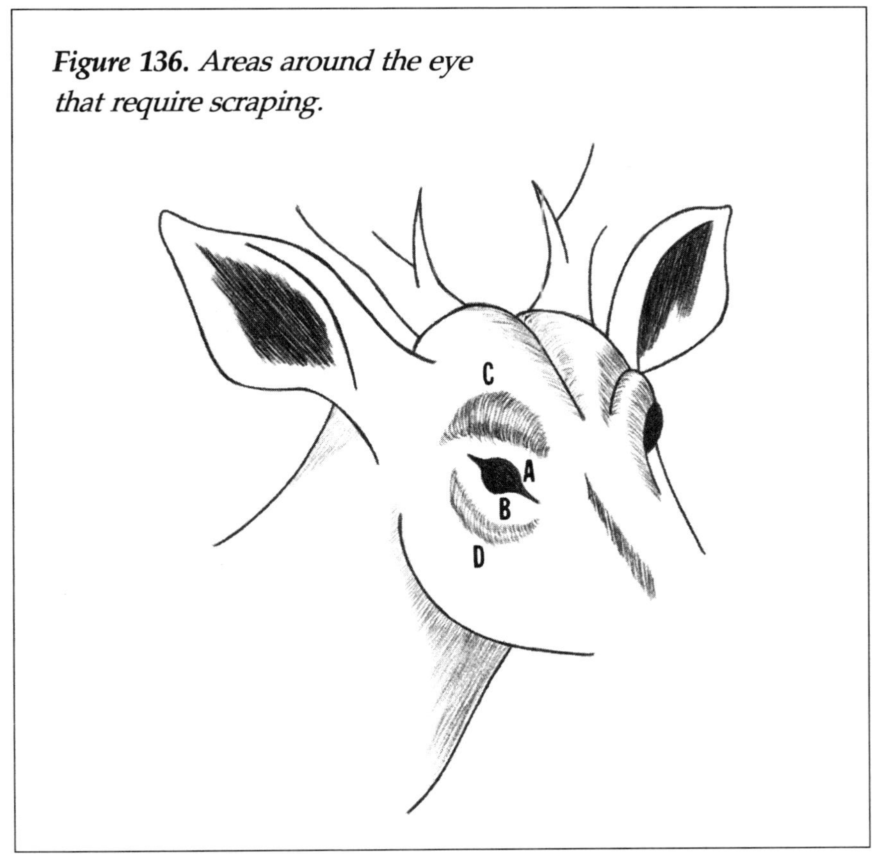

Figure 136. Areas around the eye that require scraping.

10

GALLERY OF FULL-SCALE DESIGNS

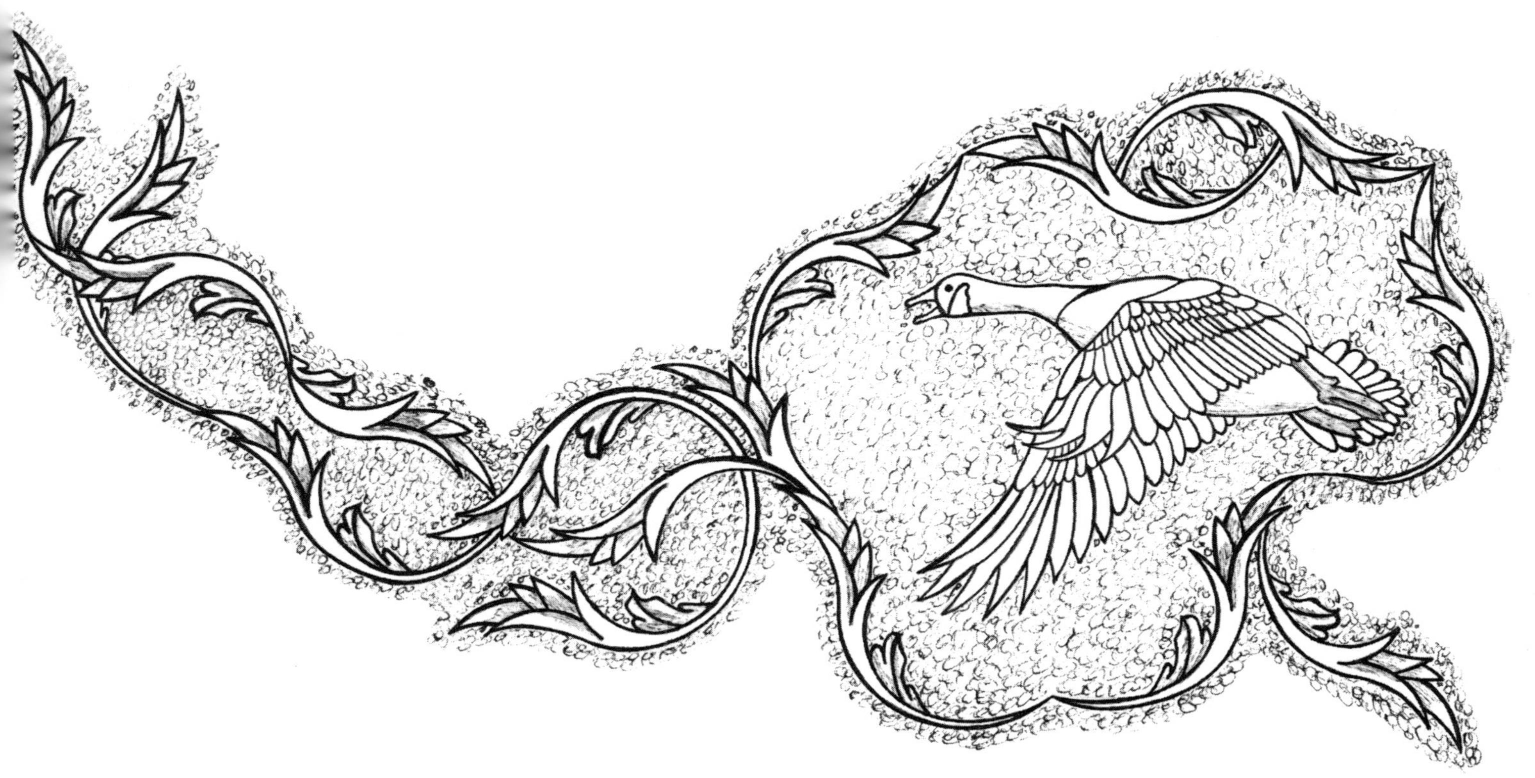

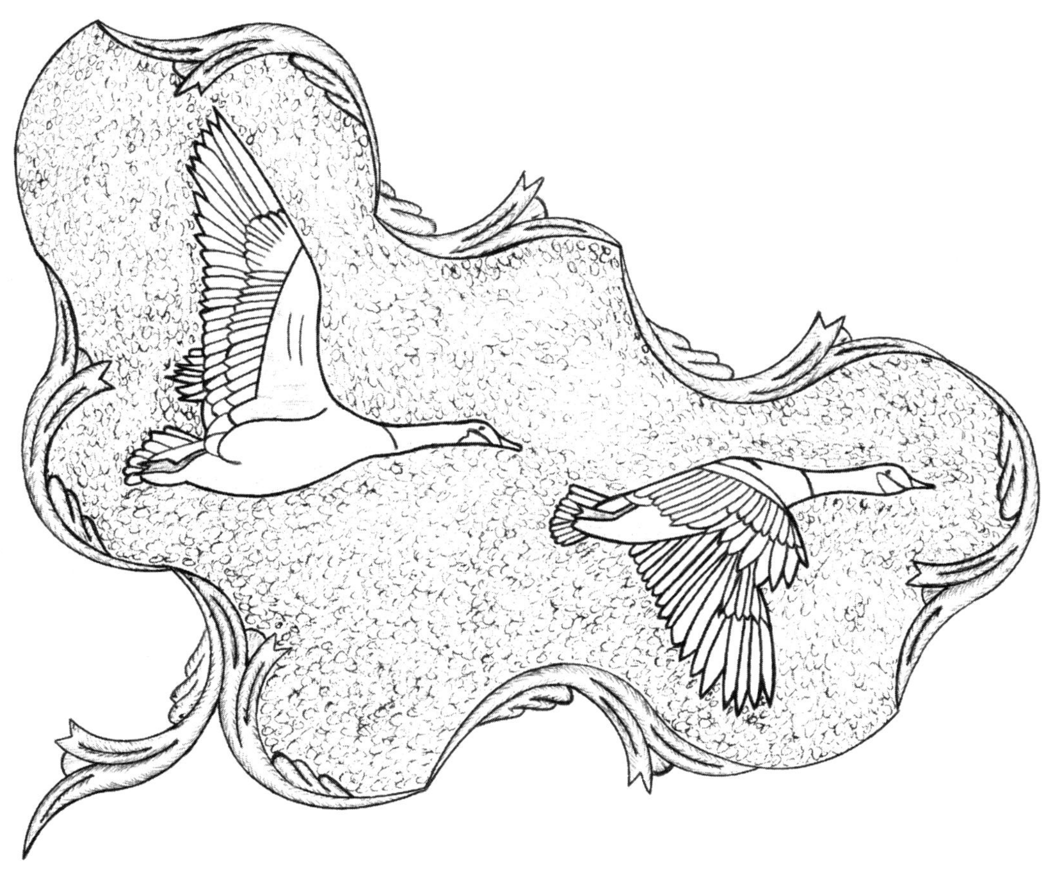

Oak Leaf and Acorn

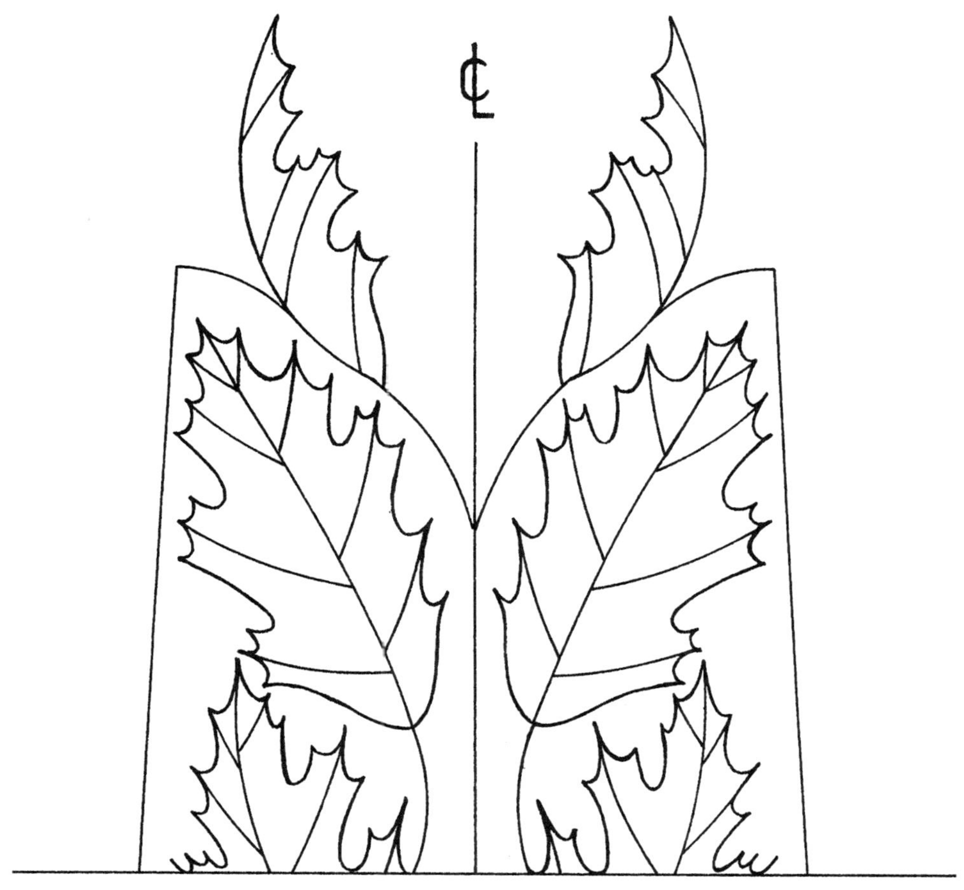

Oak Leaf and Acorn

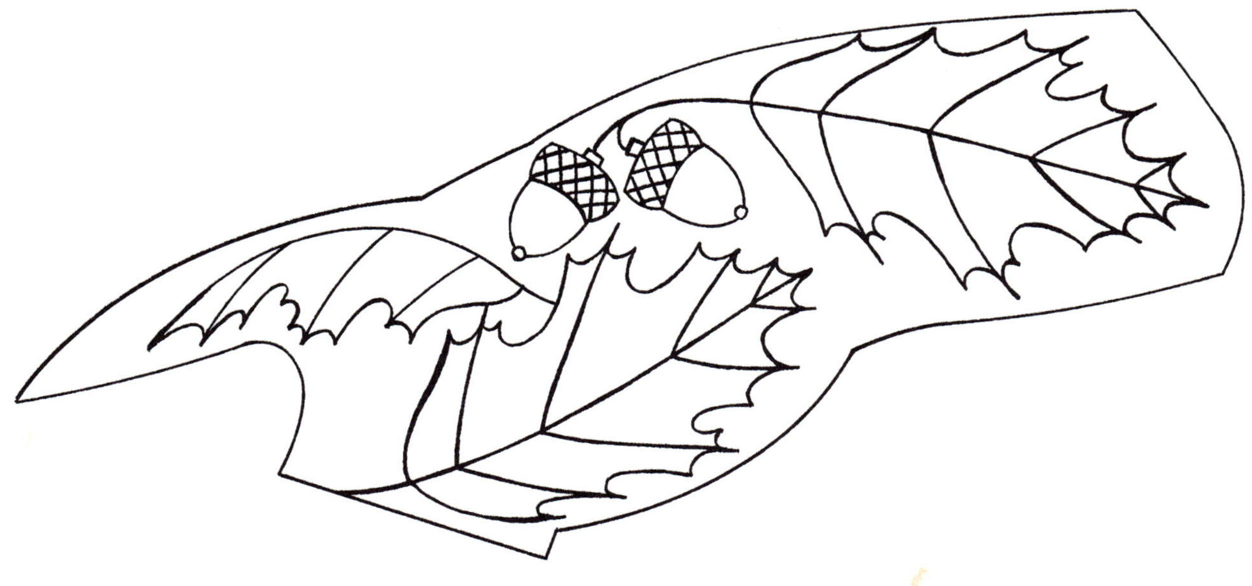

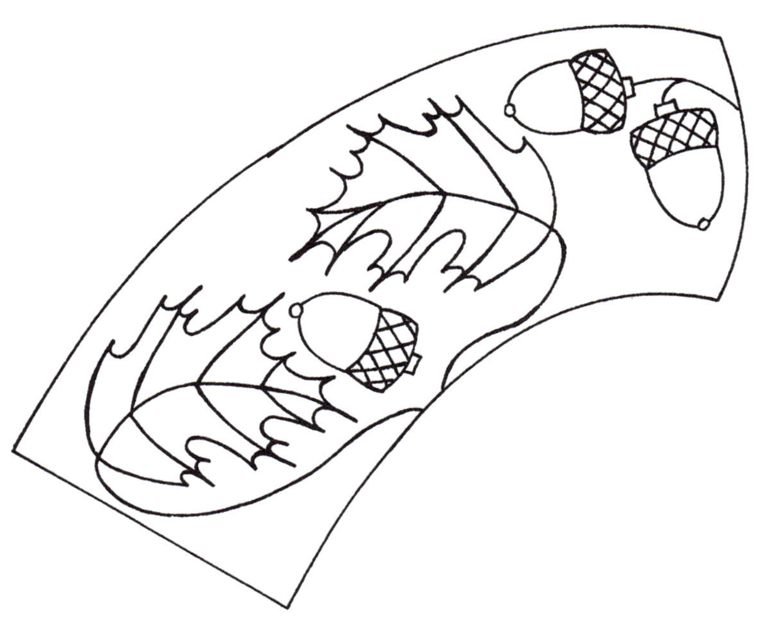

Oak Leaf and Acorn

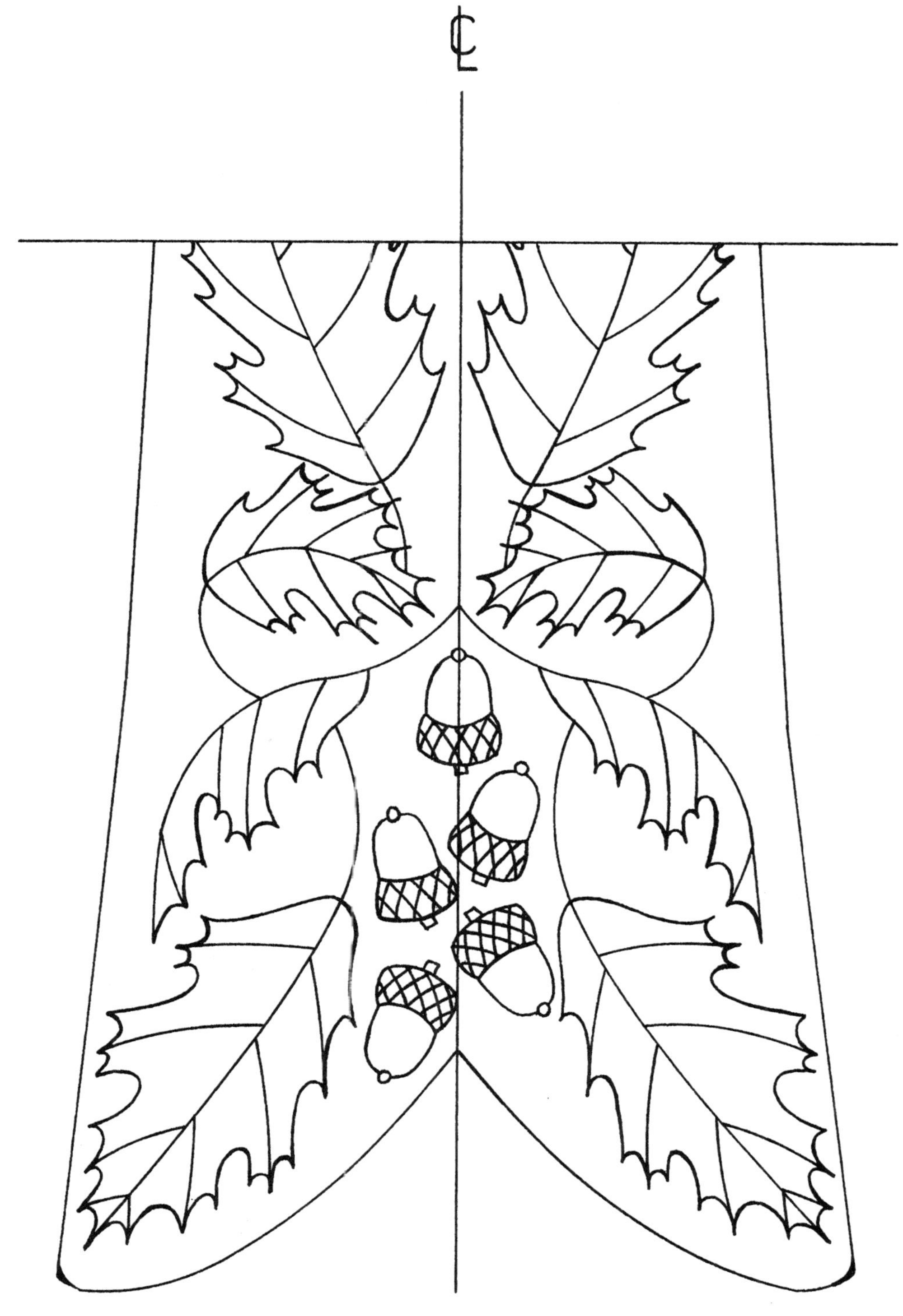

Random Rococo

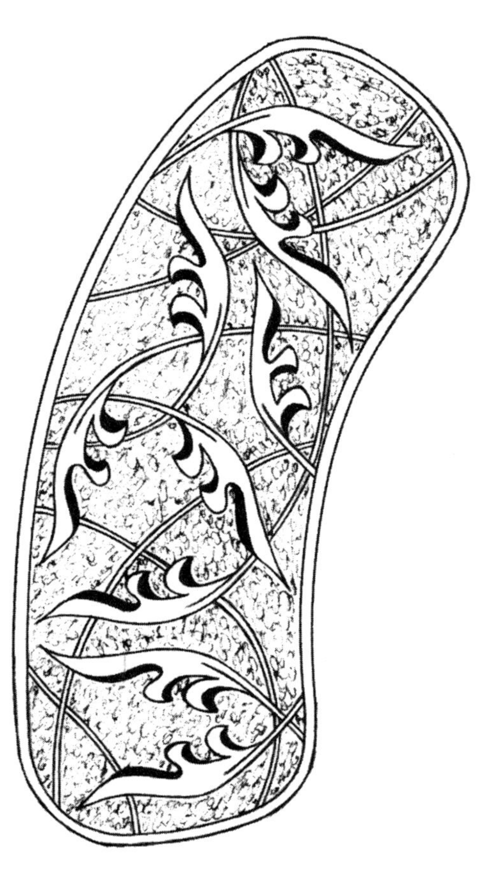

Black Walnut

Morning Glory

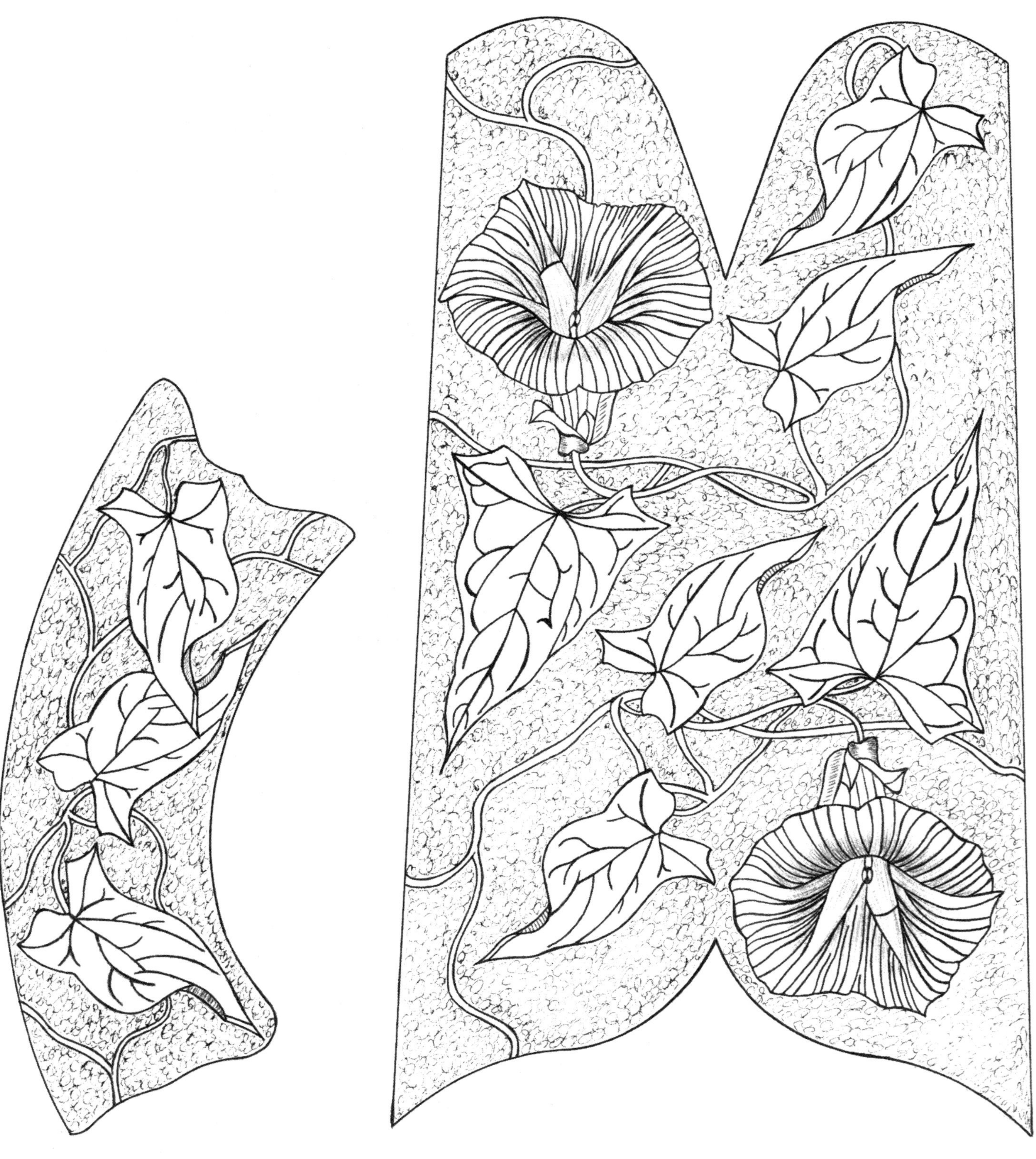

Maple

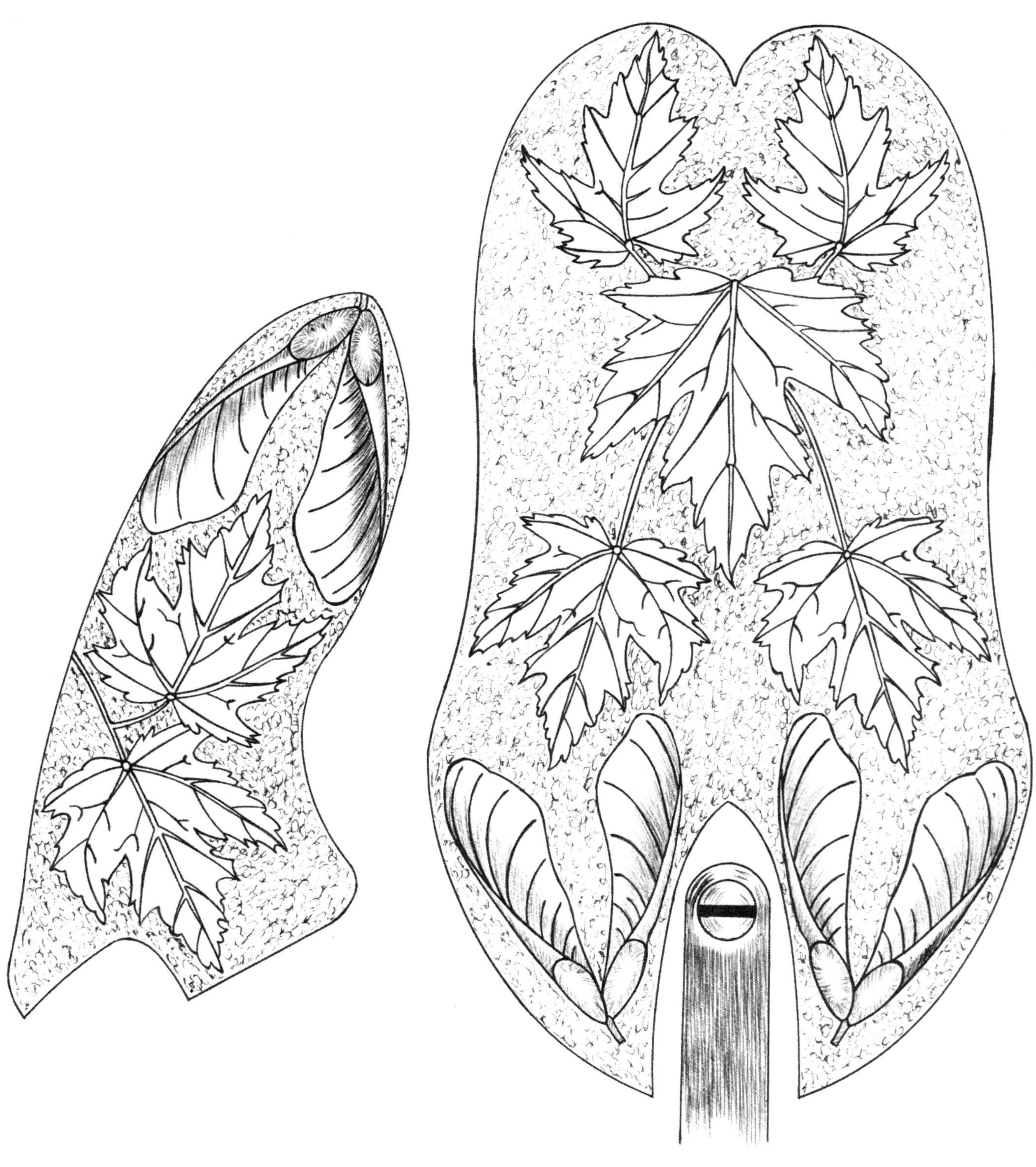

Rosette

Flowering Maple

Basket Weave

Ram

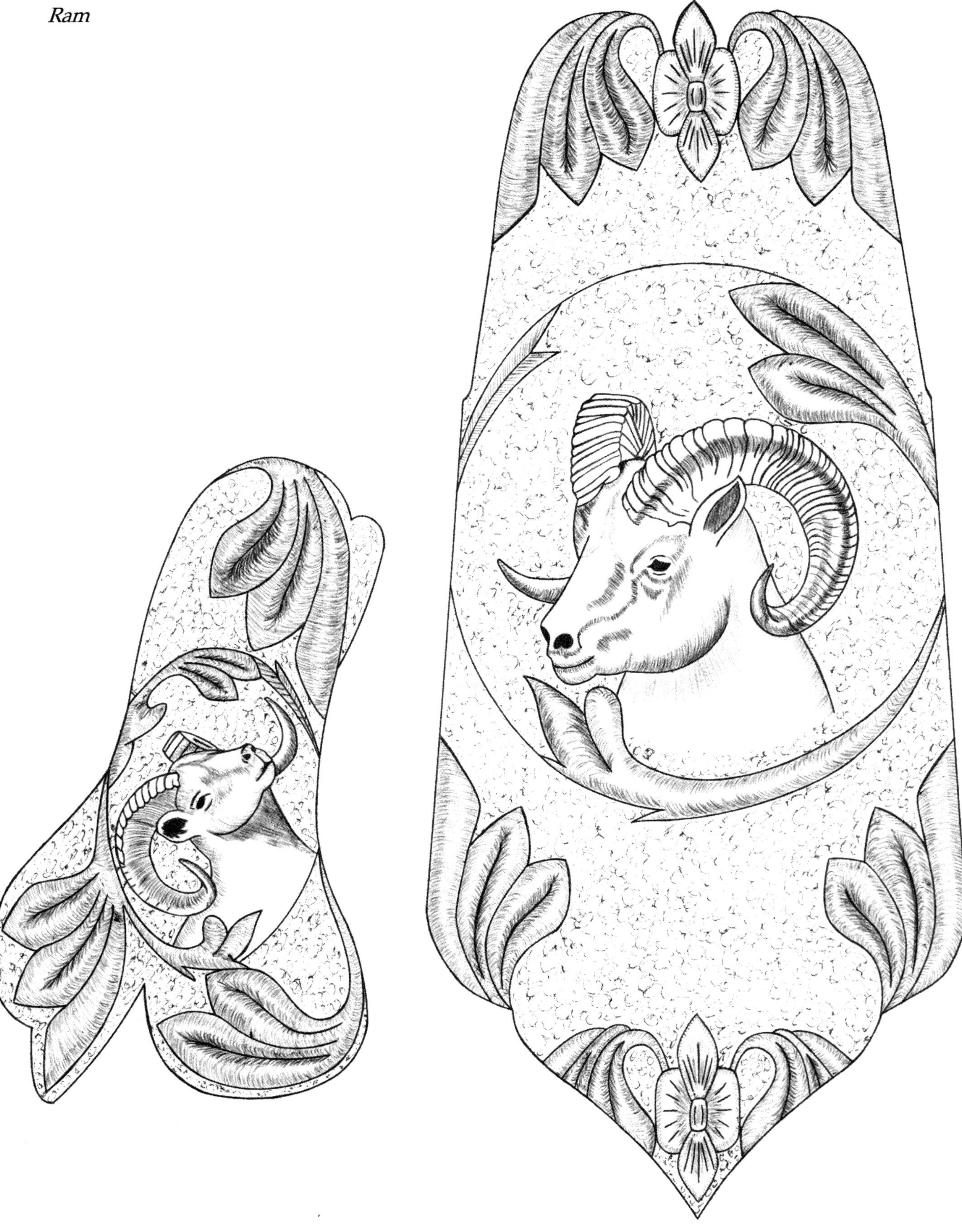

California Black Oak and Mule Deer

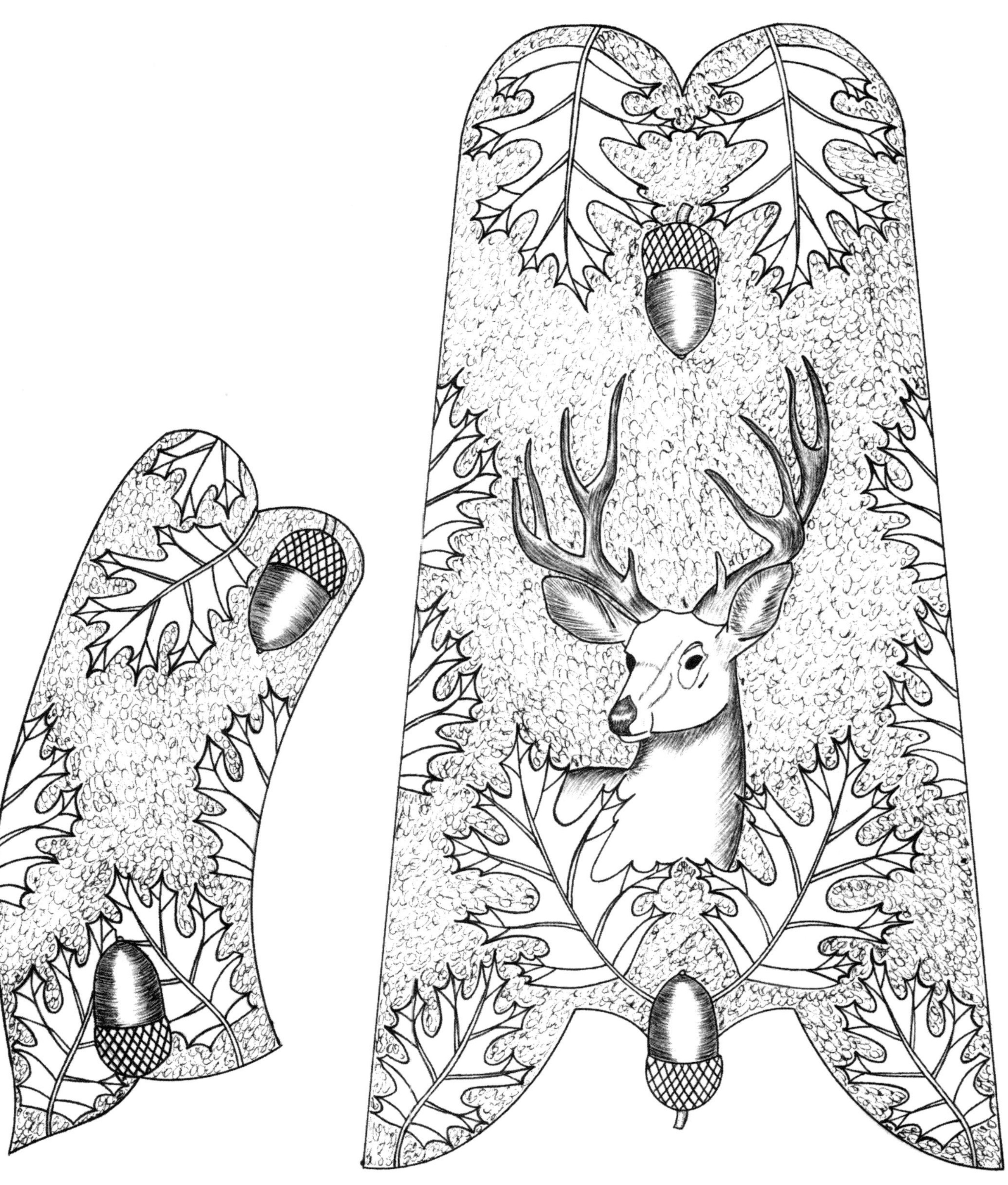

Grape Ivy

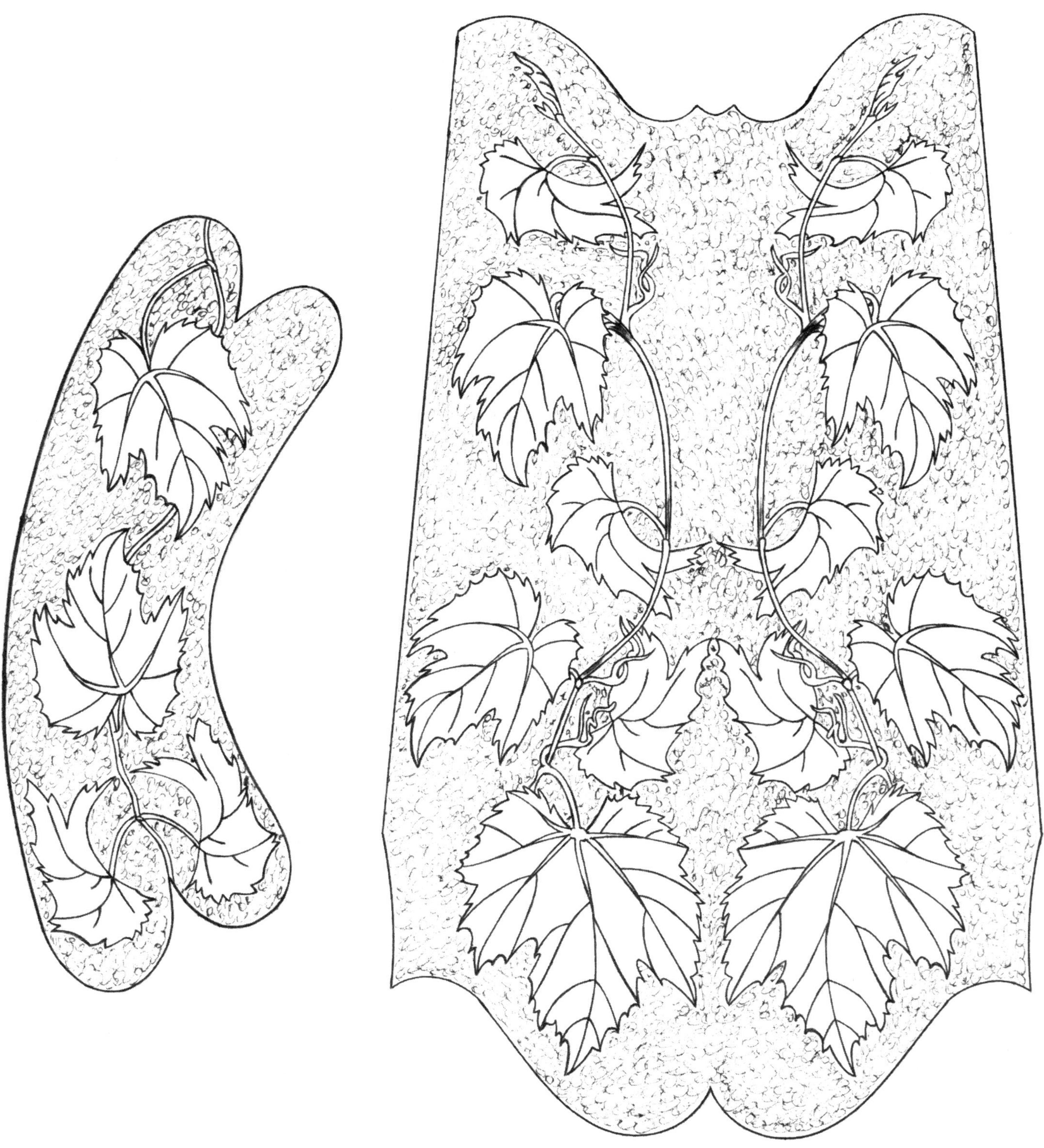

Pointer

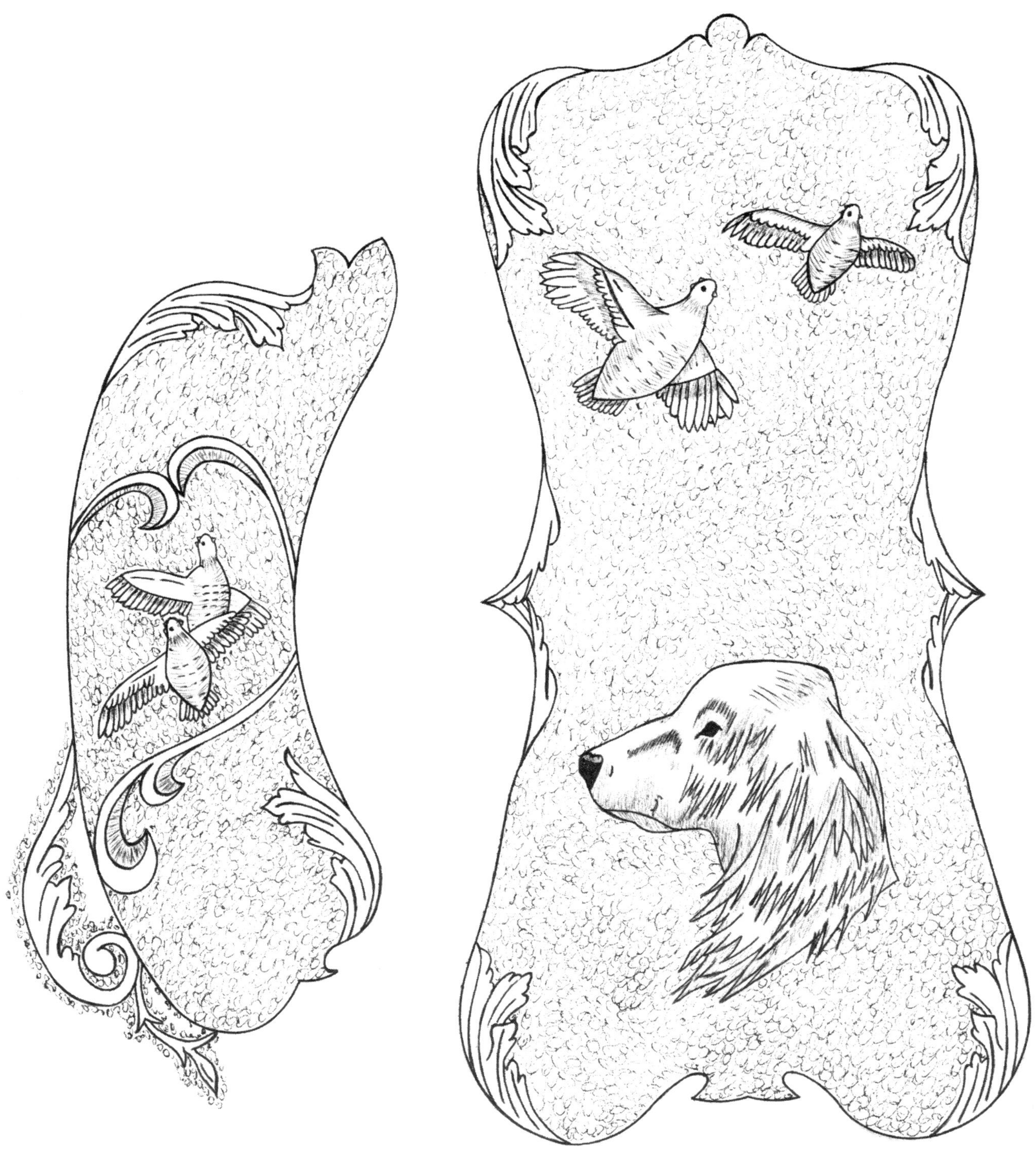

ACCENT CARVINGS

Accent carvings are those placed to enhance a specific area or feature of a gunstock. They may stand independent of other carvings, be incorporated into a larger design, or be the only carving present. Others refer to such carvings and drawings as intaglio or finials. According to the dictionary, intaglio is incised or engraved carving, and a finial is a crowning ornament or detail. Each can correctly be used to describe gunstock carvings.

Accent carvings can be applied in many ways. One of my favorites involves the use of inlays, especially diamond-shaped inlays of mother-of-pearl. The inlay shown here has a black border, although not all inlays of this type are presented with a border. An accent carving used to enhance an inlay does require that some wood be left around the perimeter of the inlay so that the inlay's embedded side edge will not be exposed. This would detract from the overall appearance and leave the edge of the inlay exposed to subsequent damage. Raised portions of the carving can be placed to serve as the outside edge of this thin wood strip. When this is done, the lower background level of the carving is generally stippled to a point that leaves the line of the thin strip clearly visible and in harmony with the space of the raised portions. The black border in the drawing can be used as a reference for the recommended amount of wood to be left between the inlay and the carving. With an inlay that does feature a border, leave a line of wood between the outer edge of

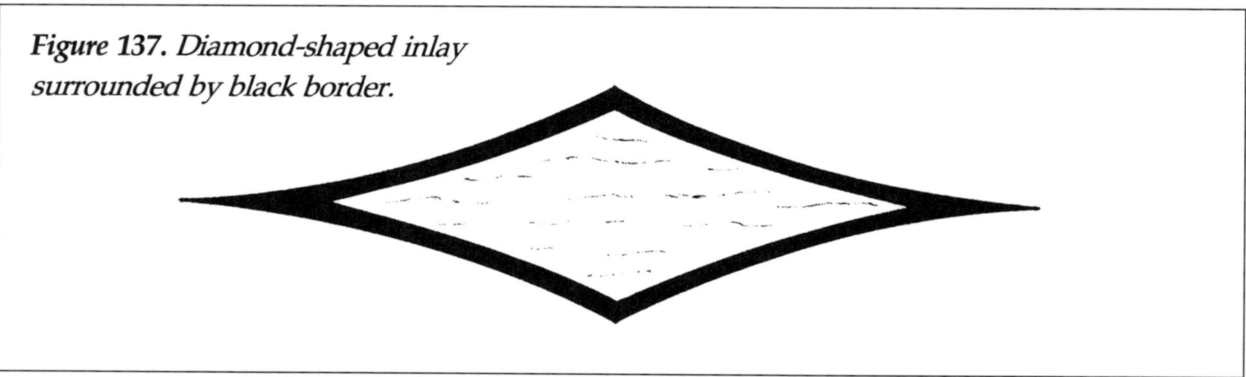

Figure 137. Diamond-shaped inlay surrounded by black border.

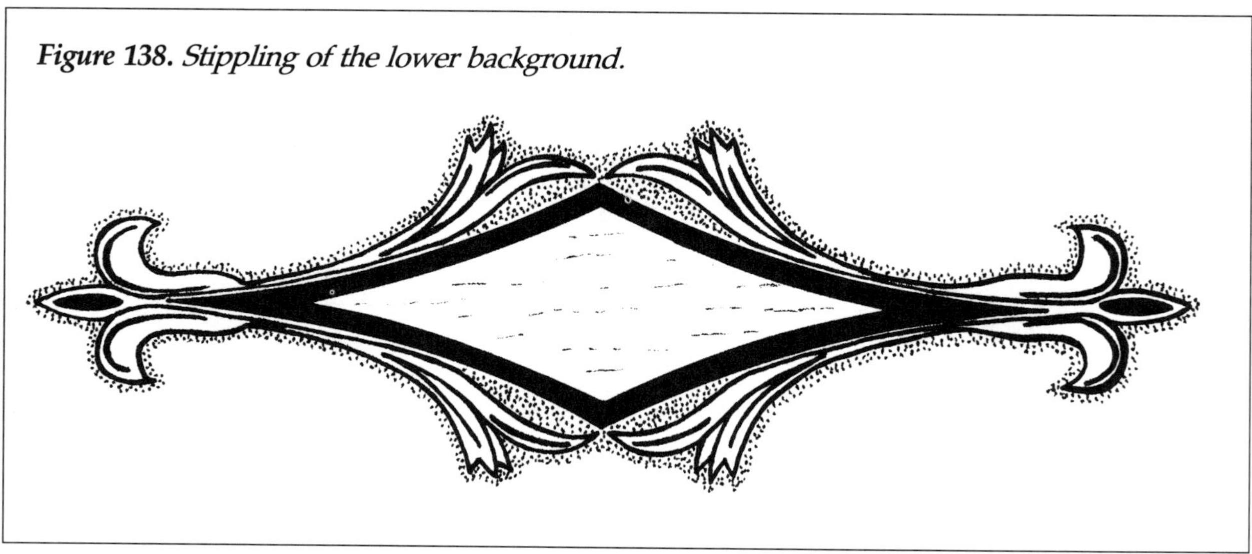

Figure 138. Stippling of the lower background.

the border and the carving. In this case, the line of wood can be much narrower. Never run a carving into the black border area.

Fleur-de-lis designs of varying sizes and shapes are often found as an accenting design on rifles and shotguns. Most who have more than an occasional association with firearms have become so accustomed to the fleur-de-lis that it no longer possesses the appeal it once had. Many are requested to be removed and replaced with something more original. On occasion, however, a client will request one, or several, to be incorporated into a design when it can be placed in harmony with the overall layout. For this reason, several types are included with the accent carving designs presented here.

Some accent carvings serve to enhance the border of existing checkering that is to be left intact. To be most effective, an addition of this nature must appear as close to being a part of the original layout as possible. Added carving must never appear to have been tacked on as an afterthought. The most common mistake that creates a tacked-on appearance is to leave a space between the cut line of the border of the checkering and the newly applied carving. Most checkering will feature a border cut at or very near the same depth as the checkering. A truly fine job of checkering is one that lacks a border altogether, as a border is generally placed to conceal checkering overruns. Only on very rare occasions will a carver be called upon to place a standard checkering-type border around existing checkering. Most who have a truly fine checkering job without overruns will not want it changed in any way.

Occasionally, a second border line will be present around checkering. This second border will lie $1/16$ to $1/8$ inch outside the line of the first. Its depth will generally be approximately half that of the checkering, or even less. All added carving should be placed to run to the inside border, which is generally cut to the same depth

as the checkering. Should a second border be overly deep, the connecting point of the carving will have to be placed to the outside border. If it is not, the line of the second cut border will be clearly visible through many areas of the carving. This is to be avoided.

Checkered layouts often incorporate varying degrees of carving. Most often, the carving is featured running with the border. In an original manufacturer's checkering layout that incorporates carving, the checkering stops at the very base of the carving. With manufacturers' layouts, the outline of the carving is "set in," or the carving completely finished, before the application of checkering. Some of the more imaginative layouts extend portions of the carving into the area of the checkering. This cannot be done when adding a carving to existing checkering unless a section of wood is inlaid and then carved. In such an instance, any excess wood beyond the perimeter of the carving will have to be leveled even with the top of the checkering and then itself checkered to match the existing checkering. The inlaid wood should match the wood of the stock and be placed with the grain running in the same direction. Such a project is generally not tackled unless it is a major repair job and is not recommended for anyone not proficient at checkering and carving. It would be less expensive and much easier to purchase a new stock and start from scratch if you wanted to run a carving into the area of the checkering.

When you add carving anywhere near checkering, take care to prevent damage to the high points or chipping out checkered squares altogether. The deepest parts of a carving placed to enhance areas along the line of the checkering should be no deeper than the grooves of the checkering itself in order to properly blend, and the outside perimeter of the carving should be no more than half that depth. If the design has open or flat areas between portions of the carv-

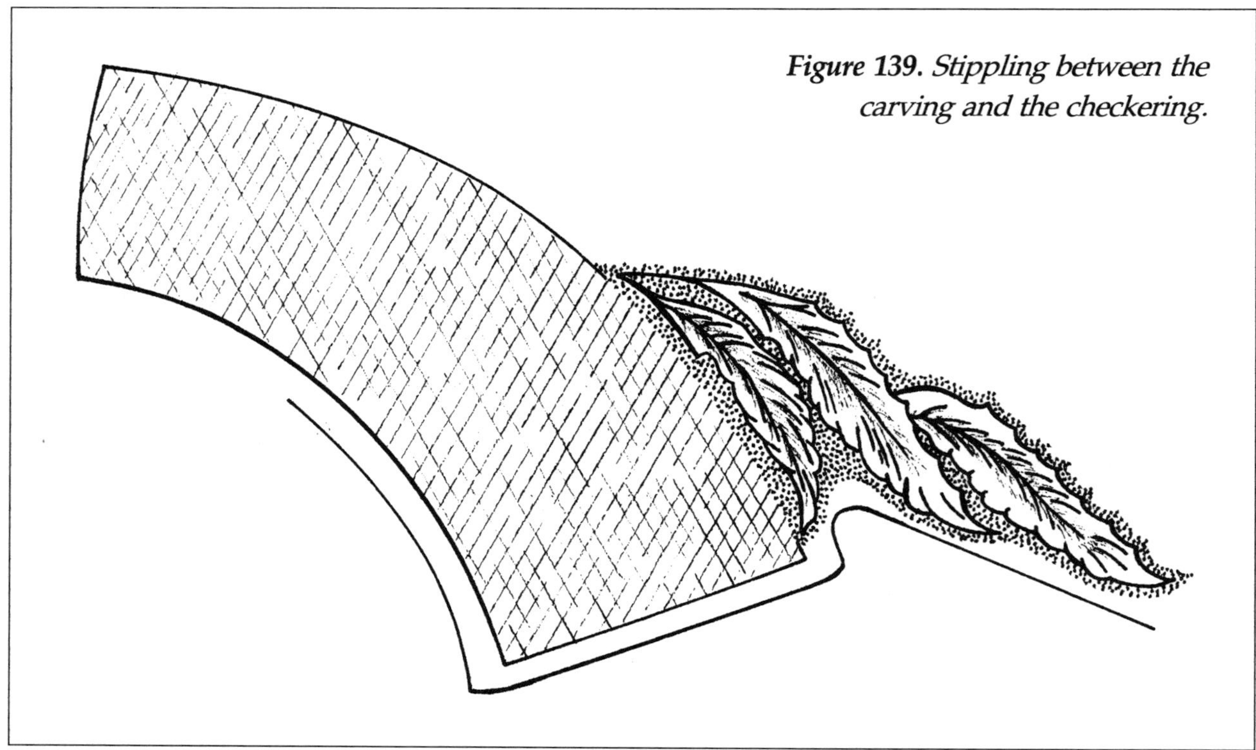

Figure 139. Stippling between the carving and the checkering.

ing at a lower plane adjacent to the border, stipple these areas up to the checkering, as well as any other open areas in the design, after the carving is complete.

Accent carvings that stand independent of other carvings are generally placed at one, two, or all three principle areas, which are just be-hind the receiver inletting at the top of the pistol grip, or wrist; at the forearm tip when the tip consists of the natural wood of the stock; and just below the bolt release (fig. 140). Occasionally there is a small ledge below the bolt release. The side portion of such a ledge lends itself nicely to carving.

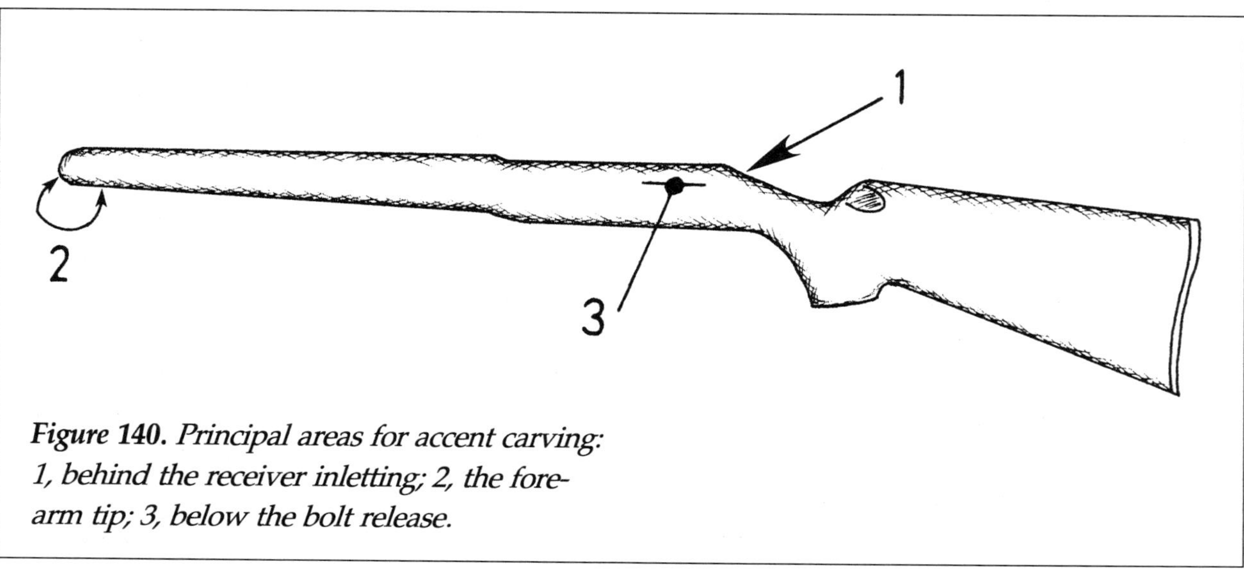

Figure 140. Principal areas for accent carving: 1, behind the receiver inletting; 2, the fore-arm tip; 3, below the bolt release.

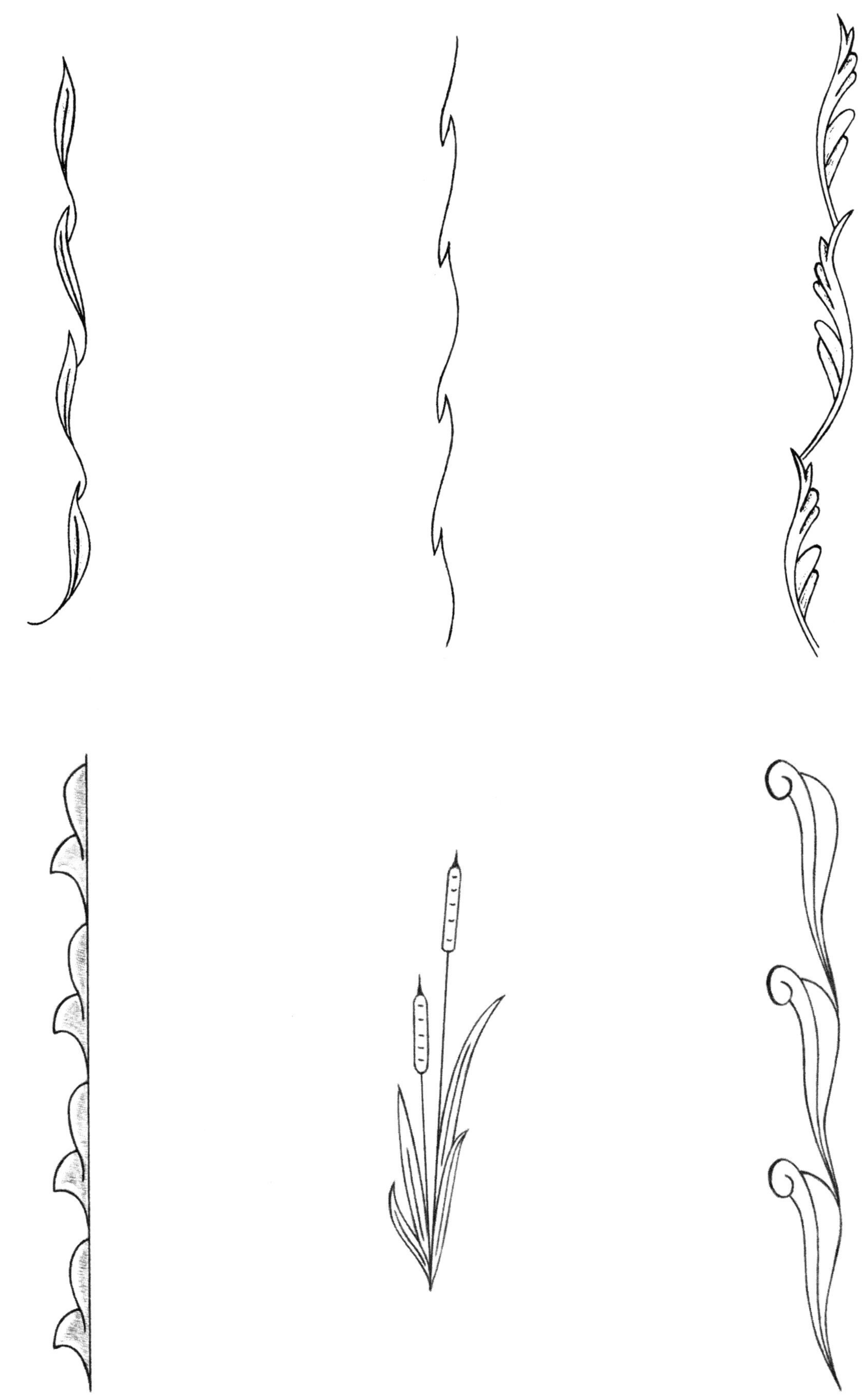

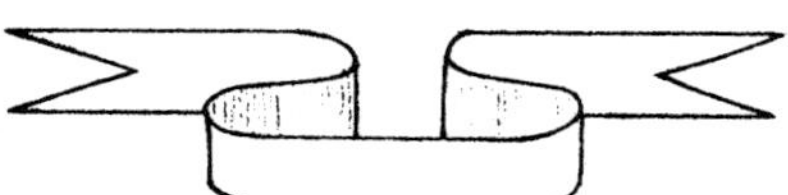

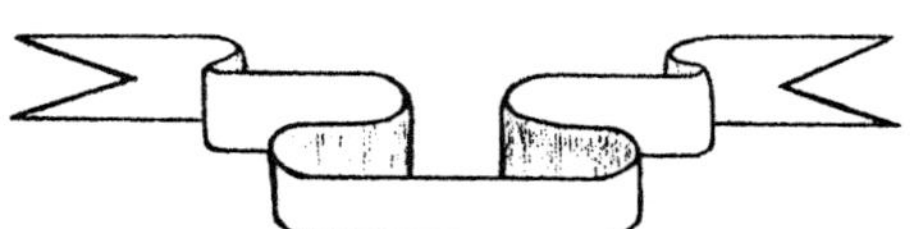

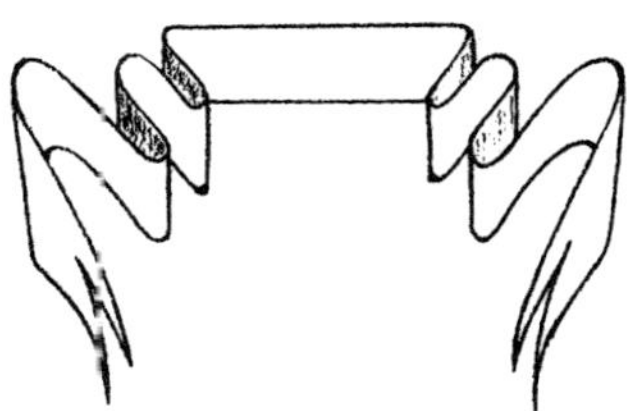

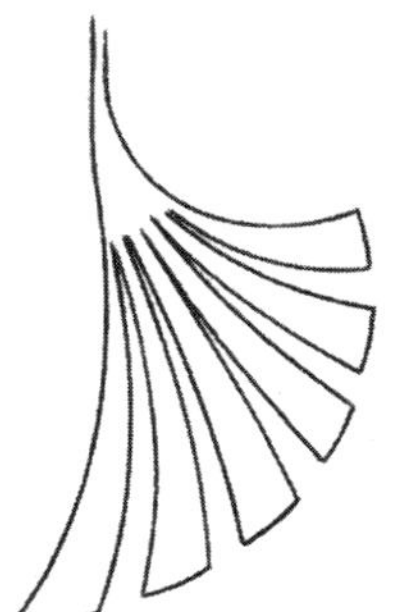

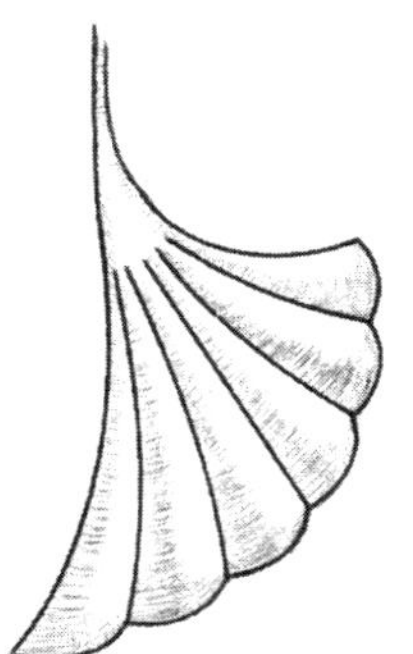

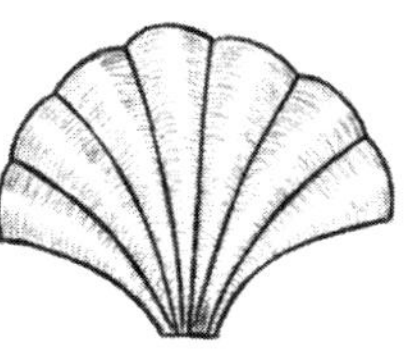

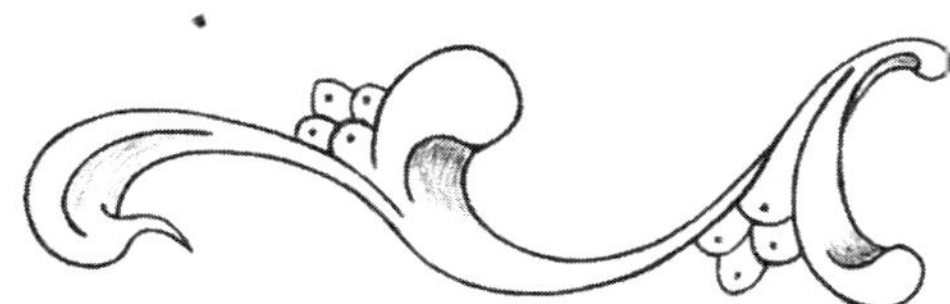

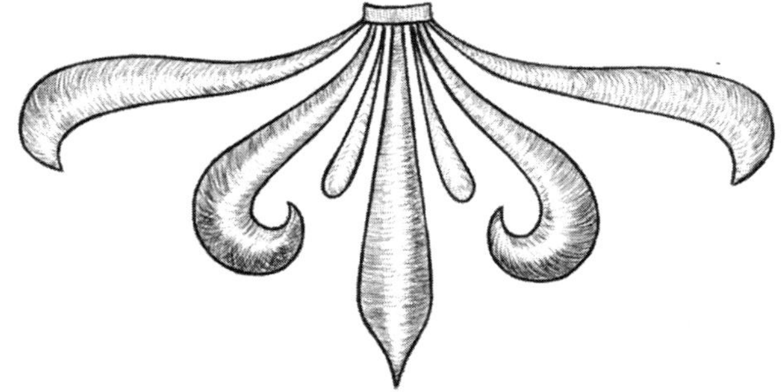

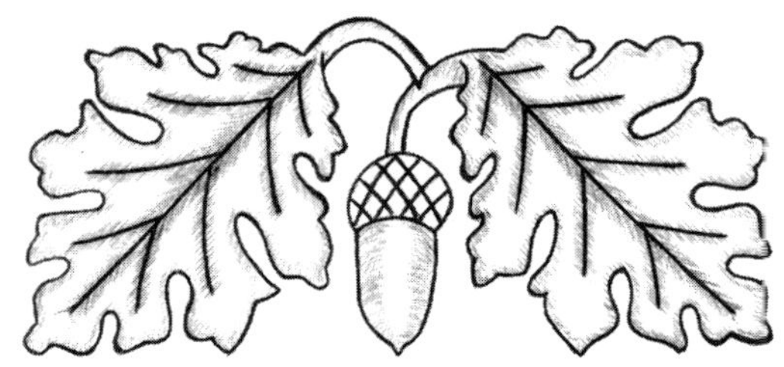

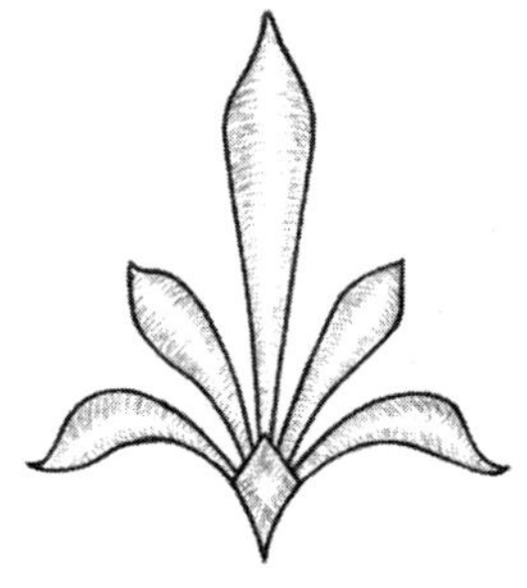

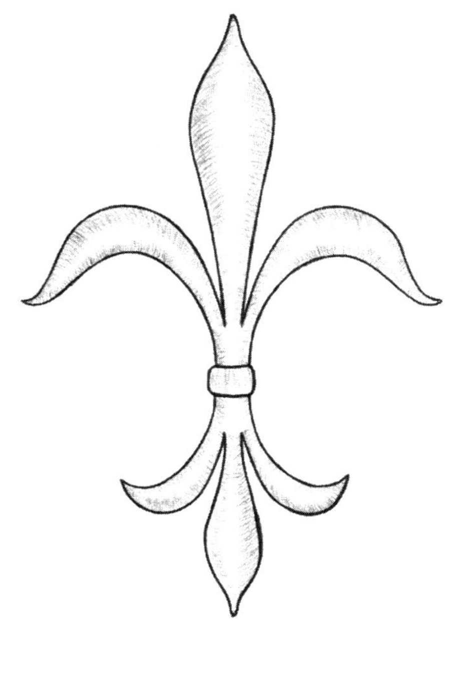

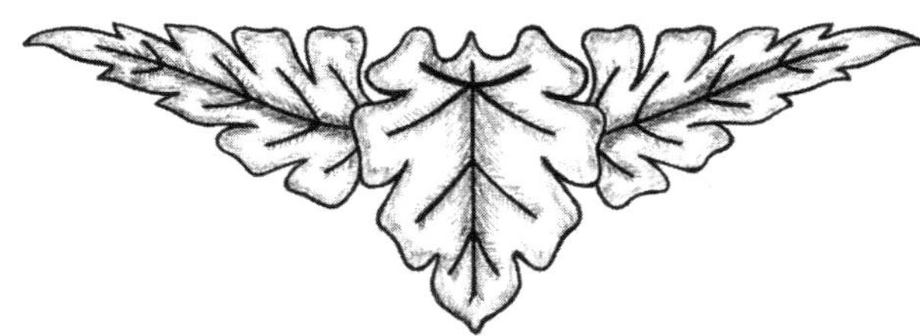

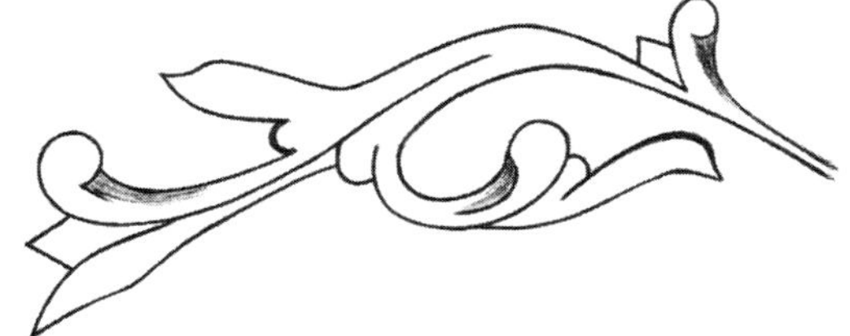

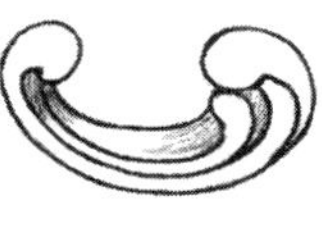

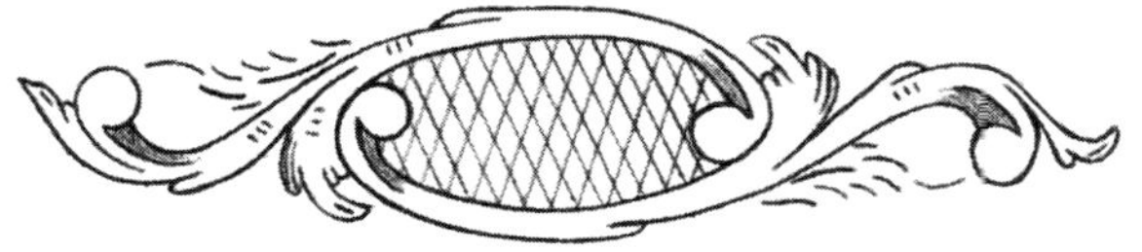

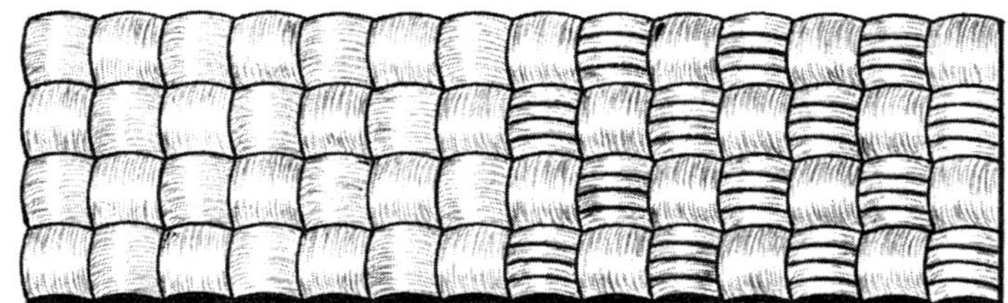

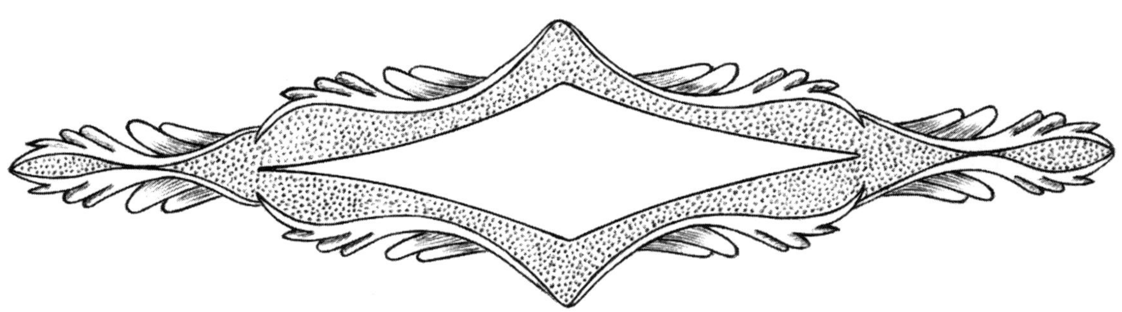

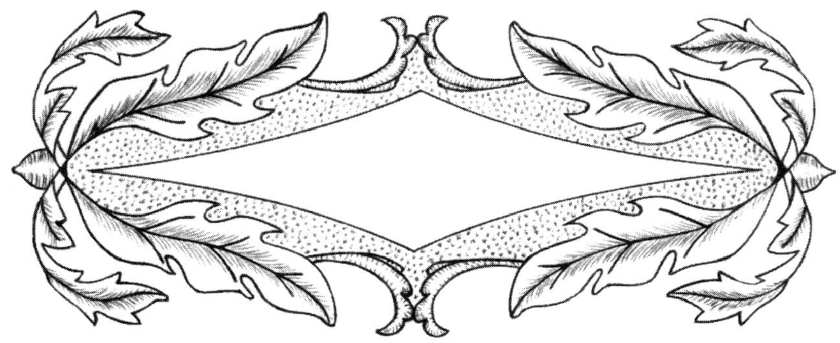

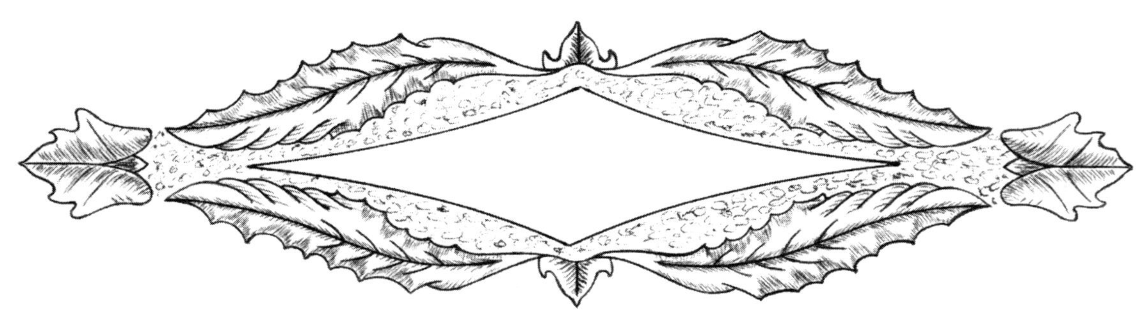

Accent carving. Carving that is used to enhance a specific area. Generally stands alone, but can be part of an overall design, such as an embellishment for a border layout.

Area available for carving. Area upon which carving can be placed without interference to, or from, stock configurations or inletting.

Ball-of-thumb recess. The recessed portion below the forward base of the comb that allows for a more comfortable grip.

Barrel channel. The elongated groove in the forearm portion of the stock for seating of the barrel.

Base coat. A thinned substance that is applied to the stock to provide protection and/or as a base to which subsequent applications of finish will adhere.

Bent chisel. A seldom-used chisel with a spoonlike configuration near the cutting edge.

Breakaway. A portion of wood that separates or chips out from the carving.

Buttplate. A thin steel, plastic, or hard rubber plate attached to the end of the buttstock that is pressed to the shooter's shoulder and that protects the end of the stock from damage and prevents slippage when the gun is fired.

Buttstock. The thickest portion of the stock, encompassing the area between the rear portion of the receiver inletting and the buttplate.

California stock. A style of rifle stock with exaggerated pistol grip, comb, and raised cheekpiece areas.

Centerline of stock. The midway point of the thickness of the stock.

Checkering. A series of parallel cut lines that aid in the gripping of the stock. Generally found on both the forearm and pistol grip of long guns, but occasionally on the pistol grip alone. On handguns, one panel on each side of the elongated grip.

Cheekpiece. The raised area of the buttstock rested against the shooter's cheek when firing.

Chip-out. Similar to breakaway, but generally applied to smaller portions that separate from the design itself during the course of carving.

Comb. The entire upper edge of the buttstock, from pistol grip to buttplate.

Cross-hatching. A series of narrow cut lines similar to checkering, used as ornamentation or fill-in for large areas within a design. More often found on flintlock and percussion-type firearms.

Crossover. Refers to portion of a design giving the illusion of lying atop or running over another while continuing on its path.

Design transfer tool. An instrument with a needlelike point used to puncture the lines of a pattern to transfer it onto the wood of the stock.

Dremel tool. A small, elongated, motorized hand tool used as a drill, grinder, engraver, polisher, and cutter.

Drop-of-comb. The downward slope of the upper edge of the buttstock from front to rear. Though incorrect, the term more generally is used to refer to the forward area of the comb that curves sharply downward to the grip.

Filler. A substance used to fill in the pores of the wood of the stock.

Finger groove. An elongated depression found on both sides of the forearm grip of a shotgun; runs parallel with the length of the forearm, and affords the shooter a firmer grip, specifically with the fingertips.

Finger rail. The flat area on each side of a barrel at the top of the forearm grip, running from the receiver inletting to the tip of the forearm. Predominant on rifles.

Finial. In a broad sense, a finishing touch or crowning detail to a design. Also refers to a carving that stands alone and is used to enhance the top portion of an overall design within or as part of the border.

Finish. A substance, such as oil, lacquer, or polymer, that when applied to a stock protects it from moisture and other damage.

Fleur-de-lis. Ornamental design of French origin, frequently used on firearms.

Forearm. The grip portion of a long gun forward of the receiver area.

Forearm release tang. A portion of the locking mechanism used to hold the forearm grip to a shotgun.

Gouge. A type of chisel with a rounded cutting edge, used for cutting grooves or extensive wood removal.

Grain. The direction of wood growth and texture.

Grip. The part by which is gun is held when firing, such as the forearm and pistol grip or wrist on a long gun, or the elongated extension for holding a handgun.

Grip cap. A plate attached to the underside of a pistol grip for protection or decorative purposes.

Groove. A recess or trench at the base of a design caused by improper squaring or pointing up of side walls. May be deliberately placed to give a greater sense of depth to a design or for contouring within a design.

Guide cut. A shallow cut made before the actual cut to define its path and help keep it from deviating.

Incised carving. Carving in which design lines are cut straight into the stock at far deeper levels than usual. Predominantly found on flintlock-era long guns. Also known as intaglio.

Inlay. Pieces of a material set into the wood of the stock to make a design that is generally flush with the surface.

Inletting. Mortised areas that allow fitting of metal components.

Intaglio. See incised carving.

Layout. The completed form of a design, or the act of forming a design.

Levels. The various heights within a design that create a three-dimensional appearance.

Locator mark. A line drawn on a placed piece of tape to serve as a guide in positioning a completed design for transfer to the stock. Used to establish exact pattern sheet positioning before removal for design tracing.

Match line. A line drawn from one segment of a sectional pattern sheet to another to aid in the correct overall placement of each segment when reassembling the pattern onto the stock for design transfer.

Match-line pattern. A pattern consisting of two or more segments to make up an overall design, with match lines on each segment for correct alignment.

Monte Carlo stock. A type of stock that has a sloped rise toward the rear of the comb that drops off sharply near the end of the buttstock.

Outline cut. The vertical cut made to the lines of a design to separate interior detailing or the overall design from surrounding portions of wood.

Over-the-top. Pistol grip design that continues from the top of a side panel over the top of the grip to connect with the top of the opposite side panel.

Over-under. A descriptive term used for the type of shotgun or rifle on which one barrel is directly atop another.

Parting-line cut. A sloped, trenchlike cut made in conjunction with the outline cut to further separate all or part of the design from the surrounding wood.

Parting tool. A chisel with a V-shaped cutting edge, sometimes used for detailing, but in stock carving generally used for parting-line cuts.

Pattern sheet. Tracing paper on which a design is traced. Can consist of one or more segments.

Pistol grip. Curved finger rest portion on the underside of the stock, at or about its midpoint between the action and main body of the buttstock. The gripping point of the trigger hand.

Point-up. Final shaping or smoothing of rough areas before final detailing, such as done to the side walls of a design.

Pores. Minute openings in the wood surface, found in greater or lesser degrees depending on the texture and density of the type of wood.

Pump action. Action found on single-barrel shotguns and rifles. When the forearm is slid to the rear, the shell is ejected and the hammer cocked; when slid forward, a new shell is fed into the chamber by the forward movement of the bolt, and the gun is ready to fire.

Push cut. A cut made away from the body.

Recoil pad. A thick pad, generally made of rubber, attached to the rear of the buttstock to absorb recoil shock that a standard buttplate cannot. Serves also to prevent the firearm from slipping from the shooter's shoulder when firing.

Relief carving. A form of carving in which shapes and figures are distinguished from a surrounding plane surface. There are three types of relief carving: high, middle, and low. In high- and middle-relief gunstock carving, the design projects beyond the surface plane of the stock. For such carvings, additional wood must have been left in appropriate areas during initial shaping of a stock. In low-relief carving, wood is removed from around a design, and the design's high points while at stock surface level appear to be raised from that surface.

Ridge. A rise or peak that is formed from angular parallel cuts sloping away from each other.

Riffler. A file or rasp available in various sizes and shapes. File types are used for fine delicate work, and rasp types are for bulk removal of wood. The latter are far too harsh for gunstock carving. File types are also used for leveling off and smoothing rough cut areas, such as side walls, design features, and background areas.

Round off. To round or soften sharp edges.

Rub. An imprint taken by rubbing the side of a pencil's lead across paper lying flat over a design that is being copied.

Scratch awl. A pointed tool used for scoring lines, punching holes, or with stock carving, applying stippling.

Sectional pattern. A layout of two or more segments that make up patterns for a complete design.

Set in. To make outline cuts that separate individual features or a full design from surrounding wood.

Shank. The stem of a tool between the handle and the working end.

Side-by-side. A double-barrel shotgun on which the barrels are parallel on a horizontal plane.

Single-barrel. A shotgun with one barrel. May be single-shot or semiautomatic.

Single side panel. A single checkered or carved panel on each side of a grip.

Skew chisel. A flat chisel with its cutting edge set at around a 60-degree angle to its stem, rather than 90 degrees, as is the cutting edge of the straight chisel.

Skip. Refers to a cutting tool losing its bite and overriding into another area.

Sling swivel inletting. Inletting that allows metal parts for attachment of a sling retaining ring. On long guns there are generally two, both on the underside of the stock, one near the buttstock shoulder end and the other near the forearm tip. Some firearms have only one, which is at the buttstock end with a retaining ring assembly attached to either the barrel or the loading tube beneath the barrel.

Stippling. A series of shallow indentations made on the background area to enhance the overall appearance of a design. Stippling is sometimes applied to areas of the design interior for decorative purposes.

Stop cut. Cut made to prevent overrunning of another cut.

Straight chisel. A chisel with a flat cutting edge at 90 degrees to its shank.

Straight stock. A stock that has no pistol grip. Sometimes used for a stock that is level from front to rear of the comb.

Sweating out. The heating of a stock in order to bring oil to the surface of the wood so that it can be wiped away.

Transfer holes. Holes made by the transfer tool, at a depth barely through the finish and into wood.

Transfer hole connecting cut. A lightly made cut along a line of transfer holes to serve as a guide for a deeper second cut.

Transfer tool. Tool with a needle point for transferring a design by making minute punctures along its lines through the paper into wood.

Transition area. An area immediately behind the lower rear portion of the pistol grip, where the shape of the grip flows into that of the underside of the buttstock.

Trench. Small V- or U-shaped groove around the base of a design to give an illusion of greater depth. Sometimes inside or part of the design.

Undercut. A trench or groove between the background and design as a result of too much angular penetration with a cutting tool or file. Can cause the vertical side wall of a design to be ragged.

Whiskers. Hairlike wood fibers dislodged by cutting, sanding, or moisture.

Wrist. The grip area of the stock between the action inletting and the forward severe drop of the comb. This grip is straight, having no extension or curve like the pistol grip. Also called the small of the stock.